CORRESPONDENCE OF
CATHERINE THE GREAT

THE GRAND DUCHESS CATHERINE

AFTERWARDS EMPRESS CATHERINE II OF RUSSIA (THE GREAT)

Correspondence of
CATHERINE THE GREAT
When Grand-Duchess, with
SIR CHARLES HANBURY-WILLIAMS
And Letters from
COUNT PONIATOWSKI

Edited and Translated by
THE EARL OF ILCHESTER
and
MRS LANGFORD-BROOKE

THORNTON BUTTERWORTH LTD.
15 BEDFORD STREET, LONDON, W.C.

First published 1928

CONTENTS

ILLUSTRATIONS

INTRODUCTION
By M. Serge Goriaïnov
(Written in 1909)

Among the Archives of the Empire is deposited the correspondence in French of the Grand-Duchess Catherine Alexéievna with Sir Charles Hanbury-Williams, British Ambassador at the court of the Empress Elizabeth from 1755 to 1757.

This correspondence, which covers the period from July 31st, 1756, to June,[1] 1757, is composed of two portfolios, one of which (letters) contains sixty-five letters from the Grand-Duchess and three from Williams ; the other (answers) eighty-four answers from Williams and five letters from Catherine, in all a hundred and fifty-seven documents. According to several of these letters, the Grand-Duchess's notes were generally returned to her by the same messenger who brought her Williams's answer. But the latter, it appears, took the precaution of having the letters which he received from Catherine copied, before returning them to her. Nevertheless, a few originals remained in his possession. Of the answers from Sir Charles, the greater portion are in his own handwriting, the others in a strange hand.[2] It can be assumed that Catherine returned them to Williams at the time of his departure from St Petersburg in 1757, and that he took them with the copies of the Grand-Duchess's letters to England, where he placed them in charge of a trustworthy person; for until now this correspondence has remained unknown.

The binding of the two portfolios is ordinary boards. The paper used in the correspondence is mostly gilt-edged. The portfolio containing Catherine's letters had been tied up with a dark green ribbon, the ends of which were fixed to the portfolio with red sealing-wax, bearing the impression of a signet ring. Above the shield is a crown, imperial, as far as can be seen, and below is a suspended sabre. The papers are arranged in no

---

[1] July.
[2] No doubt the letters dictated by him during his illnesses.

chronological order ; the letters and answers are even bound in such a manner that letters from Catherine are to be found in the portfolio containing Williams's answers, and vice versa.

By order of the Emperor Alexander II, this correspondence was placed in the Archives of the Empire, on May 10th, 1864, by the Vice-Chancellor, Prince Gortschakov, and remained deposited there, sealed by the Prince's seal, till October, 1865, when the Emperor expressed his desire to see it ; in consequence of which, on October 4th, it was handed to His Majesty by Prince Gortschakov. By a supreme command, Count D. Bloudov, State Secretary, was instructed to undertake an historical work on the period of residence of the English Ambassador Williams at St Petersburg during the reign of Elizabeth Petrovna, and on his correspondence with the Grand-Duchess. At the death of Count Bloudov, this memoir, drawn up in French, was incomplete; and for that reason His Majesty deigned to entrust it to Count V. Panin (head of the Private Chancery). The latter, after reviewing and correcting it, handed it to the Emperor.

On March 10th, 1866, all the preparatory notes for Count Bloudov's work were deposited in the Archives of the Empire ; but the original correspondence was only replaced there on September 15th, 1881, in a packet bearing the seal of His Majesty's private library. It was found among the papers of the Emperor Alexander II, and was handed to his successor by his own orders on September 29th, 1881, with the first and second parts of Count Bloudov's work in the rough draft. In 1893, the Emperor Alexander III replaced the original correspondence and the memoir by the Count in the Archives of the Empire, to be kept there under seal.

His Imperial Majesty has now deigned to accord us authority to publish this correspondence. In arranging this publication, we have turned to good account the preparatory work of Count Bloudov, who in his memoir had fixed the dates of the letters and answers, and had thrown light upon many of the facts related in this correspondence. It is worded as if it emanated from people of the masculine sex, without any indication of who the writers were, and without signature, except one letter signed by Catherine. The letters were generally dated with the day of the week ;

sometimes the time of day is noted. The dates will follow those indicated by Count Bloudov, who has numbered all the letters and answers in the order in which they are bound. As already stated, Catherine's letters are not originals, with three exceptions. But although they only reach us in the form of copies, there can be no doubt of their authenticity, both from the subjects with which they deal, and from the fact that the style and phraseology are entirely characteristic of Catherine. For that reason, therefore, they can be looked upon as one of the works of her pen—one which comes down to us from the first years of her youth, and forms a complement to her memoirs. The wording of most of Catherine's letters is careless, sometimes even obscure, with mistakes in spelling and omission of words. These mistakes, however, may partly be attributable to the person whom Williams employed to copy the letters of the Grand-Duchess. In any case, one may conclude from their wording that Catherine wrote them in haste, expressing her thoughts in the first words that came. Williams wrote with greater care, but since, as he says himself, he only knew French imperfectly, many mistakes and defective, sometimes even unintelligible, phraseology are to be found in his letters.

After this preliminary information regarding the documents which we publish below, let us say a few words about Sir Charles Hanbury-Williams. Descended from an ancient family in the county of Worcestershire, he was born in 1709.[1] In Parliament he belonged to the Whig Party, and was a loyal member of the administration of Sir Robert Walpole. He did not shine in eloquence, but rose to notice by the sprightliness and subtlety of his conversation, his caustic replies and the great elegance of his manners. He was further celebrated for his satirical poems.[2] He was a man who loved life and knew how to make the most

[1] His father, Major John Hanbury, of Pontypool, was the head of that branch of the family which had its residence in the county of Monmouthshire. One of eight brothers, Charles became heir to the fortune left him by his godfather, Charles Williams, of Carleon, an old friend of his father, and adopted his name. For further details of Sir Charles's life we may refer our readers to his *Life*, which will be published during the next few months, by the editors of this volume.

[2] These were published in three volumes in 1822, after several previous editions in a smaller form.

of it. In 1747 he entered diplomacy[1] as Minister to the court of Saxony at Dresden, where he knew how to make use of his social talents and his power of observation. He had the gift of interpreting most diverse characters, and of profiting in the course of a negotiation by the weak spots in his adversaries. His despatches were written in a style both brilliant and forcible; he excelled in the art of writing "portraits," and those which he made of the best-known people showed great resemblance. In his letters to his friends, he described, as an astute observer, the minutest events of life abroad.

After some years at the court of Saxony, Williams passed on as Minister, in 1750, to that of Berlin; but his sharp tongue and his caustic remarks displeased King Frederick. The Prussian Government asked for his recall, and in 1751 Williams was again transferred to Dresden. During Sir Charles Hanbury-Williams's prolonged stay at the court of the Elector of Saxony, Augustus III, who was also King of Poland, Williams went on several occasions to Warsaw, where, after becoming friendly with the family of the Czartoryski Princes and their brother-in-law, Count Stanislas Poniatowski, Castellan of Cracow, he took under his protection the latter's young son, Stanislas-Augustus.[2] When Sir Charles was appointed, in 1755, British Ambassador to the Imperial court of Russia, he proposed to Count Stanislas-Augustus, who, at the age of twenty-three, had received from the King the post of Stolnik of the Grand-Duchy of Lithuania, to accompany him to Russia as secretary of embassy. This proposal was accepted by the young Count, who arrived at St Petersburg at the end of June, 1755, when Williams had already been received, on June 12th, in solemn audience by the Empress Elizabeth Petrovna.[3]

[1] After the death of his close friend and companion, Thomas Winnington, in 1746, Williams felt that life in England had temporarily no pleasures for him, and sought employment abroad.

[2] This is not accurate. Sir Charles first met young Poniatowski in Berlin, soon after his arrival there as Minister in 1750.

[3] During his stay in St Petersburg, Poniatowski lived with Williams in the house of Count Scavronski, which the British Embassy occupied on the Quai de la Neva. On its site now stands the house of the Ratkov-Roshnov, facing the Marble Palace.—G.

L'Hôpital, the French Ambassador, mentioned that he took over Sir Charles's house on his departure. He spoke of it as belonging to the

Williams took an active part at the Imperial court in all the events which preceded the Seven Years War. George II, King of England, and at the same time Elector of Hanover, with a view to the defence of his German possessions against the attack of Frederick II, King of Prussia, had instructed Sir Charles to conclude a treaty with Russia to secure this. Williams quickly adapted himself to the court life of St Petersburg, and succeeded in a short time in carrying out the orders of his Master. A treaty was signed as early as September 19/30, by which Russia, in return for an annual subsidy of £500,000 sterling, undertook to equip a corps of troops of 55,000 men, for the defence of the possessions of George II in Hanover. In the letters which we publish, the first payment of this subsidy is frequently mentioned, because of the £100,000 which the Imperial court obstinately refused to touch.[1]

The ease with which Williams obtained this first success turned his head. He over-confidently imagined that he had gained enough influence over the Grand-Ducal court and the Great Chancellor Bestuzhev, to direct by their means the politics of the Empire in the sense most favourable for English interests. But his triumph was of short duration. It faded as quickly as it had arisen, and in the struggle which Williams had to maintain against a series of disappointments, he began to drift: and at the end of his sojourn was attacked by a mental illness, which later carried him off.[2]

The first thing which caused him to get out of his depth at the Russian court was the news of the alliance which the King of Prussia had contracted with the King of England, at the very moment when the latter had just prevailed on Russia to guarantee the protection of his Hanoverian possessions against any possible attack by the King of Prussia. On January 16th, 1756, the

Prince de Cautemir, and said that he was paying 3,000 roubles a year for it. (*Archives des Affaires Etrangères*. Paris. *Russie*. September 15, 1757.)

[1] This account of the treaty is somewhat misleading. £500,000 per annum was to be paid from the time of the first movement of the troops. But besides this, England contracted to pay four annual subsidies of £100,000, the first payment of which was due upon ratification. This was to continue until the larger payment came into force.

[2] Sir Charles's maladies before leaving Russia were far more physical than mental.

Treaty of Westminster was signed in London, by which treaty Frederick II and George II concluded a mutual guarantee of their possessions, and made a reciprocal arrangement to defend their territories in Germany against any incursion of foreign troops. This treaty was aimed, on the one side, at Russia; on the other, at France, who had at that time drawn nearer to Austria in order to defend herself against Prussia, and concluded with the court of Vienna, some little time after, on May 1st, 1756, the Treaty of Versailles, which was renewed a year later. Williams vainly exerted himself to secure the extension of the guarantee, provided by the treaty of September 19/30, 1755, and promised by Russia with regard to the possessions of King George II in Hanover, to the defence of that territory against an incursion of French troops, now that the danger of an attack directed against Hanover was no longer to be feared from the King of Prussia.[1] Williams in vain proposed to pay the £100,000 sterling, as a first payment of the subsidy which the King of England had bound himself to pay for the guarantee of his possessions in Germany. This guarantee against France Williams could not obtain, nor could he induce them to touch the £100,000 sterling which he offered.

Once allied to the King of England, Frederick II found at the court of St Petersburg a zealous defender of the interests of Prussia in the person of Sir Charles. The King of Prussia entrusted him with secret commissions, and especially with substantial sums for the Great Chancellor Bestuzhev. He held aloft, to use Williams's own words, the gilded pill to the Great Chancellor, who had the eye of an eagle for those sort of things. But what raised his value most of all in the estimation of Frederick II, was Williams's intimacy with the Grand-Duke, and, above all, with the Grand-Duchess.

Having quickly acquired friendly connections at the court and a knowledge of the general position of affairs, Williams centred his attentions principally on Catherine Alexéievna. By her

[1] This may have been the Russian view of the convention, but it is hardly in keeping with its actual terms, as laid down in Sir Charles's despatches in the Record Office. (See *Life*.) The Russian Minister did indeed seek after ratification to limit the general scope of the clause by a Declaration, but the British Government refused to accept it.

talent, her pleasant disposition and her good inclinations towards England, this charming princess of twenty-six succeeded in captivating the Ambassador, who, notwithstanding his ripe age[1] and blasé manner, was a man of strong passions, capable of allowing himself to be led on. She found in him a gentleman with perfect manners, highly cultured, a diplomat, trained to business and all kinds of intrigues, an agreeable conversationalist, and an assiduous courtier.

In his despatches Williams wrote that, owing to the failing health of the Empress, the throne of Russia might soon become vacant, and that, as the Grand-Duke Peter, who would succeed, was incapable of reigning, the reins of government would pass into the hands of Catherine. For this reason, Sir Charles made every effort to gain the complete confidence of the Grand-Duchess, and to acquire unlimited influence over her political views. At this moment the court of Versailles had undertaken certain steps to secure the re-establishment of diplomatic relations with that of St Petersburg, which had been interrupted since the year 1747. On October 4th, 1755, there arrived at St Petersburg a Scotsman, Mackenzie Douglas, as agent for the secret diplomacy of Louis XV. The Empress Elizabeth, herself, was favourably inclined to France ; and in full sympathy with her wishes for a reconciliation were the favourite, Ivan Schuvalov, and the Vice-Chancellor, Count Michael Voronzov. The Great Chancellor Count Bestuzhev, however, was looked upon as belonging to the party which favoured the alliance with England. On his side was the Grand-Duchess, while the Grand-Duke never concealed his goodwill towards the King of Prussia.

The task of the English Ambassador was to frustrate the success of the designs of the court of Versailles, and to maintain the alliance between Russia and England. With this aim in view, he set to work to influence the Grand-Duchess, by reminding her of the intrigues of the Marquis de la Chétardie, the former French Ambassador, and by inspiring in her a fear of her future in the event of a closer union with the court of Versailles, after the renewal of diplomatic relations with France and the arrival of her representative. Williams cited as proof of his assertions the

[1] He was but forty-six.

B

example of Sweden, where the French Ambassador upheld the
party who was acting against King Adolphus Frederick, the
Grand-Duchess's uncle. At the same time, Sir Charles pointed
out all the advantages which Russia would receive from the
alliance with the King of England, who was ready to second the
views of the Grand-Duchess, and who through his intervention
had lent her sums of money. When George II became the ally of
Frederick, Williams set himself up as champion of the latter's
interest at the Imperial court, and was commissioned by him to
propose to Elizabeth Petrovna that she should arbitrate between
the King of Prussia and the Empress-Queen Maria Theresa.

While employed in moulding the ideas of the Grand-Duchess
upon the general political situation in Europe, Williams advised
her on questions which concerned the private affairs of the
Princess and her husband. Catherine asked for the assistance
of the Ambassador in the negotiations with the King of Denmark
for the exchange of Holstein for the Duchy of Oldenburg.[1]
The Grand-Duchess took no step in her relations with the members
of the Empress's court, and during the struggle which she maintained with them in order to defend herself against their plots
and intrigues, without taking his advice and strengthening
herself with his counsels.

Williams's designs were greatly furthered by the liaison which,
under his auspices, was growing up between Catherine and his
pupil, Count Poniatowski, secretary of his embassy, who lived
with him.

Williams was not the only man who looked upon the Grand-
Duchess in the light of the future regent of the Empire and consequently set to work to acquire her favour. The Great Chancellor,
Count Bestuzhev-Riumin, the only man of those in power at the
time who was endowed by nature with the capacity of a states-
man, of strong character but artful and greedy, had fallen,
even earlier than Williams, under the charm of Catherine's
intellect and of her extraordinary talents. Like Sir Charles, he
looked upon her as the future sovereign, and for some time before

---

[1] The Grand-Duke Peter's father was Charles Frederick, Duke of
Holstein-Gottorp, who had married Anne, elder sister of the Empress
Elizabeth, both daughters of Peter the Great. The Duke died in 1739.

his advent had enjoyed her full confidence. But by then the position of Bestuzhev at the court had become precarious. A supporter of the alliance between Austria and England, he had been forced little by little, to yield, through a feeling of self-preservation, to the current of thought led by the Vice-Chancellor Voronzov and Ivan Schuvalov, one which was favoured as well by the Empress Elizabeth. This current led to the alliance with France and the rupture with England. Having lost ground and being in continual dread of losing his position, Bestuzhev was in no position to offer Catherine the solid support which she needed to thwart the court intrigues, which encircled her like a net now that the Empress was constantly ill, and which threatened the Grand-Duke, and the Grand-Duchess as well, and even their son, with the loss of their right of succession to the throne.

Catherine's only devoted and faithful assistant was Williams. He alone desired her success without ulterior motive, both as a devoted friend and as the ambassador of a Power who was interested in securing the future Empress as an ally of her sovereign. Williams, besides, was in a position as intermediary to procure for Catherine pecuniary resources, which she had need of for the success of her enterprise. At the same time he could give a guarantee of the future of the friendly relations of England and Prussia, which were necessary for the Grand-Duchess's cause, in order to counterbalance the evil intentions of the Cabinets of Vienna and Versailles towards the Grand-Duke and the Grand-Duchess, the avowed opponents of the Franco-Austrian party of the Schuvalov.

The feeling which Catherine inspired in Bestuzhev and Williams inevitably aroused hostility between them. One became jealous of the other, first, on account of the influence to which the Grand-Duchess had succumbed, and shortly afterwards on account of the favour which she showed. Bestuzhev could not hide from himself all the advantages of his adversary's position, who had profited by the intercourse between his pupil Poniatowski and the Grand-Duchess to draw still nearer to her. May not the Chancellor also have been afraid that he might be entirely set aside by Williams, who would remain in sole possession of the

Grand-Duchess's favour and her unlimited confidence ? From another point of view, he might apprehend that the relations between Catherine and the Ambassador might prove a matter of suspicion to the Empress Elizabeth, whose affection for the wife of her nephew had never been very marked. Bestuzhev knew full well that the Grand-Duchess was surrounded by spies, and that many people were to be found only too ready to do her harm with the Empress. Lastly, suspicions might be awakened about himself, from the fact that the Grand-Duchess had often required him to communicate to her secret diplomatic documents. Influenced as much by the feelings of hatred and for his personal safety as by anxiety for the Grand-Duchess, Bestuzhev, as early as the month of January, 1756, embarked on a campaign to persuade the English Ministry to recall this dangerous rival. When this intrigue failed, Bestuzhev found another means of weakening Williams's power by removing from him Poniatowski, who, by his interference in business and by his winning qualities, was beginning to inspire envy and distrust in Elizabeth Petrovna's entourage. Poniatowski was to go away.[1] In her despair the Grand-Duchess found her only consolation in Williams's promise that her friend should return as the representative of his sovereign. Some means were necessary to establish constant communication between Catherine and Count Poniatowski on his departure. The Grand-Duchess found no other alternative but to apply to the Great Chancellor himself for his assistance. She believed him, notwithstanding his insincerity, to be still devoted to her ; and he, even in the opinion of Williams, was alone in a position to insist upon the return of Poniatowski to St Petersburg as representative of the King of Poland. It was for this reason that Bestuzhev was let into the secret of the correspondence between Catherine and Count Stanislas-Augustus.[2] In promising to do what was requested of him, Bestuzhev had

[1] Sir Charles's papers and Poniatowski's autobiography clearly bring out the fact that the latter returned to Poland at the desire of his parents, to seek re-election to the Diet.

[2] A further reason was the fact that Bestuzhev, ignorant of Catherine's growing penchant for Poniatowski, had been searching in vain for someone to replace her former lover Saltikov in her affections, and was on the point of recalling him from Hamburg, whither he had been sent as Minister.

his own personal interests in view. He felt that his position was much shaken by the intrigues of the Schuvalov and the Vice-Chancellor, the champions of the reconciliation with France. He had to strengthen his position and to secure for himself in the future the favour of the Grand-Duchess. For the moment, therefore, no alternative remained open to him but to promise his assistance in everything which Catherine desired, and at least to pretend to be on good terms with Williams. We may presume that in conforming to the desire of the Grand-Duchess, Bestuzhev took into consideration the fact that the absence of Poniatowski, which might last a long time, would weaken Catherine's affection for him. The Great Chancellor promised everything, and relied upon time and circumstances to show him what advantage he could draw from it for his own interests. As a matter of fact, after delivering Catherine's first letter to Poniatowski, he refused, on various pretexts, to forward subsequent ones ; so that, notwith-standing his promise to insist upon the return of Poniatowski to St Petersburg, Bestuzhev raised all sorts of difficulties to obstruct its realization. Yet, the stronger his resistance by delays and stratagems, the more obstinate became Catherine in insisting upon and demanding the fulfilment of his promises. She achieved her ends, thanks to her perseverance and to the help of Williams, with whom Catherine kept up an uninterrupted correspondence, which began with the departure of Poniatowski, and continued throughout his absence and a little longer.

Williams arranged for the transport of his letters to the Grand-Duchess by the agency of a certain Swallov, subsequently English Consul at St Petersburg. Swallov had been successful in gaining the confidence of the Grand-Duke through his personal attendant, Bressan. Swallov was a protégé of the Ambassador and of Baron Wolff, the resident Minister of England at the court of St Petersburg, and acted as go-between for the Grand-Duke : and had, in this way, free entrance to his palaces in St Petersburg and at Oranienbaum. The Grand-Duchess gave him her letters either herself or by Leon Alexandrovitch Naruishkin, her gentleman-in-waiting. Swallov took them himself to Williams, or sent them by his valet, who received the Ambassador's replies. Not-withstanding all these precautions, Bestuzhev got wind of this correspondence, and spoke of it to Williams, who denied the Chancellor's assertions with great pertinacity. Although this correspondence still continued after the arrival of Poniatowski at St Petersburg, it cooled off by degrees. Many letters belonging to this period have not come down to us ; the interest which brought it into life, it seemed, no longer existed. Catherine herself had not the same necessity for the advice of Sir Charles ; and he, having failed in his negotiations with the two Chancellors, who evaded all his efforts to bring them over to his side, was obliged to own to himself that he had been deceived by them. He fell ill from despair, and asked for his recall, which was granted.

His departure took place under such curious circumstances that his contemporaries plainly showed their astonishment. For a long time he could not make up his mind what route he should take on leaving Russia ; at one moment he wanted to make a start by Poland, at another by Sweden, and after having gone several stages into Finland returned, saying that his horses were bad and had broken down. He then decided to board an English ship at Cronstadt, but again obtained horses to pass through Finland and Sweden. Owing to all these astonishing delays, Williams allowed the fine weather to slip by, and when he embarked at Cronstadt at the end of October or beginning of November, 1757, he met with a bad passage to Hamburg, where he fell ill.[1] He was taken in a demented condition to England, but recovered at the end of the year at his house in Monmouthshire, only to take his own life in a fit of madness on November 2nd, 1759.[2] He was buried at Westminster Abbey on November 10th of the same year.

We publish the letters of Catherine and Williams in French, with a translation into Russian, without any alteration of the text. We have thought best to retain the peculiarity which characterizes them, that they are written as if the correspondence was carried on between people of the masculine sex, though

[1] This account of Sir Charles's journey is quite incorrect. The delays are fully accounted for by a severe attack of illness at the start, and by contrary winds which prevented him from leaving Cronstadt. He finally reached Hamburg by way of Finland, Stockholm and Copenhagen.

[2] The fact of his suicide is not supported by reliable contemporary evidence.

Catherine does not always rigorously conform to this principle. The incorrect phraseology, as well as the grammatical mistakes, in the letters and the replies, have been left as they were. The dates enclosed in brackets do not appear in the original letters, but have been fixed by the sense of the letters and by other indications.

SERGE GORIAÏNOV.

The history of the original correspondence, as told above by M. Goriaïnov, commences with the fact that the letters were placed in the Archives in St Petersburg by Prince Gortschakov, the Vice-Chancellor, in 1864. No clue, however, is given to the sequence of events which led up to the return of the papers to Russia, nor can we throw light upon the subject. There can be little doubt, however, that Sir Charles removed them with him upon his departure from that country in 1757; but the course of their wanderings from that moment is shrouded in mystery. That they were brought back to England seems clear, for reference is made to them in 1824, by Miss Caroline Bowles, subsequently Robert Southey's second wife, in a letter to her future husband. She had seen the collection of letters, which she describes, at a house near Lymington in Hampshire, belonging to the Roses. There is nothing to show where the letters had been reposing all those years, or how they came to be in the hands of the Rose family.

During the Great War the late Czar spoke to Sir John Hanbury-Williams, who was Chief of the British Military Mission with the Russian Armies in the Field, about this correspondence, in which he took great interest, and told him that when the War was over he must return to Russia and have access to the manuscripts.

It may be desirable at this point to give a very brief account of the position of affairs in Russia which led up to the period of these letters.

Peter the Great had been succeeded by his second wife, who ascended the throne in 1725 as Catherine I, and died two years later. Her grandson, Peter II, died in 1730, and was followed by the Empress Anne, daughter of Peter the Great's elder brother,

Ivan V (1682-7). At her death in 1740, her great-nephew, an infant, survived for a few short months, and was then deposed by the youngest daughter of Peter the Great, Elizabeth, whose elevation to the throne was largely due to French influence. She survived until 1762, notwithstanding the illnesses of which we find such frequent mention in these pages. The chief events of her reign which are to our purpose to note were, the dismissal of the French Ambassador, La Chétardie, on account of his continual intrigues, a year after the Treaty of Abo, in 1743, between Russia and Sweden : a defensive treaty between Austria and Russia in 1746 : and the treaty between England and Russia concluded by Hanbury-Williams during the autumn of 1755, but which, as we shall see, never really came into action owing to England's subsequent treaty with Prussia in January, 1756. Elizabeth, in 1743, chose for her heir, her nephew, Duke Karl Peter of Holstein-Gottorp, who was known in future as the Grand-Duke Peter : and in the following year arranged a marriage for him with his cousin Sophia, Princess of Anhalt-Zerbst, who took the name of Catherine on entering the Greek Church. The Great Chancellor of Russia under Elizabeth was Count Alexei Bestuzhev-Riumin, whose power over his Imperial mistress had been for some time on the wane, and was considerably diminished at the period touched upon by this correspondence.

It must be recollected that, though the letters were originally written in French, one writer was a German, the other an Englishman, while Poniatowski, whose letters are now printed for the first time and were unknown to M. Goriaïnov, was a Pole. Consequently, we have throughout attempted to follow the text as closely as possible, retaining in most instances the long periods and somewhat confused phraseology which was often characteristic of the various efforts of the writers at French composition. To have eliminated these, and to have freely translated the whole in a style which might have been permissible had the authors been writing in their mother tongue, would, in our opinion, have destroyed the character of the letters. We have retained the arrangement of paragraphs as in the French text.

At Poniatowski's departure, a code was arranged between him and Sir Charles, comprising the names of various individuals who were likely to be mentioned in the course of their correspondence. A copy of this is amongst Sir Charles's papers; and it seems likely that the Grand-Duchess was also supplied with one. When these code words appear in the text, the proper name will be found inserted in round brackets.

We have retained M. Goriaïnov's sequence of the documents, except in one or two instances, where the new material at our disposal has thrown fresh light on the date of the letters in question. We have, however, relegated to the notes copies of other letters or papers, which appear in his text as enclosures sent with the original correspondence, as well as a number of letters from Poniatowski and his family. For these last we are deeply indebted to Mr T. Fitzroy Fenwick, who has most kindly allowed us to make use of the voluminous material in his possession, in the Sir Thomas Phillipps collection, now at Thirlestane House, Cheltenham, and also for his very active assistance. The bulk of Sir Charles Hanbury-Williams's correspondence and papers were purchased from various sources by Sir Thomas Phillipps, and are now reunited at Cheltenham. Their history will be fully related in a forthcoming *Life* of that wit, poet and diplomatist, prepared by the editors of the present work.

Our best thanks are also due to Miss Mabel Robinson, for her assistance in translating various complicated passages in the text; to Dr Hagberg Wright, of the London Library, for invaluable help and advice; to Mr Warner, of the Newport Public Library, where copies of the Mitchell Hanbury-Williams correspondence are to be found; to Prince Vladimir Galitzine; and to Viscount Powerscourt for so kindly allowing us to reproduce his portrait of the Grand-Duchess Catherine.

The dates of the letters are in the Old Style, unless indication is given to the contrary. Proper names follow as far as possible the forms adopted by the best-known English writers. Notes signed *G.* are those of M. Goriaïnov: the remainder have been inserted by the present editors.

From Sir Charles Hanbury-Williams

Wednesday [*July* 31, 1756].

Monsieur,

As it is my duty to inform your Excellency of all that comes to my knowledge on the affairs of Europe, and as I shall always take pleasure in proving to you my inviolable and everlasting devotion, I take the liberty of telling you that I have received a courier with orders to inform this court, on behalf of the King, my Master, that the King of Prussia has declared to him, that the armed preparations which he has been making in his dominions were only intended to insure his own security and that of his dominions,[1] and that, so far from thinking of taking offensive action against Russia, His Prussian Majesty is very anxious to enter into most friendly relations with Her Majesty the Empress, in conjunction with the King, my Master. These are the words which I am ordered to speak to this court, and it is full time that some declaration of the sort was made ; for one of the artifices which our enemies make use of at this court for maintaining a coolness between the King, my Master, and Her Imperial Majesty, is every day to retail to the Empress falsehoods against His Prussian Majesty. I shall soon take the liberty of sending your Excellency my views on the present state of affairs, and particularly upon the King of Prussia. I believe that I shall soon send off a courier, who will pass through Dantzig ; so your Excellency can write freely and with complete safety, for I shall instruct our consul to send a trustworthy man from Dantzig to Warsaw to deliver the letters with his own hand to your friend.[2] I commend myself to the continuation of your kindness and protection.

My devotion to your Excellency will end only with my life, and there is nothing in the world that I am not ready to undertake for your service.

[1] Frederick shortly afterwards proceeded to forestall the plans of Austria, and launched his attack upon her through Saxon territories.

[2] Stanislas Poniatowski. He had left St Petersburg a week or so earlier.

From Sir Charles Hanbury-Williams

Friday, August 2.

I yesterday received the enclosed from Poniatowski, and send it you, as I believe that the perusal of it will give you pleasure. I beg you to send me word of any news which may reach you.

From the Grand-Duchess

[*Saturday, August 3.*]

It is a sort of comfort to me to be able to write to you, who esteem our absent friend as much as I do and wish him well. Here are two pieces of news for you, which are better than nothing. The friendship which you have shown leaves me in no doubt that you will continue to give me your counsel, which has been so useful to me up to now. My gratitude for it will end only with life. I feel more than ever also the need of advice as sound as yours, for the disagreeable situation in which I have been for the last eight days makes reflection difficult. This is how matters stand. B. (Betski)[1] who had come to take leave at M.,[2] accompanied by Prince and Princess Troubetskoï, brought P. (Peter Schuvalov),[3] in the course of a conversation on many other subjects, in a roundabout way into the discussion, and said how much annoyance he, Peter, had expressed to him at the manner in which he had been blackened in my sight: that he had only tried to help me, that he had thereby sometimes even done

[1] Ivan Betski had been a lord of the Bedchamber to the Grand-Duke since his marriage. He was an illegitimate son of the celebrated Marshal Troubetzkoï by a Swedish lady. The Grand-Duchess mentions in her *Autobiography* that Betski had arrived at Oranienbaum shortly before leaving Russia for foreign parts. She speaks of him as accompanied by Prince and Princess Galitzin. The Princess was daughter of the Princess of Hesse-Homburg, née Troubetzkoï. The Prince Troubetzkoï mentioned in the text, was Nicetas, his half-brother.

[2] Mourzinski, the country house of Alexei Razumowski, where the Empress was staying.

[3] Peter Schuvalov, general in the army and financier, brother of Alexander Schuvalov, the Grand Inquisitor and governor of the Grand-Ducal establishment. Ivan Ivanovitch Schuvalov, the Empress's favourite at this period, was their cousin.

himself harm, but that there had been many occasions on which
he dared not do so : that if his relations failed me, it was without
his knowledge, and that he hated the greatest of his relations
and his wife[1] as much and more than I did.   I only replied with
smiles and questions, to which answers could not but give the lie
to the apologies that P. had attempted.   When he saw that
I was little moved by what he said, he threw himself at my feet,
and begged me, if I believed him to be an honest man, never to
believe that P., whom he protested was his intimate friend, had
failed me.   He entreated me to rid myself of the bad opinion
which I had formed of the man whom he was justifying, and
entered into details of several things that he had done, which
are too long to repeat.   Bored with this scene, and astonished
to see it played in this theatrical manner, I said to him : " In
order to do you a good turn, I will let P. know that you have
spoken to me, and all that you have done for him.   He knows
that I have always had a regard for you, and will not fail to
think that you have made an impression on me.   By that I
shall kill two birds with one stone.   I shall help you and myself
as well."

On Tuesday morning I was scarcely up, when I saw B. (Betski)
taking a walk under my windows.   I made him come up.   He
repeated what he had said on the previous day, and begged me
earnestly to look favourably upon the ruling family.   At last
I bethought myself of telling him what no doubt our absent
friend[2] had communicated to us, and what I had intended to
propose to them through the General Minouci (the Hetman, Count
Cyril Rasumowski), that, if they were willing to assist me,
without knavery or bad faith, in the manner and at the time
I should ask, I would try to alter many things which I knew were
disagreeable to l'électeur (Peter Schuvalov),[3] and would arrange
everything in such a way that he would be satisfied now and in
the future : that I hoped that their relation[4] would ask and follow

[1] Alexander Schuvalov.

[2] Poniatowski.

[3] A code of words had been arranged at Poniatowski's departure between him and Sir Charles.   Catherine seems also to have had a copy.

[4] Ivan Ivanovitch Schuvalov, the Empress's favourite, at this time
26 years of age.   He had been at one time page to the Grand-Duchess,

my advice, and would help me with everything whenever I desired it; and that these services would be their guarantee for the future. He put that in writing, and told me that when he went away he would call at *Nymphenbourg* (Tsarskoïe Selo), and that he would make use of it. These are only words, which will have little or no results. I have paid them, I think, in their own coin.

When speaking of other subjects, B. asked me what book I was reading, and hearing that it was a history of the secret intrigues of France, he said to me, " England's story does not in the least fall short of it," and promised to send it to me, which he has done. Then, speaking of the affairs of Sweden, I flew into a passion and said that it was shameful of Russia to allow a French Ambassador to dethrone a King whom she had set up. He agreed. After some time had elapsed, I asked him whether it was true that his travelling companion was going to France.[1] He assured me that he knew nothing of it, but thought it was desirable that harmony should be re-established; for, said he, the arts and sciences are more necessary to us than anything else. But how, I replied, would an Ambassador help towards this, will he give public lectures ? His answer was, " The French, if assured of protection, would establish themselves here and would cultivate the arts and sciences. To introduce these the Ambassador would be useful." " That is all very fine," said I. " If the advantage is not great on the exchange of goods, we shall anyhow have bales of wit to our credit." He answered that one need not always have money nor be led by self-interest. I contented myself with replying, " Our dandies will profit most ; they will have someone to set the fashions for them." He began to laugh, and said, " I am a bad politician." I changed the conversation, and made him talk gardening, and I shall follow his advice on that subject with pleasure and with more profit, I think, than on the preceding one. All this goes to prove what bad reasoning is made use of, apparently as better than nothing, by those who are imbued with it.

who by her kindly treatment seems to have laid the foundation for the high favour which he was then enjoying.

[1] M. Goriaïnov's Russian index speaks of Betski's travelling companion as being the celebrated Chevalier d'Eon, who was in Russia at this time.

To come to the second point.   You will, I think, have heard of
G. (Glebov),[1] the favourite chosen by P. to arrange his introduction to me.   I had hardly arrived in town when he sent me
back two letters, which I had written to his late wife during the
period when she was falling in love with him, and in which he and
his protector were drawn from life.   The public utterances of
the latter vouched for the character of his protégé.   Attached
to them was a very long letter on a folio sheet in very minute
handwriting, in which he strives to convince me, by his eloquence,
talent and good style, of his devotion to me ; and he ends by
saying, that all the evil designs of his protector, very far from
finding a seconder in him, will only serve to prove to me the
candour and sincerity of his conduct in the end.   In addition,
he swore to all this solemnly.   I sent him thanks by word of
mouth for having returned my letters.

I will write down in future anything which appears to me worthy
of your attention, believing that I have no friend more faithful,
more sincere, and at the same time more enlightened than you.
A certain person's health[2] is in a worse condition than ever ; and
I think that she will attend her devotions on Tuesday next.   I
have just received the letter which you sent me ; it gave me the
very greatest pleasure.   In answer to those which you have
written about the orders that you have received to announce
the sentiments of His Prussian Majesty towards this court, I will
tell you the good news that a motion was brought forward and
unanimously approved at the conference held yesterday, to
guarantee the defence of Hanover, and to publish it abroad.   It
has not yet, however, been committed to paper, and it still lacks
the final approval of the Empress.   This is news which reaches
me from the Chancellor.   The suggestion was made by him, and
the others agreed.   The future will show what it is worth.   I
am going to make every effort to remain in town.   The story
goes that her head doctor wishes to leave in three months' time,
as the prospect does not appear to him any laughing matter.

---

[1] Alexander Glebov, General Attorney of the Senate.   Catherine speaks
of him at the time of the Empress's death as a rascal and one of Peter
Shuvalov's minions.

[2] The Empress.

During her stay at M., she tried witchcraft without his knowledge to cure herself ; and an old woman, who was employed, has, it is said, succeeded in putting an end to the discomfort from which she was suffering. It is, however, quite certain, that she has water in the lower part of her belly. I hope to have the pleasure of seeing you to-morrow. I write this, six o'clock on Saturday evening.

From Sir Charles Hanbury-Williams

[Sunday, August 4.]

What do you wish for, Monsieur, in reply to your letter ? Do you wish for protestations, assurances, and even oaths, or do you prefer a frank, sincere, and straightforward answer, the advice of a humble, faithful and disinterested friend—in short, a continuation of my past conduct towards you ?

My devotion to you, Monsieur, has no limits, save that of a higher duty. That is how the faithful Minister should speak. The private individual may speak differently : my services, my life, as a private individual, are yours to command.

These are preliminaries ; and I do not like such things. Rely on it that this is the last time that you shall be troubled with anything of the kind. Betski's plot was transparent ; but I defy a man of the world to have answered him better than you have done. The account of your conversation has enchanted me. Your answers were worthy of the good sense of Richelieu and the genius of Molière. You ask for my advice, and I shall obey you ; but remember that though I am loyal and sincere, I have not your knowledge of this country.

It is certain that to rule, one must create divisions. If you can separate Ivan Ivanovitch from Peter Schuvalov, their party would be the weaker, and you the stronger. But the danger of acting with such people is ever before my eyes ; and what foundation can be built upon unmistakable bad faith? Continue, therefore, Monsieur, to listen to all their proposals, but let your answers be ever polite and indefinite. It appears to me that this mission of Betski is a last effort, and proves very clearly the danger of his patron from the ill-health of another. It is true that Betski is not a great politician; but he and his travelling companion are fully convinced that their astuteness is worth more than genius, and that their tricks take precedence over good sense. All that you said, Monsieur, upon the introduction of the arts and sciences on the heels of the French Ambassador is admirable. I know of no dish so agreeable as good sense seasoned by ridicule, when a conceited ignoramus or false confidence produce such fare. Monsieur Betski, retired into private life, a philosopher, a man of culture and of letters, and one who never meddles in business, plunges headlong into matters of the greatest importance, enters the closets of princes, and sways Europe.

These are the words and actions of the Jesuit. I have been told that that order was banished from Russia; but I own to you, Monsieur, that I find many people who resemble them very closely indeed, except that they have neither their knowledge nor their intellect. I am delighted, it is true, to see the masterly way in which you fathom their artifices and despise their weakness. My advice to you on the whole Betski affair is to sit quiet, to let them come to you without ever giving any decided answer, and one day to appoint Betski Grand Master of your gardens, but never to let him inside your house. He will arrange a flower-bed much better than a plan, and will produce a drawing better than a scheme. Experience counts for everything in business—that is what gives knowledge; thus an adviser and a doctor without practice will only make a mess of things and murder patients.

I was enchanted with the story of Glebov, and still more by the manner in which you have recounted it. There again is the plan of a false knave, badly thought out and still worse executed. The man offers to help you against his patron. If he was in earnest, he would be a rascal; but as we know that it is untrue, because his patron who drew up the plan has certainly seen the letter, he is only a liar. I do not know if there is much spirit in his epistle, but I am sure that there is no good sense in it, because there is no truth.

I am very credibly informed that Glebov has already whispered to people, who have repeated it to me, that he had written to you, and that he had sent you some papers for which you had asked him. It seems to me that he had better not have boasted

c

so soon of his fine scheme, because I do not believe that he is as certain of what he says as he or his patron imagine.

You did very well not to answer his letter, for, as he has begun by deceiving you, he will end in the same way. You can nevertheless listen to him, but it is not worth while trying to humour him in any way, because you will only get lies out of him.

I have noticed something, which I am going to put to you. It appears to me that all the kindness which you have shown to the Schuvalov has never produced any good, and has only helped to increase their vanity and their pride. Minds of a very low order are ruled by fear alone ; and, rely upon it, you only owe Betski's last mission to the dangerous state of the health of another. This then is my advice on the two points mentioned in your letter. But to tell the truth, neither your words nor your actions require advice.

All that I could tell you about Prussian affairs would at present be premature, but in ten days I shall tell you a deal about them. How can I thank you for the news of the resolution passed at Friday's conference ! The Grand Chancellor had already sent me word that all was going perfectly well ; but I knew no details. The Vice-Chancellor[1] said many things about me, amongst others that the King of Prussia was so annoyed with me that he would ask my court to recall me. You will soon judge if this be true, because this secret will be in your hand and never in those of any-one else. He complains that I have received two couriers without informing this court of the contents of our despatches. He is a poor creature. Is it possible to inform this court of anything, without it becoming known to the Vice-Chancellor ? And does he think that the confidant of M. Douglas[2] will have my confidence ? The two Chancellors and I sometimes act as a triumvirate, and I raise no objection to the Grand Chancellor being Augustus, but I desire at least to be Antony, and during my stay here, Monsieur, the Vice-Chancellor shall only be Lepidus.

---

[1] Count Michael Voronzov. He had spent some months in Berlin in 1745 and 1746, and became on friendly terms with King Frederick, who was said to have paid his expenses in the country.

[2] Mackenzie Douglas arrived for a short period in 1755 as secret agent of the French. He returned in April, 1756, with proper credentials, and was now in the position of *chargé d'affaires*.

Thank God, the bad weather to-day will prevent any thought of your return to the country. I am entirely of your opinion, Monsieur, that your presence in town is very necessary. All that you have told me about the illness of a certain person agrees exactly with everything which reaches me from various quarters.

She offers up her prayers to-morrow, but how can devotions and witchcraft work side by side? There is short shrift for those who have water in the belly; and I know at first hand that the cough is returned, with great shortness of breath. I was assured yesterday evening that the Empress is seriously annoyed with Peter Schuvalov, on account of a feast which he recently gave to some peasants, on the occasion of a festival or the consecration of a church, and that she flew at him in the presence of one of our friends.

I was very vexed to hear that the Grand-Duke has been angry with Naruishkin.[1] I like Naruishkin very much indeed, and implore him to humour his Imperial Highness, and to allow the Holsteiners to speak their bad French with impunity.

Truly, I am ashamed, Monsieur, of the conduct of this court towards the King of Sweden; and, believe me, the abandonment of this Prince, in the way in which it is being done here, will give a very bad impression of the court of Russia throughout Europe.[2]

I implore you to tell me everything that you hear about the

[1] See *Introduction*, p. 22.

[2] In 1743, Prince Adolf Frederick of Holstein-Gottorp, at that time Prince Bishop of Lübeck, a nephew of King Charles XII of Sweden, was elected Crown-Prince of that country, and successor to the reigning king, Frederick I, by the influence of the Empress Elizabeth of Russia. Indeed, his election was one of the conditions of the peace of Abo, between Sweden and Russia. Adolf Frederick was uncle of the Grand-Duchess and great-uncle of the Grand-Duke. He ascended the throne in 1751, having married Louise Ulrica, a sister of Frederick, King of Prussia, who was as brilliant and domineering as her husband was weak and easy-going. Notwithstanding his obligations to Russia, he came under the influence of the pro-French party, at that time in power, but shortly after his accession, spurred on by the Queen, he quarrelled with his Council. So strained did their relations finally become, and so active a part did the Queen take in public affairs, that she tried to make the court masters of the situation by arresting the Government. The plot, however, was discovered, and Count Brahé and other conspirators were executed. The Queen was tried for her share in the attempt and was severely rebuked by the judges, while the King was forced to sign an Act, which reduced his power to a mere semblance of monarchy.

health of a certain person.   There is nothing in the world which interests me so much.   I realise all that I owe you ; and my gratitude knows no bounds.

It is a fact that the Empress has sent a snuff-box worth 4,000 roubles to Poniatowski.

After the resolution of the conference on Friday, the arrival of a French Ambassador at this court will not do me much harm, but I always fear for you.   His arrival is the one thing most fatal for your interests.   Think this over, and send me your reflections. I will then send you mine as to the best means of parrying this thrust.

From THE GRAND-DUCHESS

Monday [August 5], 4 o'clock in the afternoon.

Betski brought me yesterday the answer to my proposals, made through him.   The person to whom they were addressed almost threw himself at his feet, and said that to tell him that I wished to renew my intercourse with him and his relatives, was to restore him to life ; he gave assurances that they will consult with me on everything which happens and that they would inform *le notre* (Alexander Schuvalov) of the confidence which they intended to place in me.   There's something to talk about !

Another achievement !   When Alexander Schuvalov brought a memorandum to be signed by the Grand-Duke, in which the exchange of embassies with France was said to be necessary in the present condition of affairs, the Grand-Duke flatly refused, and based his refusal on the present French intrigues in Sweden, " which are openly conflicting with my interests (he added), both as Grand-Duke and as a good kinsman to the King of Sweden." " I am not sufficiently pleased either with the Vice-Chancellor," he said, " or with Douglas, with whose plots I am fully conversant, to grant them this pleasure."

Alexander Schuvalov tried to persuade him, but he answered, " How long is it since your brother Peter changed his tactics ? He maintained in my presence that an alliance with France must not be allowed.   In a word, I will not be forced.   I will not sign what in my conscience I know to be wrong."   They tried to point out to him that matters were already under negotiation, and that they were too far advanced to be withdrawn. " So much the worse," he answered, " if my opinion is asked after a thing is done, I refuse to sign." I bade Bernardi[1] tell you all this. I do not know if he will have given you the true story ; he assured me that he had dined at your house, and that he was returning there immediately. I gave him a tiny note for the Chancellor, containing just a few lines in Russian. "My friend has refused to sign the *doklade* for the exchange of embassies with France : the present intrigues in Sweden have provided him with the excuse. I beg you, in the event of the death of the Great General of Poland, Branicki, to promote to the office of Little General, the Great Chamberlain Poniatowski[2] and to recommend him at once. I have still to ask you how the guarantee of Hanover stands. Is it in the same *doklade* as the French business ? "

I practically wrote this note in Bernardi's presence, and told him that haste was the excuse for its confused state. But, in reality, I am very glad to put this last point in the form of a reproach, in view of the fact that he sent me word that the guarantee was as good as settled, and instead of that out comes that cursed *doklade*. If you have any news of our absent friend, I beg you to send it to me. Is it true that he received by a messenger a present worth 4,000 roubles ? I have only to renew the assurances of that friendship which I bear you in my thoughts.

From Sir Charles Hanbury-Williams

Tuesday [August 6].

Every day, Monsieur, you give new proofs of your kindness to me! It is a fact that they did not pass a resolution at the conference

---

[1] Catherine wrote : " Bernardi was an Italian jeweller, who was not lacking in talent, and whose trade opened every house to him. I think that there was no one who did not owe him something, and for whom he had not done some little service or other. As he was continually going and coming everywhere, people gave him commissions as well for one another. A line, carried by Bernardi, would arrive quicker and more safely than by the servants."—(*Autobiography*.)

[2] Casimir, an elder brother of Stanislas-Augustus.

on Friday last to defend Hanover; and I cannot understand what object they had in giving you that information.

Bernardi told me briefly that the Grand-Duke had refused to sign the *doklade*; that was all. This morning he called here to tell me that the Schuvalov were to approach you to persuade him to sign. It appears to me that you should not be always doing the business of people who do nothing for you. If the Grand-Duke does not remain firm this time, they will not bother their heads about his signature in the future.[1] He said the right thing to Alexander Schuvalov.

I had a two hours' conference yesterday with the Great Chancellor. He owned to me that they had not passed any resolution guaranteeing Hanover; and it appears to me that they will not even take the £100,000.[2] To tell you the truth, from his manner of treating the matter, I begin to think that you are my only friend here. I shall be pleased to see his reply to the question which you put to him in your last letter on the subject of this guarantee, for I do not understand it at all. I send you an enclosure—a paper which Wolff will take to him from me to-morrow morning, and which will explain to you the whole of my present difficulties. I own that what happened yesterday makes me more than ever afraid of the arrival of a French Ambassador; for amongst other things, I have been begged to live on a better footing with the Vice-Chancellor. What can he mean by that?

The moment that I have any news of my friend I will send it to you. But I do not think that I shall receive any before Saturday.

The Great Chancellor assures me that I shall soon have a conference with him and the Vice-Chancellor about the answer which is being prepared for my court. But alas! I foresee that the answer will be vague and in no way conclusive. I will send it to you the moment that I receive it. I cannot imagine why the Schuvalov are so anxious for the arrival of this Ambassador. There must be some mystery in it, some hidden design, and perhaps a secret known to that family alone. You would do well

---

[1] This was exactly what did happen.   See p. 201.
[2] See *Introduction*, p. 15.

to tell the Hetman[1] to extract all he can about this matter from the Vice-Chancellor, for they are on very good terms.   But I do not believe that the Vice-Chancellor knows the whole secret, and I should much like to know on what footing he is with the Schuvalov.

The Chancellor confided to me last night the proposition regarding England.   He wished to begin by the renewal of the ancient alliance between the two Crowns, to be followed by a new treaty between the Empress and the Elector of Hanover on the same footing as that with Saxony.   After that, he would like England to declare the price which she is willing to pay for Russian troops, when she requires them.   These matters should not be difficult to arrange ; but it all means time, and the present time brooks no delay.

I shall explain all this better to you, when I have had my conference.   My paper is at an end   My gratitude to you, Monsieur, will never end.

From THE GRAND-DUCHESS

Thursday [August 8].

I am ashamed to write to you after reading your letter.   It is not very astonishing that the King, your Master, should give his attention, when all that he has to read is as agreeable as it is full of good sense, wit and determination.   Either you excel all others of your nation, or you are one of the least.   If the latter is the case—a thing unbelievable, especially to me in whose estimation you stand so high—what a triumph for England, and what may she not expect !   If you are among the former class —and that is more easy to understand—what do I not owe to the providence which sent you here like a guardian angel, to unite me with you in ties of friendship?   That I know you feel for me.   You will see, if one day I wear the crown, that I shall partially

---

[1] Count Cyril Rasumowski, Hetman of little Russia, and younger brother of Alexei Rasumowski, the former lover and reputed husband of the Empress.   The Hetman had been deeply in love with Catherine, though she never realized the fact until many years later.   He was sprung from quite a humble origin, but made the most of the opportunities afforded him by his brother's position at court.

owe it to your counsels. Without you, I should have been the ward of the Great Chancellor ; over whom I believe that I have some influence. Finally, without recapitulating all my obligations to you, and without wearying you with assurances and long speeches, be assured that I feel them as I ought to do : and I thank you for the preface to your reply.

You should have received the sequel to the Betski story. I sent it to you on Tuesday by Swallov. I do not deserve the praise which your friendship lavishes on me. I see through your purpose ; you try to encourage me.

Here is something new. After Alexander Schuvalov received the Grand-Duke's refusal to sign the French paper, he appeals to me, apparently in accordance of the instructions of his cousin, founding his hopes upon my friendly proposals, and points out that the refusal to sign would vex the Empress, and that in any case the matter would be none the less settled, because the Vice-Chancellor's secretary[1] and Michel (Bestuzhev) had been in France for three months. " What ? " said I, " Do they ask you for an opinion after it is all done, and force you to sign it whatever happens ? " He replied, " The Empress can do what she pleases ; and if she gives someone secret orders, what can we say ? " " Then your opinion," I answered, " is quite useless ? " " True," he said. " What is the good then of pressing the Grand-Duke to do something which answers no good purpose ? " " To comply would be best for him." " I will speak to him about it," was my answer. He thanked me. " This is a great mark of friendship," I continued, " for I never meddle in matters of which I understand nothing and know nothing : and I am in absolute ignorance of the pros and cons of this business." He attempted to make me understand it, and pretended, in the

[1] Feodor Bekteïev, who was *chargé d'affaires* in Paris before the arrival of the Russian Ambassador, Michael Bestuzhev, in 1757. The latter was brother to the Great Chancellor, and had held diplomatic posts in Dresden and Vienna. But M. Goriaïnov appears to be mistaken in believing that the second reference in the text was to him. He seems to have been in Russia at this time. More probably that shadowy character, Michel de Rouen, the merchant who supplied the court of Versailles with information from St. Petersburg during the period when they had no Ambassador there, is here indicated. He was moving to and fro at this time. (See *Recueil des Instructions, etc., Russie, ii.* 28).

first instance, that, to guarantee the frontiers of Turkey against invasion, there must be a French Ambassador here, who, seeing himself made much of, would be in a position to prevent trouble, owing to the influence of his court with the Turks. " Yes," I said, " but they have so many internal complications of their own, that at present they are not thinking of war. I have heard it said that they never break a peace." " Poland is included in our treaty with the Turks," he replied, " and the least necessity for sending troops there might afford them a pretext." " You all take a long view," I answered, " and decide accordingly. But I, who do not understand these things, can only see one more intriguer in one more Minister." That made him laugh, and he said, " Powers which are anything but friendly place them at one another's courts, and why should we not do the same ? " He then begged me to persuade the Grand-Duke to sign. I promised to speak to him about it, and said that was all I could do, that further I promised him assistance in our domestic affairs, but that it was not expedient for me to enter into public business; and therefore in a similar situation he must not appeal to me again.

He returned Wednesday to ask me what I had accomplished. My answer was that the Grand-Duke had been offended at my magnanimity towards him [Alexander], and that I was firmly resolved to have nothing more to do with matters of which I understood nothing. When Apraksin[1] saw the Grand-Duke at the ceremony of the kissing of hands by the officers of the Preobrajenski[2] last Wednesday, he entreated him to sign, and said, " The blame for it will fall on the Great Chancellor and me." But the Grand-Duke refused. Bernardi and someone sent by Apraksin came to ask me the same thing. I have advised the Grand-Duke, and they are notified of it, to announce in public that Apraksin had implored him to sign, but to remain firm. Alexander Schuvalov muttered to me on Wednesday, " He will sign in the end, anyhow."

The Chancellor confirmed the guarantee about Hanover, but said that the *doklade* was not yet drawn up. I am going to warn

[1] Stepan Fedorovitch Apraksin (1702-58). Field-Marshal, and Commander of the army in Livonia.
[2] One of the regiments of Guards.

the Grand-Duke of the plots against the Hetman. They spoke at a conference the other day of sending him to the Ukraine. But I shall get someone to speak against it. Glebov has sent to entreat an interview, claiming to have matters of great consequence to bring forward. I replied that the only way for him was to address himself to Alexander Schuvalov : otherwise I could not see him. Your remarks on the Schuvalov are very sound. They must be treated as inferiors. What I am doing at present is only, in case the decease is very imminent, to postpone, by lesser evils, projects which might be accelerated by despair. If you do not agree with my reflections, or if you find them wanting in vigour, pray point me out surer methods.

The confidence which you clearly desire to place in me on Prussian affairs can only inspire me with the intention of fulfilling your expectations. Rumour has it that a certain Lieutenant-General Winterfeld, is in your house, sent by the King of Prussia. It is further said that he has come incognito.[1] I would welcome some apparition of this kind, were it only to counterbalance Douglas in that vile ascendancy which the Seigneur Lepidus[2] has allowed him to obtain over him. The words of a miserable creature like Douglas are not worth your attention, certainly not your belief in them. It is confidently stated that the court will return to the country in a week ; but there is little probability that the people, who, on Tuesday, for want of breath, could not go the whole way from their room to the church, can be in a condition to trudge off again to the country, and in this weather. It would be difficult to reconcile devotions with witchcraft, if thirteen years' experience had not convinced me that to disordered minds the same thing can appear as black and white at

---

[1] This story was incorrect, and no doubt came from the same source as that referred to by Sir Charles in his letter to Mitchell of August 18th, n.s. (*Frederick Political Corres.* xiii. 269). A Minister was then reported to be on his way. Some suggestion of the kind had been made at the end of July, and a council was held to discuss it in Petersburg. Since then, the matter had received further favourable consideration, and Sir Charles offered his services to forward it. Frederick, in replying to Mitchell, who had sent him on the letter, said that he would discuss arrangements with him as soon as he received final news of the attitude of the court of Vienna.

[2] Voronzov.

the same time.   Naruishkin is more in favour than ever with the Grand-Duke.   I feel indebted to you for taking an interest in the man who in all this nation is the most loyal to me.   He will in future allow anyone to mutilate the French language, who wishes to do so.   My heart aches when I think of Sweden.   My imagination is so much worked up by it that I dream of it every night. My sincere devotion to Russia, the discredit which it brings upon her, my friendship, inbred from the cradle, for the King of Sweden, all combine to cause me regrets, which increase as I realize that I am powerless to help matters.

The martyrs have caused me suffering which is renewed each time I think of them.   If you have any accounts from thence, I beg you will pass them on to me.

It is not possible to understand the present which was sent to Count Poniatowski.   I might be inclined to ask you, what does it mean ?

I look upon the arrival of a French Ambassador with great dislike, and will tell you quite plainly that my understanding is not sufficiently keen to discover the best means of avoiding the harm which he may do me.   Your reflections will decide my own.

I return your letter with regret ;   the composition is good enough to print.

From Sir Charles Hanbury-Williams

Friday, two o'clock in the afternoon [*August* 9].

I have nothing but bad news for you.   It is almost certain that instead of guaranteeing the safety of Hanover, as you were led to believe, this court will not even accept the £100,000 sterling. The French Embassy is a settled fact.   When talking this morning to my best friend here,[1] he suddenly exclaimed,   " Ah ! how I pity their Imperial Highnesses.   The arrival of the Ambassador will prove their ruin and destruction."   I begged him earnestly to explain himself, but he said that the blind alone could fail to see the reasons.   When France and Austria were united, they

[1] Baron Wolff.

would dispose of the succession as they liked.[1] In the end he said to me, " I know that you are devoted to their Highnesses. Warn them in time, tell them to persuade all their friends to ward off this thrust. I know this country. I have seen all the intrigues of Rabutin[2] and La Chétardie.[3] I am fond of the Grand-Duchess. Only enemies can put forward or commend such a proposal. She should try to win over Ivan Ivanovitch. Anyhow, she must move heaven and earth to parry this thrust." This is what my friend Wolff said to me this morning. I will try to extract more from him. Certain it is that he knows this country very well, that he is very devoted to the Grand-Duchess, and that he knows far more than he says. How could they tell you that they wished to guarantee Hanover ? I know their plan (and it is the Great Chancellor's plan), to propose a new negotiation so as to spin things out and gain time for the arrival of a French Ambassador at this court, without giving any assurance of assistance to the King of England, or even of good news from Russia. I am myself, Monsieur, so convinced of all that I have just told you, that I must absolutely change my batteries. I ask for your good judgment, your advice and your assistance. I ask for them on my knees. I must have new friends. Point them out to me. But I am very much afraid that you may also need some yourself ; for if the Chancellor is already in the hands of Austria and France, I am much afraid that he will go still further.

Perhaps my love for my Master and my devotion to you, Monsieur, help to increase my fears. But I am convinced that all I have said is true, and I am resolved never to hide the truth from you. It is also true that Wolff's words have made a serious impression on me.

Tell me frankly whether you believe that the last message which Betski brought you was to be relied upon, and whether

---

[1] It must be remembered that the Czar Ivan, deposed in his infancy when Elizabeth was placed on the throne, was still alive, imprisoned in the Castle of Schlüsselburg.

[2] Count Bussy Rabutin, Imperial Minister at the court of Russia from 1725 to 1727.

[3] Count La Chétardie (1705-58) was originally in the French Army. He was French Ambassador to Russia from 1739 to 1742, and again in 1743 and 1744, until he was expelled on account of his intrigues.

Ivan Ivanovitch would be ready to give you a proof of his wish
to deserve your favour.   If you think it feasible, send him word
that you ask him, as a proof of his devotion, to prevent the arrival
of a French Ambassador, adding that it is the thing which the
Grand-Duke has most at heart, and that he will be much obliged
to the person who will help him to parry this thrust.   But I leave
you to judge of all this.   I beseech you to answer me as soon as
possible.   From you alone I look for support and comfort.
Poor Poniatowski !   If he were here, he would be in great anxiety.

From THE GRAND-DUCHESS

Friday, August 12 [*August* 9].

Your despondency has completely infected me, and your fears
partly.   I have only one consoling thought, that for the next
three months our enemies' plans will not be sufficiently well
arranged for one single event not to upset them.[1]   You will
say, " I give her facts, and she repays me with nonsense."
That is true ; but granted also the worst of designs towards me,
what moment do you suggest for their execution ?   During the
life-time ?   You know the impossibility of strong resolutions, the
universal discontent, particularly amongst the soldiery, added to
the fear of having three or four living pretenders (a point that has
much influence with her) to whom she would prefer her relatives.
Anyhow, the little certainty which she can build on the destiny
of a child of two years old, in addition to her timorous disposition,
will, I am daring enough to hope, prove safeguards during her
life-time.   Afterwards, within two or three hours, every dirty
trick will certainly be played ; yet whether they wish to exclude us
or to tie our hands, they will not be able to do it alone.   There
are but few officers who are not in the secret ; and, provided that
my arrangements for being informed in time do not fail, and that
even only one among eight people gives me warning, it will be my
fault if they gain the upper hand.   Be assured that I shall never
play the King of Sweden's easy-going and feeble part, and that I
shall either perish or reign.   I do not, for all that, make light of
the French Ambassador's arrival.   I look upon him as an enemy,

---

[1] The Empress's death.

armed from head to foot, especially in alliance with Austria, who seems still more formidable than ever to me from the confidence they place in her, and whose support would impress the Empress. The Chancellor's dislike for Esterhazy,[1] the harm which the latter tries to do him, his own natural pride, his talent, even the welfare of his country, his hope of office, money, honour, all prevent me from believing him to be allied to or in the hands of France, or of Austria for France. I leave you to think whether he can be suspected of it, and whether even the blame which is laid at his door for the Grand-Duke's refusal to sign is not a proof in his favour. Consequently, I have no need myself of new friends. I believe that the proposals of Ivan Ivanovitch made by Betski are sincere, as far as those people can be so. They would hardly believe that one would trust them, and that makes them more suspicious. Anyhow, it may be that they have been acting more straightforwardly from fear due to the bad state of health. Naruishkin will go to Ivan Ivanovitch to-day, to tell him that it will be a proof of his devotion to the Grand-Duke if he prevents the arrival of a French Ambassador. I believe that he is too far involved to draw back, and that his answer will be, that the Empress wishes it, and that he can do nothing.

The Empress sent yesterday to ask the Grand-Duke who had dissuaded him from signing, and said that it was a matter which she had decided ; to which he replied angrily, asking if they took him for an idiot in not seeing that it was a bad business, that they must only expect intrigues here like in Sweden, and that they would never force him to play the part of a dishonest man by putting his signature to anything of which he did not approve. He added that he was not in the humour to please the Vice-Chancellor without either rhyme or reason.

As to your own affairs, I shall reply, " Make me Empress, and I will give you comfort." If you will not or cannot do that, I shall tell you that the Chancellor's advice to humour the Vice-Chancellor is not so bad. If you are still averse to so mean a course, nothing can be so needful here and so efficacious as an envoy from Prussia. He will counterbalance the infatuation

---

[1] Count Nicholas Esterhazy, the Imperial Ambassador at the Russian court.

of the Seigneur Lepidus for Douglas ; and you will have a second to fight for you, a new-comer who will attract attention, and who, as such, will be made much of and humoured.   If he has the wherewithal to grease palms, so much the better for him.   Who knows if he may not even lessen the Vice-Chancellor's ardour for the French.   If it could be arranged that the German paper,[1] which you are sending to the Chancellor, should reach the Empress, it appears to me that the reasons contained in it are convincing. Ask an answer to it.   But a truce to absurdity, for that it is for me to pretend to guide you in things which you know by heart ; it is your own fault for leading me into temptation by your requests.   I would have answered you yesterday, but it was impossible for me to do so.

You have put me off till Saturday for news of our friend. Have you any ?   His anxieties would have increased my own. You cannot think how pained I am at not being able to lessen yours, and at not giving you the comfort which you ask for and deserve.   I wrote yesterday to the Hetman for the secret of the extreme eagerness for this Embassy.   Let him extract it from the Vice-Chancellor, if he can.

From Sir Charles Hanbury-Williams

Saturday, seven o'clock in the afternoon [August 10].

I thank you, Monsieur, for your two letters.   The one which I received yesterday enchanted me.   I read it ten times over, and it is with deep regret that I return it to you.   There must always be comfort for me in your letters, for I feel a delight at opening them even before I read them.   Nothing can make up for the obligations which I owe you but my gratitude.   And alas, it is a barren gratitude, which can never produce fruit worthy of you. The Grand-Duke played his part well.   He honoured me by sending word by Swallov what he had done ; and I am very proud of this mark of his kindness and confidence.   The interview between you and Alexander Schuvalov is certainly well described in your letter.   I should have much liked to have seen your face while he was lecturing you, and when he was putting out the

---

[1] The King of Prussia's *Mémoire Raisonné.*

whole power of his intellect to prove that he had none. Can it be possible that he thinks it necessary for the safety of Russia, that the King of France should whisper a good word for her in the ear of the Grand Seigneur ?[1] It is very true, as you have properly remarked, that this great Minister takes a long view of things. No one has looked so far ahead ; and that, I imagine, is how things have become so confused.

I was a little surprised to hear that Apraksin had spoken to the Grand-Duke about his refusal to sign ; but he is a man who is devoted to you, and that reassures me. Your suggestion to make public the fact that Apraksin has spoken to him about it was very wise. You have provided me with a great deal of comfort by the confirmation which the Great Chancellor gave you of the guarantee about Hanover. If that is so, I shall be perfectly happy.

It appears to me that Glebov goes ahead at a great pace ; the moment after the first letter he asks for an interview. Evidently Alexander Schuvalov will do anything to get him admitted to your presence ; and I allow that I shall be curious to know what may be these matters of great importance, which he has to produce. I entirely agree with all you say about the conduct of the Schuvalov. You see how they press you. They must have secret reasons for that, and the only good one is the bad state of health of another, of which they know more than anyone else.

If there was a Prussian Minister in the town, and if I knew of it, you would have heard of it within a quarter of an hour of his arrival. I am quite sure that there is none in my house. I asked my servants if anyone was hidden in my house, and they assure me that there is no one. Nevertheless, I am told that they are convinced at court that there is a Prussian Minister in this town, and that they are resolved to turn him out ; and also that they will not allow General Winterfeld to remain any longer at Mitau. God knows if he is there ; as far as I am concerned, I swear to you that I know nothing about it.[2]

It certainly seems to me impossible that the court can return to the country. The effort made to go to the church proves

[1] Turkey.
[2] General Winterfeld was in Berlin at this time. *See Frederick Pol. Corres.* xiii. 245, etc.

terrible weakness. An experience of thirteen years may prove
that the same people practise witchcraft and their devotions.
But you must admit that to sacrifice to God and the Devil is a
little contradictory, and that the same person should not worship
God and Mammon. I am surprised and annoyed that I have no
letters from Stockholm. I have long pitied the King of Sweden,
but since I have known how fond you are of him, I feel quite
differently towards him, and share your distress. The moment
that I receive any letters from Sweden, I will send them to you at
once.

With regard to the present which Poniatowski received, I
understand no more than you do the reason for this proceeding.
What I imagine is this : and you can then judge for yourself.
A secretary of the Chancery, who took the Great Chancellor's
letters to him, was treated by him to a beautiful gold watch, and
another, who took him the Empress's letter to the King of Poland,
received a still better one. Therefore, as everything is known
at your court, is it not possible that the Empress, hearing this
news, may have been stung by his generosity, and may have
wished to outdo it ? You may perhaps think this idea very far-
fetched ! You should know also that when the person, who was
sent after him with the snuff-box, handed it to him at Riga, he
made him a present of a gold watch and a hundred ducats. I
imagine that this touch will please you, for a noble spirit loves a
generous heart. I have already given you my suggestions for
preventing the arrival of a French Ambassador. My fondest
hopes are founded upon the great event which will soon occur,
notwithstanding the Devil, the witches and the witchcrafts. All
my friend's letters will be sent to you immediately. Mon Dieu !
What a pleasure it is to be able to give you pleasure.

I now come to your second letter. What a heart, what firmness ! I admire you, I adore you more and more every day. I
have no guide, no protector but you. All that you say about the
thoughts and actions of a certain person[1] is striking and convincing. I am partly recovering from my fears, but believe me,
Monsieur, my worst were more for you than for myself. I do my
duty, and have nothing to fear. " I fear God, dear Abner, and

[1] The Great Chancellor.

naught else." You are my law-giver. I shall never change my friends, unless you so ordain it. Here is a new idea, which I submit to you like all my others. Prince Troubetskoï, from what I have been told, is faithfully attached to you. He is a member of the conference; and your orders to the Hetman, to bid him to send you an exact account of all that happens there, would be at once obeyed by him. That would keep you fully informed of all that happens there, and would be, in my opinion, of great use to you.

Remember, Monsieur, that in my first letter I told you that in dealing with the affairs of this country your own judgment must decide.

You are born to command and reign, and old age alone will kill you. You have my best wishes for this, from the bottom of my heart. In obedience to your orders I shall live on better terms with the Vice-Chancellor than I have done up to now ; but it will cost me some effort. I deceive no one, and I am ashamed of being deceived a second time. All the answers made by the Grand-Duke to Alexander Schuvalov, to Apraksin and to the Empress, are good and decided. Ivan Ivanovitch is too far involved in the intrigues with France to draw back, though in the present state of health of another he must fear the future, and he certainly does fear it. I am entirely of your way of thinking about the arrival of a Prussian envoy. He would be very useful ; and in the present state of affairs, the King of Prussia is ready to throw himself into the arms of Russia and to become (as Osterman[1] said Prussia should be) the nag of that Empire with regard to the rest of Europe. But in a very outspoken conversation which I had Monday last[2] with the Great Chancellor, he told me quite frankly that they would never tolerate a Prussian Minister at this court. I tried by most persuasive methods to move him, and to win him from this prejudice. But I own that it was all in vain. His palms (as you put it) might be well greased. But a higher power holds him back. It is mysterious; for my offers were very large. He said to me, " Begin by the Vice-Chancellor, he is pro-Prussian, he will assist you ; and when he has opened

[1] Count Andrei Ostermann (1686-1747), the favourite Minister of Peter the Great and the Empress Anne. He was exiled in 1742.
[2] The same interview which was mentioned in his letter of August 6th.

up the road, I will support him." I replied that I had no orders regarding the Vice-Chancellor, and that I wished to address myself to no one but him. But another time I shall increase my offers, and you shall know the effect. The Hetman tells me that he promises that Troubetskoï will obey all your commands, and that he is ready to carry out all that you bid him to do ; and the Hetman will be delighted to take your orders on the subject.

What thanks should I not express for those words to me ? You cannot believe how it distresses me not to be able to lessen your distress. Ah, Monsieur, my heart is smitten. I kiss your feet : I am yours entirely.

Forgive this scrawl and the length of this letter. I have just written a still longer one to Poniatowski, and am exhausted. I shall take the liberty of writing a few words by Swallov to the Grand-Duke, to-morrow or the next day, to thank him for his kindness, and to tell him something which I am sure will give him pleasure. Your orders are my law ; your protection is my ambition.

From THE GRAND-DUCHESS

[Sunday, August 11.]

Alexander Schuvalov returned to the charge on Saturday, both with the Grand-Duke and with me, on the subject of the signature. He told me amongst other things that he had not known what reason to give to his colleagues or to the Empress, that the Grand-Duke had not ordered him to say that he would not sign because everything had been done without him ; that the Empress had taken this very badly, and in the sense that the Grand-Duke was desiring to dictate to her that she should do nothing without him. Apraksin sent to tell me that there would be a conference on Monday, at which the Empress would ask the Grand-Duke before everyone for his reasons. His answer to her will be, that it was impossible for him conscientiously to sign what he feels is hurtful, that a French Ambassador can only come here entrusted with intrigues ; that an example of this was Chétardie, who, although loaded with her favours, nevertheless continued to show himself ungrateful to her; that when he affirmed that they had done everything without him, he had implied those who were specially interested in this affair, and that he was neither foolish nor mad enough not to recognise that her will was law. The Vice-Chancellor has made friendly proposals through two different channels. Buturlin[1] has done the same; and each side has shown mistrust and dislike of the intentions of the Schuvalov, without, however, giving any explanation. I wait with impatience to hear what the Hetman may have succeeded in extracting from the first-named. I am disturbed because we receive no news from our friends. I am busy arranging, setting up and winning over all sorts of tools for an event which you desire; my head is swimming with intrigues and negotiations. The words of a toast which is drunk in Russia are, "May God, quickly, nay very quickly indeed, give us our desires." I hope to write to you to-night, but I think I may well be as despondent as you appeared to me to be from your last letter. I forgot to tell you that Bernardi came to me on Saturday to persuade me in your name to procure the signature. This touch will make you laugh, call it what you please.

From Sir Charles Hanbury-Williams

Sunday [August 11].

I am born, Monsieur, to obey you. You ask me for news of our friend. I send it to you at once, and I flatter myself that the letter for you will afford you much pleasure.[2] A faithful English merchant sent it to me by his confidential servant from Riga, and I have received it safe and sound. I flatter myself that the two enclosures will make my letter agreeable to you. Be assured, Monsieur, that my own business here goes very badly. They will not accept the £100,000 pounds sterling, and without that I look upon the treaty as broken; for by the nature of our Government it will be necessary for Parliament to intervene. I already know the new requests which this court proposes to

---

[1] Field-Marshal Count Alexander Buturlin.
[2] Poniatowski's letter to Sir Charles is among the Phillipps MSS, but has no special interest here.

make to mine, and I can tell you in confidence that we shall agree to them all ; but before anything is done, this money must be accepted.

I must speak to the Vice-Chancellor on this point to-morrow morning, and if I do not move him, things will go badly ; for the Great Chancellor either does not, or is determined not to understand me.

I assure you that our whole business may be ruined by this stupidity, and I know that our Ministry, who are ready to agree to everything, will not be able to take a step forward.

This is very annoying to me, and puts me in a very bad temper with all the world but you.

From THE GRAND-DUCHESS

[Monday, August 12.]

Take my word for it.   There is nothing treasonable in these two sealed letters against the King, your Master, nor against your country.   One is from Naruishkin to Horn,[1] in answer to one from him which he wished addressed to Mitau ; and the other is from me to our absent friend.   Be so good as to forward them. The request which he makes you, to send him word that I love him, emboldens me to tell you that you are confirming for him a truth of truths.   His letter gave me sincere pleasure, and I own that your own, though valuable, lost nothing by accompanying that welcome enclosure.   I am much obliged to you for it. Tormented yesterday by the Great Chancellor and Apraksin, the Grand-Duke appended his signature this morning, saying to Alexander Schuvalov that it was from a desire to please the Empress, and not in any way because he approved.   Ivan Ivanovitch's answer to Naruishkin's mission was that it was too late, that had he known how distasteful it was, Douglas should never have set foot in his house.   Then, after much other talk, he said that only success would come of it, that the Empress would mediate between England and France, that therein lay

[1] Count Horn, an envoy from the Swedish King, who had recently left St Petersburg on his return to his own country, in company with Poniatowski.

the Chancellor's plan, and that he could not understand what circumstance or what person could have inspired us with such fear of a French Ambassador. Between his teeth he muttered some words about forbidding Douglas to enter his room. Apraksin told me yesterday (Sunday) that the two Schuvalov, Ivan and Peter, had scolded Alexander for not having stated the Grand-Duke's strong reasons, which would have prevented the anger of the Empress and all this muddle. He added that it was the Vice-Chancellor alone who had pushed on this affair. Subsequently, he begged me to humour and flatter the Schuvalov, especially Peter, because they had designs which might be stopped by these means. He was continuing his conversation, when the Empress's departure prevented us from finishing. But this morning I sent to the Chancellor to find out from him what these designs were. I gave Bernardi to understand that if they did not guarantee Hanover, it was possible that I might change my mind about the Holstein affair.[1] " Why ? " said he. " From caprice," was my answer. It was childish, I know ; but when one has no good reasons, one gives bad ones. Your proposed letter to the Grand-Duke will have a very good effect ; and all said and done he has well deserved thanks from you, were it only for his good intentions. I doubt whether Glebov will obtain admittance through Alexander Schuvalov.

I have a different reason to give for the present to Count Poniatowski, but perhaps it is far-fetched. Yet it is quite possible that it may be true. The Chamberlain Voronzov,[2] suspecting Count Poniatowski of being what he is, will have given a hint to his brother : and he, to curry favour for himself, thought of this present. I should tell you that I like to connect everything possible with myself. I thank you for allowing me to do so. Let me tell you, that from no one but you would I readily without complaint accept the numerous flatteries which you shower on me. But from you, I take them as a proof of friendship.

Your plan about Prince Troubetskoï is very good, and I shall make use of it. The Hetman has asked me for an interview ; he wishes to come to me here. If you approve, and do not think

[1] See ante, p. 18.
[2] Count Roman Voronzov (1707-83), the Vice-Chancellor's brother.

that it will be an insult to our absent friend, I shall not refuse him. It is in some degree necessary at the present crisis, for I am never able to speak to him at my ease, and have thousands of things to arrange with him, in case certain eventualities should arise.

The prejudices against Prussia will be easy to remove from the Vice-Chancellor's mind, I think, and especially with one's hand in one's pocket. I am annoyed that your affairs are so perpetually held up, but am very flattered that your bad temper is diminished as far as I am concerned. When shall I be able to put you in a good one ? Meanwhile, my good wishes and my affection are always with you. Forgive this scrawl, and the poor arrangement of this scrap of paper.

From Sir Charles Hanbury-Williams

[*Tuesday*, 13 *August.*]

I send you back two of your letters, Monsieur, with a thousand thanks. The enclosed for the Grand-Duke is under flying seal. Will you have the kindness to read it, and, if you approve, hand it to him.[1] But I beg you to return it to me. I will speak to

---

[1] From Sir Charles Hanbury-Williams to the Grand-Duke.

Monseigneur—I have begged the Grand-Duchess by Swallov to hand this letter to your Imperial Highness, and at the same time to make my excuses for the liberty I take in writing to you.

I am fully aware of all the great obligations that the King, my country, and I owe to your Imperial Highness. My Master is in a position to show your Imperial Highness proof of his friendship, and he is very desirous of doing so. My country, allied without interruption to Russia for two centuries, will always retain a deep sense of gratitude ; and for my personal feelings, my devotion and strong affection for the person and interests of your Imperial Highness will only end with my life.

After the unworthy manner in which the French Ambassador and the French party in Stockholm have treated the King of Sweden, your uncle, I have not been surprised to learn that your Imperial Highness has opposed the measures concerted to bring a French Ambassador to this court. The ministers of Versailles intrigue ; they push themselves forward in every court, and have given sufficiently astounding proof of this at St Petersburg. As the views of your Imperial Highness about them are now known to the public, you cannot too much mistrust those who would persuade you to look on that nation or its ministers as friends of Russia. And if France to-day makes a pretence of again seeking the friendship of the Empress, it is more with the intention of injuring Great Britain than of obtaining any advantage for this Empire.

you in a few moments about the Grand-Duke's signature. You shall complain no more of flattery. Things done, and badly done, by our friends should be forgotten. But for future use let me give you a piece of sound advice, to weigh things well and carefully before coming to any important decision. But once you have made it, never change. Now this suggestion becomes all the more necessary, because after this affair I know people who will think that they can always influence the Grand-Duke. When the Schuvalov wish to carry a point against the wishes of the Chancellor, they will have only to threaten him with the anger of the Empress, if he does not persuade the Grand-Duke to agree to their measures. In this last instance the Grand-Duke had spoken well, and the reasons which he gave were strong and unanswerable. He might have made an impression at the conference, and would perhaps have raised himself in the opinion of the world. But he yielded to please his friends, and to harm his country ; for to-day I believe that his opposition would, perhaps, have put an end to the affair, or would at least have greatly weakened the French plans and their party at this court. This I must tell you. The commencement of this affair has proved the resolution and sound sense of the Grand-Duke ; and the result has proved to his friends the kindness of his heart towards them Thus the impression which he has made is anything but a bad one. But, notwithstanding all that, it is a part which he cannot play twice without loss of reputation.

As I know that your Imperial Highness honours Swallov with your patronage, I can assure your Imperial Highness that he is a young man of good sense, and devoted to your service. This last merit is a great recommendation to me, and I have thought of a means which may some day make his fortune. Baron Wolff is the King's consul at this court. He is old, and, if he were to die, I have enough influence at my court to arrange that Swallov should succeed him, especially if the King knew that this would be agreeable to your Imperial Highness. The appointment would be worth from three to four thousand roubles a year to him. I hope that your Imperial Highness will forgive the liberty I take in approaching this question, but I shall always believe it to be part of my duty to assist (in any way that I can) those whom I know to be devoted to your service.

I have the honour to be, with an inviolable attachment and the most respectful submission, Monseigneur, your Imperial Highness's very humble, very devoted, and very obedient servant,

St Petersburg, *August 13th*, 1756.   HANBURY-WILLIAMS.

There is no question of flattery. I never flatter you, and I pray God that I may never tell you anything but what I think. What advantage should I have in deceiving you ? Should I ever by that means attain my sole object with you—to gain your esteem ? So you approve of the plan about Troubetskoï. If Buturlin knew that he would curry favour with you by opposing the French party, would he not do all you wish ? I am sorry that Glebov has not had his interview with you ; you might have been able to extract things from him. But I hope that in the end Alexander Schuvalov will be persuaded to do him this service. Ivan Ivanovitch dined here last Monday, and in conversation, after some compliments, said that he was leaving my house well pleased, and promised to do me a small favour which I had asked of him.[1]

I quite approve of your interview with the Hetman, because he is and always has been the friend of our friend. How can anyone know and suspect you at the same time ? I cannot have respect for those whom I mistrust, and what I feel for you surpasses respect—it is almost an adoration, an adoration founded on all the good sense and power of reasoning which God has given me.

I shall take great care of your letters for Mitau and Warsaw, and have no more suspicion of their contents than I have of you. For six years I have been, so to speak, guardian and instructor to our friend, and he is certainly under some obligations to me, but none which can compare to the service which I shall now render him, when I tell him the truth of truths, that you love him.

You see, Monsieur, that Naruishkin's mission has shaken Ivan Ivanovitch's French leanings. Follow it up ; and when Naruishkin calls upon him on other business, let him whisper in his ear as a friend and tell him that the essential way to put himself on good terms with you is to curb his zeal for France. Believe me, Monsieur, you do not realize your real power ; for these last intrigues at court about the Grand-Duke's signature, prove clearly that you have a great deal. I shall, at some other time, send you my views upon the Russian mediation between England

---

[1] Sir Charles had been able to further himself in the favourite's good graces by helping him to buy pictures and statuary in Rome, through the agency of the painter, Mengs.

and France.   There is another idea which seems to me useful to raise the Grand-Duke in the eyes of his friends, who are perhaps rather vain at the victory which they have gained.   His Imperial Highness, on the first day at court, might well say to the Grand Chancellor, and, if you please, to Apraksin : " You see how far my obedience to the Empress goes, and you likewise see how readily I complied with your advice on this occasion· But remember that in changing my resolve I have not altered my opinion, and that, if I see French intrigues gaining ground at this court to the prejudice of the interests of our friends and true allies, I shall oppose such measures by every means in my power.   I shall do my duty by my country, as every good Russian should do, and I shall never change."

God knows if the Vice-Chancellor is the only culprit.   Following your advice and that of the Grand Chancellor, I met him on Monday last, and if he fulfils all his promises, he will earn my gratitude.

Perhaps your reason for the present which Poniatowski has received is more probable than mine ; but I am very glad that he received it.

As to Prussian affairs, I am resolved to have nothing to do with them till those of my Master are finished : and I shall not speak of them to the Vice-Chancellor, unless the Grand Chancellor refuses to have anything to do with them.   The Vice-Chancellor asked me last Monday, why the King of Prussia now seemed anxious for the friendship of the Empress, after having neglected it for so many years.   I replied that during the whole of that time he had been in alliance with the enemies of Russia : but that now, having reverted to the friends of this Empire, it was but natural that he should again seek to be on good terms with Her Imperial Majesty.   It is true that the treatment which Great Britain receives here annoys me : long delays on perfectly reasonable proposals show ill-will, to say the least of it, and they will continue to play this part until the alliance is broken up by trifles and ill-humour.   Adieu, Monsieur, I send you all the good wishes for Prince Paul Petrovitch which you can desire.   Be so kind as to seal the letter for the Grand-Duke before giving it to him.

FROM THE GRAND-DUCHESS

Sunday [*August* 18].

You have allowed me to call you my friend. Your title awes me, but as my designs are in no way criminal, I make so bold as to communicate to you and to ask your advice upon the thoughts forced upon my mind by the increased indisposition of certain persons during the last twenty-four hours. This is my dream. After being informed of her death, and being certain that there is no mistake, I shall go straight to my son's room. If I meet, or can quickly get hold of, the Grand Master of the Hunt,[1] I shall leave him with him and the men under his command. If not, I shall carry him off to my room. I shall also send a man that I can trust to warn five officers of the Guards of whom I am sure, who will each bring me fifty soldiers (this is understood at the first signal), and though perhaps I may not use them, they will serve as a reserve in case of any difficulty. (N.B.—They will take no orders except from the Grand-Duke or me.) I shall send orders to the Chancellor, Apraksin and Lieven[2] to come to me, and meanwhile I shall enter the death chamber, where I shall summon the captain of the guard, and shall make him take the oath and retain him at my side. It appears to me that it would be better and safer if the two Grand-Dukes were together, than if only one went with me ; also that the rendezvous for my followers should be my ante-chamber. If I see the slightest signs of commotion, I shall secure, either with my own people or with those of the captain of the guard, the Schuvalov and the adjutant-general of the day. Besides, the lower grade officers of the bodyguard are trustworthy ; and, though I have had no communication with all of them, I can count sufficiently on two or three, and on having enough means at my disposal to make myself obeyed by everyone who is not bought.

As my friend, correct me and point out any defect in my views and anything that I have not foreseen. Much will depend on the

---

[1] Count Alexei Rasumowski, Elizabeth's late favourite and reputed husband.

[2] General Count Lieven, a supporter of Catherine. He was in ill-health at this time.

general aspect, or on the view which I shall take of things. Pray Heaven to give me a clear head. The extreme hatred for the Schuvalov, which all those who do not belong to them feel, the justice of my cause, as well as the easy sequence of everything which runs its natural course, make me hope for a happy issue. You must tell me, and that clearly; it is for that reason also why I place it before you. The novelty of the whole thing, and the haste with which I communicate it to you, have necessitated a very great effort of imagination on my part.

Monday.

I delayed my answer, in order to have something to tell you. For various reasons our interview with the Hetman only took place yesterday, Saturday, at 11 o'clock in the evening. Here are the main points of our discussion, not in their proper order, but just as they come into my mind.

(1) The Hetman will speak from me and from the Grand-Duke to Prince Troubetskoï, to repeat what we have already told him by Bressan, the Grand-Duke's valet, who was formerly a servant of a brother of Troubetskoï, and to know whether, as he has shown his goodwill on many occasions and has again quite recently deserved our esteem and confidence, he will give proof of it, not only by informing us of all that passes at the conferences (up to this point the message sent by Bressan), but also by opposing all connection with France in every possible way. To that I added in the Hetman's ear, and I think convinced him by them, all the reasons which my zeal for Russia and my personal welfare suggested and indicated to me. If he speaks to Troubetskoï with the eloquence which I used to him, that man may be looked upon as gained to our side. Through Bressan Troubetskoï has shown every possible good intention. Naturally, I have no answer yet upon the further point put forward by the Hetman. The latter fears that the other may tie himself up with the Schuvalov, who are running after him. He will try to dissuade him from any such weakness.

(2) I pointed out to him that, in the event of the death, I insisted that his brother should warn me, and should take charge of my son and be answerable to me for him as well as for those under his command. This he promised me, and added, " He will

not wait for the end to warn you of what is happening, I can answer for it : he will undertake any instructions that you care to give him."

(3) I asked him if he was sure of his regiment in case of necessity. He replied, " As sure as you could possibly wish." I said to him, " You quite understand that these enquiries only relate to the future, after the death has taken place."

(4) He was as reassuring as he could be about the plans of the Schuvalov, and said, " Have no fear ! We shall defend you at the cost of our lives. Your friends are the strongest and the most numerous."

(5) He undertook to cool the enthusiasm of the Vice-Chancellor for the French, and asked if he might dare to speak to him as from the Grand-Duke and me.   Knowing him to be fairly prudent, I gave him power to use our names as he thought fit, and as he thought the case required. He added that the Vice-Chancellor hated the Schuvalov almost as much as we did.

(6) I also instructed him to persuade Buturlin to thwart all French measures and to uphold the honour of his country, which would vanish if the treaty with an old and faithful ally was broken ; for in that way he would gain the goodwill of the Grand-Duke.

(7) I begged him to go to the Chancellor and make common cause with him, because I wished all our friends to be united, and because I considered the Chancellor to be one of the most sincere of them.

(8) I told him how Douglas was trying to form a party, by saying to all the young men whom he thought well-inclined : " The King is aware of your good intentions and only seeks an occasion to prove it to you." Amongst others, he approached Naruishkin with this expression of civility, who laughed in his face and closed his door against him next day.

Point 9 should have been to borrow five thousand roubles from his brother for me ; but shame won the day, and it was not mentioned. Thank you for counselling the Grand-Duke to stand firm. He is writing you a note in answer to your letter ; return it to him, and he will do the same with your letter. He hesitated about writing to you, fearing that someone would hear of it ; but

I positively assured him that you would immediately return him anything that he wrote. Buturlin sent me a warning by a third hand, which seemed to infer that the Schuvalov were holding Prince Ivan[1] at Schlüsselburg, 60 versts from here. I know that two months ago the Chamberlain Voronzov wished . . .

(The end is lost.)

From Sir Charles Hanbury-Williams

Sunday, August 18.

Monsieur, I am very astonished and annoyed to learn that the Vice-Chancellor has had the rashness and insolence to raise the question of your succession to this crown. Can he have said to Peter Schuvalov that he was surprised that the Grand-Duke acted in the way he did, when he must have known that Prince Ivan was not far from here ? If that could be clearly proved, the Grand-Duke, in justice to himself, to you and to his child, should demand signal satisfaction.

Is it the coldness of your friends that encourages this boldness in your enemies ? I confess that I do not understand how they dare hold such language. A man who is capable of such remarks is fully capable, when the time comes, of doing everything against your interests : and an announcement like this seems to me to be the forerunner of other schemes. They have done their best to comfort me, by saying that, in the event of the death of the Empress, all would be assured. If they are conspiring against you, they will not wait for that death to execute their plots—at all events some portion of them. I am told that the Empress has always a soft spot for the Grand-Duke ; but if she never sees him, if she is never told his Imperial Highness's real words and real actions, if his enemies alone have the ear of Her Majesty and always speak against him and you, the same story told and re-told time after time will have its effect, and will stifle the tenderest feelings.

A further piece of news, which I hope and trust will prove to be without foundation. I am told that they wish to move Alexander Schuvalov from your establishment, and to put the elder

---

[1] The Czar Ivan VI, deposed in 1740.

Chernuishev[1] in his place. New spies are always anxious to make a hit in their vile employment ; and it is better to continue to be rather uncomfortable than to change with no prospect of improvement. I am assured that Lieutenant-Colonel Brown,[2] who is in the Grand-Duke's suite, is devoted to Peter Schuvalov, and that Ismaïlov is under Apraksin's thumb. These are matters of little consequence, but I deem it my duty to warn you of everything.

What follows is an extract of a letter from Colonel Yorke[3] (a great friend of Poniatowski's) from The Hague.

" When Bekteïev was presented to the King of France at Compiègne, the King did him the honour of speaking to him, and consequently all the courtiers decided that Russia had already acceded to the treaty lately concluded between the Courts of Vienna and Versailles. But up to now there is no confirmation of this ; and it is said that the Russian Ministers, even those who agreed with the French system, insist before everything else that France must guarantee the succession of the Empire and of the conquered provinces to the House of Holstein. But France, who wants everything for herself, and who thinks little of the good of others, at once raised difficulties, because a step of this kind would in no way agree with her views on Poland nor with her pledges to Sweden. Besides all this, you may be sure that Douglas has no orders from his court to open his mind to the Great Chancellor. But he will soon have them, to declare to that Minister that France is very anxious to forget all his past behaviour and to do him no harm, provided that he will second her schemes at the court of St Petersburg."

This is what he writes me. I am personally very tired of the part I play here. Never an answer, always delay, and very little hope of success even at the finish.

Your letter left here in safe hands, but I was obliged to change the route suggested to me, for they intended that your letter

---

[1] Zachary Chernuishev.
[2] George, Count Brown (1698-1792), a Russian officer of English extraction.   Later Governor of Livonia.
[3] Yorke was British Minister in Holland.

should be put in the post at Riga, and that I do not wish. I always leave as little to chance as possible, and I act for my friends as I would for myself. So I gave orders that a trustworthy man should be sent from Riga to post the letter at Memel. I shall pay all the couriers, and when you are Empress I shall send you the bill.

I am a little impatient to know how the Grand-Duke received my letter. Continue to give me your protection ; it is the only thing which prevents me from asking for my recall.

From SIR CHARLES HANBURY-WILLIAMS

Monday [*August* 19].

Monsieur, I have just received a courier from London. All your suggestions have been cheerfully accepted, and the forty thousand roubles are at your disposal and await your orders.[1] But I shall write to you again to-night, for the King bids me tell you the most charming things in the world, and these I shall faithfully translate. Mon Dieu ! What a pleasure it is to me to give you pleasure.

Monday. Written in haste, in Naruishkin's presence.

From SIR CHARLES HANBURY-WILLIAMS

Tuesday [*August* 20].

Monsieur, I must begin by fulfilling the promise which I made you yesterday, to inform you of the friendly manner in which the King has acceded to your request. I therefore send you two extracts from letters which I received yesterday.

" His Majesty has at once agreed to all that you asked in your last secret letter of July 9. You will place the money in her Imperial Highness's hands, and you will receive a bond in ex-

---

[1] See *ante* p. 18. The suggestions were originally made in a letter to Holdernesse, which Sir Charles had written on July 9, n.s. (Record Office). Catherine had pointed out that nothing could be done in the capital without money, and that if King George would consent to advance her some, she would promise to use it for the common good. On Sir Charles asking her to name an amount she spoke of 20,000 ducats effective, or £10,000.

change, in conformity with her proposals. At the same time, the King commands you to tell the Grand-Duchess how pleased he is with the many marks of friendship which he receives from her Imperial Highness ; and you are to assure her, in the name of the King, that he is ready, and will always be ready, to give her marks of his complete confidence and affection."

Here is another extract, which gives an actual mark of confidence. " You see how desirous the King is to grant all you ask. Would it not be possible to win over the favourite ?   We give you a free hand.   But at the same time the King commands you to take no step in this matter without the approval and consent of the Grand-Duchess." I flatter myself that these extracts will prove agreeable to you.   Before answering your letter of yesterday, I am going to tell you all that I know from the outside world.

According to the last letters from Obrescov[1] (which the Empress will have seen), he states that after the English Ambassador had notified the treaty concluded with Prussia to the Porte, the Austrian Minister asked for an audience of the Vizier to communicate the treaty recently made between the courts of Vienna and Versailles.   When the Grand Vizier was informed of this, he appeared much astonished, and said to the Austrian Minister that he would give him an answer through the Reis-Effendi : and the answer was that, since the House of Austria had never ceased for nearly a hundred years in succession to represent France as the power most dangerous to the liberties of Europe and the most perfidious and unreliable nation in all its engagements, the Ottoman Porte was surprised and astonished to learn from the mouth of its Minister that Their Imperial Majesties had concluded a treaty with such a power.   That for their part, they did not understand what it could mean ; but it obliged them to think of their own safety, and they were resolved to conclude a treaty with the King of Prussia at once.   Such are the thoughts and reasonings of the Turks.   I defy any Christians to hold more sensible views.

The army which the Empress-Queen has assembled in Bohemia and Moravia makes the King of Prussia very uneasy.   He sent to ask the court of Vienna for the reason, and has received a

[1] The Russian Resident at Constantinople.

E

reply, " That as affairs are at present in a state of crisis, the Empress-Queen had thought right to take measures for her own protection and that of her allies, which will be prejudicial to no one." But since this answer does not appear to satisfy the King of Prussia, His Majesty has ordered his Minister to ask for an audience from Her Imperial Majesty, and to tell her that His Prussian Majesty, being informed that the Empress-Queen was intending to attack him, asks for a declaration, either by word of mouth or in writing, that she has no intention of attacking him either this year or next. If the reply of the court of Vienna does not answer to the expectations of the King of Prussia, we may soon expect to see war break out.

With regard to your money, I advise you to order me to pay Baron Wolff what is due to him, because that will help your credit with him in the future. When I have done that, I shall retain the rest, which I shall pay at any time to your order, and when I have done everything, I shall send you the bond to sign

I now come to your letters. I have neither a clear head, for I sat up with the Hetman till two hours after midnight, nor much time, for it is my post day. When you call me your friend, you bestow on me a title which I covet more than any which the King can give me. Continue to use it ; I shall try to be worthy of it.

I approve of your plan in the event of the death. It would be difficult, in my opinion, to frame one better. But I own that I am not afraid of anything after her death. I am very much afraid of the men who might take action previously to it. In short, you must be on better terms with the Schuvalov or find some means of preventing them from controlling the Chancellor, for at present they control him absolutely, as much by the fear which he has of their power, as by the influence which Apraksin has over him : and Apraksin and Peter Schuvalov act in every-thing as one person.

I will shortly send you a story to prove all this to you ; and while your friends remain under the rod of your enemies, I venture to say that they are useless to you, to say the very least. And, let me tell you, they never speak of helping you, except at the time when they themselves require your protection.

Allow me, as a friend (if I dare to speak of myself thus), to picture to you the scene which you will shortly see upon the stage of Petersburg.

As soon as the French Ambassador arrives, the Schuvalov, who have been the means of bringing him, will give him their entire support. Those who claim to support the French have always been either their slaves or their dupes. The Ambassador will only be under their thumb for a few days : they will then be under his, and he will force them to discard all those who do not blindly follow his plans and who do not conform to his wishes. Judge by what you see whether the Chancellor and Apraksin will not follow them. You have already seen the Chancellor, either from force or from fear, abandon a system, which he himself had formulated, and maintained for fifteen years. Only fear could have made him act like this ; for I am convinced that he does not approve of what he is doing, and in former times he would have advised the Grand-Duke to go to the council to give his reasons for his conduct in public. He also knows full well that he has opposed France too strongly to save him one day from her vengeance. According to all rules of politics, he will be the first to fall, sacrificed to the power of a French Ambassador at this court.[1] He owns all this to his friends, but adds, shrugging his shoulders, " I cannot do otherwise." I tell you all this, Monsieur, to prove to you how much the Chancellor is at present in the hands of the Schuvalov, and how they have already drawn him into doing things against his conscience, his country, and (what is more) his own interests. I leave you to think, Monsieur, how far the Schuvalov may lead him, emboldened by the support and presence of a French Ambassador, egged on by his advice, supported by his money, and deceived by his tricks.

I shall see the Great Chancellor to-night. I shall not fail in my next letter to tell you all that passes at our interview, and after that you shall hear the story which I promised you.

Never believe anything that Bernardi tells you as coming from me. You allow me to write to you : you will find my real thoughts in my letters. I see that the Hetman is a little suspicious of Troubetskoï : he believes him to be hostile to the Chancellor,

[1] The truth of Sir Charles's prophecy was fully proved when Bestuzhev fell from his high estate two years later.

but not so hostile to the Schuvalov. You will remember that I have already told you, that when the domestic affairs or individuals of the court are in question, I have no advice to give. You know their characters and their connections better than I do.

I implore you to forgive such a badly written letter ; but as Swallov told me that he was going to Oranienbaum to-night, I told him that I should have a letter to send you. I had then forgotten that it was my post-day, and I have still to read all the despatches received by my messenger of yesterday. These are very legitimate excuses.

My desires, my good wishes, my prayers are every day united for your present safety and for your future triumph. Why have I not daily opportunities of proving to you that nobody in this world can surpass my loyalty and my devotion to you, and that I covet the title of your friend more than that of Viceroy of Ireland—and that is the highest rank to which an English subject can attain ?

From the Grand-Duchess

[Tuesday, August 20.]

The speeches of the Vice-Chancellor are like dogs barking at the moon, so indiscreet and so saucy are they. The Chancellor has sent to tell me that Peter Schuvalov will repeat his own words to me himself. He will come here on his way to Cronstadt, where he goes to inspect the artillery ; and I am asked to tell him, in order to open the subject, that I heard from General Apraksin that he (Schuvalov) was well-intentioned towards us and that he even wished to prove it ; that I had heard mention of proposals, but did not know what they were, and that I was waiting for him to tell me what had come to his knowledge. Apraksin promises that, by being rather gracious to him (Count Schuvalov), I shall get even more out of him. His self-esteem and self-confidence, loving to chatter and puff himself here, will help matters even further. Having finished these remarks, I shall hint at the annoyance I should feel, after this mark of friendship, if Alexander Schuvalov is taken from us ; for, when all is said and done, they would not be able to find anyone of whom they could be more sure : and in passing I shall demonstrate my dislike to the Chernuishev, of whose machinations, I shall add, that I am not ignorant.   I shall do all this, without unduly exposing the secrets of my heart—so that he may retain some hope of bettering himself with me ; for too great efforts at persuasion would only make him too conceited, and then I shall be neglected.   I shall also speak strongly to him on the business of the moment, and, as he is a man of intelligence, I shall perhaps have more effect on him than on his brother ; and thereby it is also possible that you will not lose your friends.   Thank you for your friendship and your anxiety for me.   It is certain that more harm could be done to us than has been done hitherto.   But these people's lack of courage, the risk—in fact the maxim of Machiavel, who says that a man is rarely as bad as he should be for his own safety—leave me more at my ease than I ought to be from the look of things. Extract for extract ; yours gave me pleasure.   I shall, I think, please you with the one which I send you ; it came from the Chancellor, just as I was leaving town.[1]   I translated it the following day.   Forgive the scrawl on the last page : I have no time to rewrite it.   I am as annoyed as you are that your affairs always

---

[1] TRANSLATION OF LETTER FROM THE GREAT CHANCELLOR TO THE GRAND-DUCHESS.

" Your note, Monsieur, has made me very happy, especially the fact that you are convinced of my devotion.   My reward is complete, for it is an assurance that my efforts will not be employed in vain.   Rest assured, Monsieur, that all my life night and day I shall think only how to make myself agreeable and useful for your service.   I shall be faithful to you, without regard for anyone else, even at the risk of my life.

To satisfy your curiosity, Monsieur, here is some news from Stockholm, by which you will see how barbarously the French intrigues operate against the Swedish nation, and even against the Queen—a state of things that we ourselves may look for after the arrival of a French Ambassador, and we should be on our guard, for they will seek a pretext.   Those who are engineering this change of system are no other than Ivan Ivanovitch and the Vice-Chancellor ; and they are now again trying to put all on my shoulders with you.   You will see whose fault it is, by the packet of papers herewith enclosed, and that the absence of the Grand-Duke's signature from the document would not have prevented the matter ; but in order to help in the future I have ordered Bernardi to speak to you in my name.   I send you also the notes on the Danish affair, which the Minister of that court handed to ours.   Hasten to conclude the agreement, to prevent the French faction from depriving the Grand-Duke of the motive of his devotion to his country."

follow the same course.   What do I not owe you for all the proofs
of devotion which you show me ?   Never will a debt be paid with
greater pleasure than the one which gives me faith in your friendship.   The Grand-Duke received your letter in perfectly good part,
as you will have seen by my former one.   My gratitude to the
King, your Master, remains as strong as ever, although I still do
not yet know the charming messages which he sent me.   I hope
to repay my debt to him more by my services than by the money,
which I hope faithfully to return to him.   I am fully aware of
the pleasure which it gives you to arrange it for me.   Have you
no news of Count Poniatowski ?

Wednesday, 8 o'clock in the morning [August 21].

Shortly after writing this I received your letter of Tuesday from
Swallov.   I am more touched by the marks of confidence of the
King, your Master, than by any other of his kindnesses.   It
flatters me ; I hope to deserve it, and I shall certainly do my
best to retain the good opinion of His Majesty.   You know that
all I do is founded on the firm belief that it is in the interest
of Russia.   I cannot say more.   Although you know the contents
of Obrescov's communication, I will not take it out of this packet.
You will see his exact words ; besides, there is the filial affection
which I feel for my translation.

Do you wish me to make you out an order for the payment to
Wolff ?   If so, it should no doubt go by Bernardi ; therefore you
will not have it to-day.   After that, do as you like, for you are
a friend such as one no longer finds.

As regards your advice to be on better terms with the
Schuvalov, I refer you to the first page of this letter.

I impatiently await your story, and am annoyed, but not
disturbed nor moved, at the part played by my friends.   I have
learnt long ago to view people as they are, and not as I should
wish them to be ; but remember that Apraksin has only become
friendly with Peter Schuvalov to help his friends and to put a stop
to something worse.

As for the scene representing the French Ambassador, you
could not show it me in a worse light than it is depicted in my
imagination, and remembering the first rule of our natural rights,

I remain silent, shrouding myself in a darkness with which I am familiar.

I hope that the result of your conversation with the Chancellor may prove satisfactory to you. Has the Hetman spoken to Troubetskoï, and what is the result? I have only to recommend you that he should above all insist on him opposing all French measures. He has a greater inclination to me than to the Schuvalov. I shall know how to soothe his fears of the Chancellor and Apraksin; it is already partly done.

When you make excuses for your so-called badly written letters, you justify me in asking how to set about writing better ones? I am only sorry when you are tired or busy, for I add to your fatigues.

Here is something quite new. A friend of Glebov has sent the same little man, who is in the service of the former and who is entirely on my side, to beg me most earnestly not to see Glebov, as he had, according to him, discovered the whole plot arranged by the Schuvalov, with whom he couples Apraksin, to make me favour Glebov. He says that they will spare neither money nor pains to succeed in this, and that if he does not get hold of me, they will find another; for, being sure of the Grand-Duke, and never having succeeded in gaining over Saltikov up to the present, nor Naruishkin (the Hetman said, "What a mistake"), they wished to introduce one of their own people into my household, not to rule me, but to ruin me; but this does not fit in with the choice they have made of their favourite, for he would be ruined as well. This new acquaintance adds, that he had often tried to discover from Glebov what it was that he had to tell me of such importance as to require an interview, but that he always received the same answer from him that it was of the greatest consequence to my welfare: that after having advised him that should anyone try to do me harm—either literally or otherwise—he could warn me by writing or by the little man, he advocated writing, but said that the other hoped for and desired an interview, and wants to come here. I sent my thanks to the donor of this advice, and begged him to get all he possibly could out of Glebov, and above all to persuade him to put in writing everything that he wishes to say to me by word of mouth. Do not speak of this to the Hetman, because he hides little from the Chamberlain Voronzov.[1] The latter has told Glebov that he knew that he had written to me. This restrains him.   Say what you please, and the Hetman too, about the Chamberlain Voronzov ; he is, and always will be, double-faced and triple-faced, and deceives those who associate with him every day.   But it is not quite necessary that he should know what I think of him.   If your good wishes, your prayers and your desires for my preservation and my triumph are granted, you might well change the title of Viceroy of Ireland for that of Viceroy of Russia.   Your advice and friendship will at least give you the right to it.

If Count Poniatowski were here, I would repeat to him the most comical confidence that was made to me this morning.   Just think! twelve fair ladies at the same time, yes, twelve at once ; that is something, is it not ?   And all of them stark staring mad, or so it is asserted.

From Sir Charles Hanbury-Williams

Thursday morning [22 *August.*]

Monsieur, I saw the Great Chancellor on Tuesday evening, and we conferred for fully two hours ; but before telling you what then passed between us, you must know that on Monday morning Baron Wolff came to my house from him, to tell me that you were in pressing need of 10,000 roubles, and to beg me very earnestly to use all my influence to find you this sum.   You can realize, Monsieur, my joy at having received a courier, a few hours before Wolff's arrival, who had brought me all you required.   I replied at once that I had the money ready and at your disposal.   But you must know that after I had informed the Chancellor at our interview of the arrival of the 40,000 roubles, he begged me at once to allow him to inform you of it.   He wanted to have the credit for it.   I told him that he could do not only that, but that he could add that it was at his request that everything had been done.   I beg you, Monsieur, not to undeceive him on this point, for up till now he does not know (anyhow through me) that we are in correspondence, and I see that he believes that I am only in

[1] Count Roman Voronzov, the Vice-Chancellor's brother.

favour with you through another ; for it is not so long ago, when I was somewhat worried at the unsatisfactory state of my business at this court, that he said to me in conversation, with rather an air of triumph, " You would give something now for Poniatowski to be here ! " Yet I have always prided myself that I stood high in your esteem, even before the month of December last.[1]

I am not pleased with the Chancellor on public business ; and the answer which I shall receive (God knows when) from this court will be such that it will be more acceptable to France than to England. It will not contain a word of any guarantee about Hanover, although this has been twice promised to you. I have made him most generous and most reasonable offers from my Master. He owns it himself, but his only answer is to shrug his shoulders, and to tell me that the power of the Schuvalov carries all before it, and that they are entirely wedded to the interests of France. This is what I have to look forward to, and it is a sad state of affairs.

To give me some comfort the Great Chancellor strongly recommended me to live on good terms with the Vice-Chancellor, and assures me that since my visit to him he had been of service to my cause, and that he was no longer so favourable to France as he had been. The Hetman also tells me that the Vice-Chancellor begins to change. I will come to closer quarters with him. I was at his house the night before last, and yesterday at his request I went to dine at his country house with him and the Hetman. That house, alas ! is on the road to Oranienbaum. I would fain have continued my journey, but as at present I am not allowed to go there, and as you are not allowed to receive me, we must put off this meeting to some more favourable opportunity, and I implore the heavens to make one soon.

Here is news which will be very displeasing to you, Monsieur, and also to the Grand-Duke. A young Englishman of good sense arrived here yesterday from Stockholm. He was at my house yesterday, and told me that everything is still in great confusion in that country, and that the party in power was meditating action which will be very humiliating to their Swedish Majesties ; for it is said that a resolution has been passed to

[1] The date of the commencement of Catherine's liaison with Poniatowski.

insist upon the Queen coming in person before the States to ask forgiveness for the offences which she has committed against the nation. In the event of her refusing to submit to such an indignity, she is to be sent a prisoner to a certain castle, where she will be confined for the rest of her life. It is said that the King is so affected by this, that he is in the depths of woe.

I must now speak to you about your money. This is what you should do, and what I shall do.

First, I shall get the money from Wolff. I shall settle his account, and after that I shall send word to you how much remains in my hands ; and you will draw that sum by Naruishkin as you require it, from time to time, for my own security demands that no one should ever be able to prove that I procured you money. After that, I will send you the bond which you have to sign for my Master ; you should copy it in your own handwriting from the original which I shall send you.

I hope that this plan will please you. I shall try all my life to please you and to help you. I own that it hurts me to think that the Great Chancellor believes that your protection is only extended to me because of another, and that your good opinion of me is only founded on the favour of Poniatowski.

I assure you, Monsieur, insignificant as I am, that I would not live with the greatest prince in the world on such a footing. My friendship is of no great value and my devotion is a small affair, but, such as they are, I am not lavish with them ; and I can honestly say that up till now no one in this world has suffered from having placed confidence in me.

You see by what I say, that I am a little hurt by these words of the Chancellor. You alone can remedy this ; and I trust to your sense of justice, to make him realize very clearly, in the first letter which you write to him, that I have your protection : yet without taking the least notice of anything which I have just told you.

I hope that the liberty I take will in no way overstep the respect which I owe you. A person who is not capable of feeling resentment is not capable of feeling devotion. I pride myself on being an honest man (I am perhaps rather proud of it), and I hope in time to convince you of it. This is how I shall set about it. I shall never be troublesome to you, I shall faithfully guard your secrets, I shall oppose everything which you propose that I consider contrary to your interests. I shall give you the best advice I can. I shall tell you nothing but the truth. I shall help you in all that in my power lies, and never shall I flatter you. In return, Monsieur, I ask you to make the Great Chancellor feel that the kindness which you accord me and the protection which you grant will be continued for my own sake and for no other consideration. Your esteem is my ambition, because I believe that the man who obtains it is worthy to possess it.

From THE GRAND-DUCHESS

Friday, after dinner [*August* 23].

Certain it is, that from the moment when I had the pleasure of making your acquaintance, I conceived a real regard for you, quite independent of any other connection, seeing that this only came into being seven months later. The Great Chancellor is the best witness of this himself : he has only to remember the jealousy which it aroused in him—perhaps the reason that there were moments when he was less friendly to you than he might otherwise have been. Your conduct to me up to now, which you propose to maintain in the future, should leave you in no doubt, as much for the consideration which I owe and feel for you as for my friendship, which is so well deserved and is based on merit superior to anything that I have ever known. You may rest assured that I shall make the Chancellor realize my way of thinking. But permit my honesty upon another point also to inform you, that my affection for Count Poniatowski and all that he owes to you do you no harm in my eyes. I imagine that the Chancellor sent to you to ask for money, upon hearing what I had told Bernardi of my need of it in the future during that certain decisive twenty-four hours of which I spoke to you. He knows nothing of our correspondence ; and this, I feel, is all the better. Nevertheless should you think differently, I shall readily fall in with your views. He will have the pleasure of believing that I am under a further obligation to him, and in his opinion, I think, the news of the 40,000 roubles is of no small importance.

Let us build a few castles in the air, as they call them.   If the Chancellor, the Vice-Chancellor, Apraksin, Troubetskoï, and perhaps Buturlin, are on your side, what unfavourable answer can you expect ?   Do not swear about the guarantee ; it might still come to pass, though you will not believe it.

If it were not cruel to wish that your horses had taken the bits between their teeth and brought you on here from the house of the Vice-Chancellor, I should have done so, whilst impatiently awaiting more favourable days.   I am always delighted that you have managed to hook your host.

When I told the Grand-Duke, as gossip, of your information about the designs against the Queen of Sweden, he said to me, " Will the King of Prussia allow them to shut up his sister ? Swedish Pomerania is at his mercy whenever he wants it." It seems to me that there is a great deal of sense in this, were it not for the fact that he has so much other work on hand.   If there is anything which affects me and could give me a knock-out blow, it would be the terrible situation of my uncle, the King.   How strongly should I support him !

Do what you will with your money, and about everything connected with it.

You are not insignificant—you are a *grand seigneur* as far as merit and honesty are concerned—and you will never live on that footing with me.   Your friendship, your devotion, even your modesty, are without price.   I maintain it to your face, and I congratulate myself on having acquired your confidence.

Bernardi has just come in with the news of the arrival of the money.   He spoke to me of 50,000 roubles.   When I told him that I wished it placed in your hands, he replied, " Will that not annoy the Chancellor ? "   " Why do you think he would be annoyed," I answered ; "it is money which I do not wish to touch, after paying off Wolff and the Chancellor, except in case of urgent necessity, and it can be nowhere so safe as in the hands of the English Ambassador."   He told me that he had some of the money with him, if I needed it.   My answer was to order him to take it back ; when I required it, I should know how to ask for it, and when I came to Petersburg I would settle everything about that money.   He also brought me a note from the Chancellor with a paper about the Denmark affair. I will send it to you translated, and will follow your advice in my reply. Volkov[1] came here with a *doklade* to be signed, in which is represented the necessity of appointing a general for the Livonian Division, which Peter Schuvalov commands, or ought to command, according to the military laws of Peter the Great, being at present General commanding the Artillery.

This house yesterday resembled an English colony, from the number of English who were here invited by the Grand-Duke. I wish I knew if they were pleased. I spoke to Gibson, who told me of Monday's scenes. Naruishkin is much flattered by your kindness to him.

From SIR CHARLES HANBURY-WILLIAMS

Friday [August 23].

Monsieur, Your interests and my duty towards you, my protector and benefactor, force me to tell you what follows. A part of your debt to Bernardi was contracted for jewels which he sold to you, but which belonged to the Great Chancellor. I know that you will be hard pressed to pay this at once. I only knew this secret this morning. Had I known of it yesterday, you would have been warned of it before Bernardi's departure for Oranien-baum. Bernardi dined here yesterday, and after dinner he gave me to understand very clearly that he knew everything, and that he has the entire confidence of the Great Chancellor. I would not take the hint. But finally he told me that he was leaving for Oranienbaum, and asked me what my orders were regarding you. I answered that I had nothing to say, beyond commending myself to your protection and assuring you that I shall never forget the obligations which I owe to you. To that he replied, " Certain people are also under obligations to you, especially when they are so opportune."

With that I looked haughtily at him, and said, " That is untrue. It is not in my power to do any favour for that person ; but when it becomes a question of shedding my blood for her, I am ready to do so."

[1] Dmitri Volkov (1718-85), Secretary to the Great Chancellor, and Secretary of the conferences.

He answered, " I see that your Excellency will not speak out."

I replied, " Yes, Monsieur, I am speaking out ; and you can repeat all that I say to my protector, for she knows that I am incapable of lying or *finesse*. If you knew her as well as I do, you would know that by that alone I have deserved her protection."

Mon Dieu, Monsieur, why let such people into the secret ? Anyhow, my secret is between you and me, for by the measures which I have taken, nobody in the world can prove that I have carried out the orders that you have given me. The Great Chancellor was really rather drunk on Monday evening, and did not understand too well all that I said to him, but this morning he sent Wolff to me with many compliments on what I had done for him at his suggestion.

Never shall I have any secret from you. It is a betrayal of friendship to keep a secret from one's friend, and still more so from a friend-protector to whom one is devoted heart and soul.

Some time ago[1] the Great Chancellor asked me to obtain a large pension for him from the King, saying that they only gave him seven thousand roubles a year here, and that with a salary like this he could not live according to his rank ; that he personally recognized the interests of his country, that he knew that they were bound up with those of England, and consequently the man who served Russia well would serve England, and that therefore he could serve the King without wounding his conscience or injuring his country ; that if the King would put him in a position to live up to the high rank he held, then his hands would be free, and he would never serve anyone but Russia and England. To this I replied, that for some time past he had certainly only rendered very small services to the King, but that I was his friend, that I had more influence at my court than he thought, and that believing that he would keep faith with me, I would promise to help him. Nevertheless, he remained incredulous. But he was much surprised on Monday, when I finished speaking to him

---

[1] A letter from Sir Charles Hanbury-Williams to Holdernesse, July 9th, n.s. 1756 (Record Office), relates this conversation. Bestuzhev suggested a pension of £2,500 a year, about 10,000 roubles.

about you, and said, " I not only serve your protector, but have also done your business.   The King will grant you a pension for life of twelve thousand roubles a year."[1]   He was astounded at this : he did not believe that I was in earnest.   He never thanked me, and, when I left, took no notice of his pension, although I had told him that it was to begin from that very day.   But yesterday he sent to tell Wolff to come to him, and related all that I had confided to him, yet showed Wolff some disbelief in my news. Wolff said to him, " Well, Monsieur, if he has told you all this, it must be true ;   you do not know the Ambassador nor the influence which he has at his court.   If you doubt the truth of the fact, I will guarantee you the payment of the pension."

" Do you think," replied the Chancellor, " that he will begin this payment at once, and that he will pay me a thousand roubles a month ? "

" I will pay you them without asking orders," said Wolff, " as the Ambassador has told you this."

Again the Great Chancellor was extremely astonished.   But he recovered himself, and said at once to Wolff, " Go at once, I pray you, to the Ambassador, to thank him from me for all his friendship towards me.   Tell him that we shall live on the best possible terms, that I will do all I can for him, that I will try to make them accept forthwith the hundred thousand pounds sterling, and that, if possible, we will conclude everything before the arrival of the French Ambassador ;   but I very much wish that *the Protector* would make some advances to the Schuvalov (the Protector is you).   Also tell the Ambassador that his court should make us good offers for our forage, and all will go well."[2]

It was one of those scenes which, though hastily described, should make a good story for a future century.   You are the sole participator in my secret.   My heart, my life, and my soul are

[1] Sir Charles appears to have been inclined to go beyond his orders, which were to withhold the first payment until there were some more favourable appearances of compliance with English demands at the Russian court.   (Holdernesse to Sir Charles Hanbury-Williams.   August 6th, n.s. 1756.   " Most secret."   Record Office.)

[2] Sir Charles wrote to Holdernesse on September 4th, n.s., 1756, that the " real occasion of the present delays " was the desire of the Russian Government to get the largest sum possible for foraging their troops, when they moved from their own territory.

all yours. I look upon you in everything as a being superior to me. I adore you, and this adoration goes so far that I feel certain that I can never be worthy of your esteem.

I must now tell you another thing, that whenever I have spoken to the Russian Ministry about the large amount of the subsidy they have always answered me by laughing at the sum. And now it all resolves itself into fifty thousand pounds sterling, more or less, for the forage.

Tell me when you answer, if my letters are too long. Anyhow they take the place of a gazette, and have one higher merit—that they contain nothing but the truth. Now it seems to me that the stories contained in this one should make it more amusing than tedious. I speak to you from my heart. I write without disparagement and my thoughts hardly get a start of my pen. I could produce finer despatches, but they would not be so ingenuous, and in certain cases this is worth more than talent. Tell me, if for this once I am not right.

The Great Chancellor wishes me to continue to live on good terms with the Vice-Chancellor. In three days I have smoothed my path with him so well, that I am nearly sure how I stand. The Hetman, whom I like very much (I beg you to take an opportunity of telling him of my feelings towards him), assists me in this connection.

When I begin a sheet to you, I must finish it. Wolff always shudders when he speaks of the French Ambassador's arrival. He remembers Rabutin and La Chétardie, and he always repeats the same story until I too begin to shudder. He is extremely devoted to you.

Again I repeat, keep what remains of your money for your pleasures ; do not pay people who have sold you their goods at double value, until the death of the Empress. I shall act as your trusty banker. The Chancellor wished it to be Wolff. I told Wolff one morning that I shall soon take away all the money from him, either in specie or bills of exchange. I think that what I said and did about it was right. But I shall not feel sure of this until I have had your approval. What a horrid scrawl !

As to the means of sending you the money when you need it, nothing is easier. Naruishkin has only to tell Swallov to bring

me a note from you, and I will send the amount to Swallov's
house by him, and Naruishkin can get it from there. Enclosed
I send you the form of bond which you must copy for the King.
You must tell me later if you wish me to pay your debt to Wolff ;
and after having done so, I will send back word of the amount
which remains in my hands at your disposal.

Saturday. I received the honour of your letter yesterday
evening by Swallov. I thank you on my knees for it, especially for
the trouble which you have taken in translating the Turkish
despatch, which is extremely interesting and which I have re-
read three times with pleasure. I think it is well translated.
You can do everything ; for your style in this translation has
quite the official tone, and is quite different from all your other
letters.

You can imagine, Monsieur, my impatience to know all that
passes between you and Peter Schuvalov. It seems to me that
the commencement promises happy results. But I will say
nothing further until I have details of that interesting interview.
I delight in that paragraph in your letter where you say that you
are more touched by the marks of confidence and regard which
the King shows you than by anything else, and I guarantee that
you will always preserve the high opinion which he has formed
of you. I assure you also that I believe that all you are doing is
in the true interests of Russia. Her alliance with England has
continued, without interruption, ever since the time of Ivan
Basilevitch.[1] I believe like you that our alliance is the natural
alliance for our two countries, and if we are mistaken on this point,
at least we share our mistake with Peter the Great.

Be assured, Monsieur, that I have always depicted you as a
person who acted according to his own lights with knowledge
of circumstances, and who had nothing in view in all his actions
but the glory and greatness of Russia : one who would take no
action without first weighing it well, but once having taken it
you would be incapable of changing.

You have nothing to sign for Bernardi or Wolff : you have only
to sign the enclosed note, which will never leave my hands,

[1] Ivan the Terrible, who died in 1584. He was one of the suitors for
the hand of Queen Elizabeth.

F

except for those of the King.   Our secret is safe between us two (I have no objection to them being suspicious, but I do not want them to prove anything), and Naruishkin will be the one and only third.   He is your sixth finger, and I know that he likes me.

As soon, Monsieur, as I have settled (if you approve) your account with Wolff, I will return you all your bonds which are in his hands and the account of the balance which he still holds.

I hope you understand me ; but if you do not understand me, I am sure that it is my fault and that I have not explained myself clearly.

You may be sure that I will not speak to the Hetman of the interview with Peter Schuvalov, nor about Glebov.   I have always mistrusted Roman Voronzov.   Do you remember that it was I who prevented him from being in the secret, and I shall always pride myself on having given you that advice and on having forced Poniatowski to follow it, for he had a great desire to confide everything to him.   I should never have consented to the Great Chancellor's knowing it ; but the departure and (still more) the return of Poniatowski made this confidence necessary.

If you knew me a little better, you would know that I have very little ambition, and that I would always rather be something than appear to be something.

This is my castle in the air, which I built some time ago and with which I very often amuse myself.   When you are settled on this throne, if I am not here, I shall come at once.   I hope that you will ask my Master for me as English Minister at your court.   I should prefer to come with the rank of Ambassador in my pocket, but do not desire to produce it, because that would oblige me to keep up a station and a ceremony which would weary me.   I pride myself that I shall then live a great deal with you as a faithful servant and a humble friend.   I should like the right to come and go and to profit by your leisure hours : for I shall always love Catherine better than the Empress.   I should ask you for the blue ribbon, in order to wear some portion of your livery, and I should ask for your portrait, which I would carry all my life and would entail on my family, that so great an honour may continue to the last of my name.   That is my ambition ; do you condemn it ?   I hope not, for it is only the outcome of the devotion which I bear you, one so strong that I can only feel it, though it cannot be expressed. One word more. Is the maxim of Machiavelli true, which you quoted me ? He says that a man is rarely as bad as he ought to be ; but I say, thank God, bad men seldom have the courage which they should have to carry out their wicked designs.

Yesterday the Grand-Duke's valet gave back to Swallov the Grand-Duke's letter, which I had returned to his Imperial Highness by Swallov. I send it back to you again for the second time.

I have taken the liberty of keeping the papers on affairs at Constantinople for two or three days. I should much like to know what the Empress said when she read that despatch.

Upon my word, I am going to tell you something which will give you pleasure—my letter is ended. The story which I promised you is of no value ; I believe it is untrue, so I shall not tell it to you. Here is the form which the bond should take. You must add the date.

" I have received by the hand of the British Ambassador the sum of ten thousand pounds sterling, which I promise to repay to His Majesty, the King of Great Britain, whenever he demands it of me. C."

From Sir Charles Hanbury-Williams

Saturday afternoon [August 24.]

My letters will become gazettes ; but it is your fault. The moment I see your paper, I burn to answer it, and even in the midst of my despatches, I cannot allow Naruishkin's servant to leave without expressing to you my gratitude for your kindnesses.

I will answer your to-day's letter at the first opportunity : for the present it is enough to tell you one thing only. I loved Poniatowski before you had seen him. For six years I brought him up. I have always looked upon him as my adopted son ; therefore I deserve no special merit in your eyes on his account, and I never lay claim to special merit where I have none.

All the English who returned from Oranienbaum are enchanted. I do not believe in spells. But they are enchanted. They speak of you, as if I was speaking. There is no more to be said. I do not understand what Bernardi means by his offer of money, or by the fifty thousand roubles which I am to pay you. He knows nothing about the whole matter. I flatter myself that the ten thousand pounds sterling should produce for you forty-two thousand five hundred roubles, but I have not yet settled the exchange with Wolff. You can rely on me to make a good bargain for you. But there are besides certain charges to be paid to our Treasury for all money which leaves it. All this will be submitted for your consideration.

Adieu, Monsieur. I shall write to you again soon, and I shall never cease as long as I live to be your devoted servant.

From THE GRAND-DUCHESS

[*Sunday, August 25.*]

A circumstance has just arisen, which if not remedied, will certainly counteract all my adroitness in persuading the Grand-Duke to come to a friendly understanding with the King of Denmark.[1] The chapter of the Canons of Lübeck has fixed the third of September for the election of the *dom-dèchant*, as they call him, and the choice will fall on a certain man named Witzendorf, in the service of the King, your Master, at Ratzeburg. This is of no account, but I mention it, because the man may be useful in partly preventing what follows. October 3 is fixed by the same chapter for the election of the coadjutor to the Bishop, who is my uncle, brother to my mother.[2] This coadjutor, they say, is to be the second son of the King of Denmark. Now the Bishopric of Lübeck has for two hundred years descended from father to son in the House of Holstein, and is looked on as an appanage for the younger son. These younger sons, without

[1] The Duchy of Slesvic was reunited to Denmark in the reign of King Christian VI. His successor, Frederick V. (1746-66) went further, and laid claim to the Duchy of Holstein, which was held by the Dukes of Holstein-Gottorp. The matter dragged on until after the Grand-Duke's accession in 1763, but, at the moment when war was about to be declared, he was deposed. Catherine then came to an arrangement with the King to exchange Holstein for the Duchy of Oldenburg, and a treaty was signed to this effect.

[2] Prince Frederick August of Holstein-Gottorp. His eldest brother, Prince Adolf Frederick, whom he had succeeded in the Bishopric, was at this time King of Sweden.

this appanage, will be beggars. They will throw themselves on the mercy of the Grand-Duke ; and I shall have the humiliation of seeing them come all this way to beg their bread from me. And you know what a family of poor German princes means, more especially in Russia.

I wrote on the subject this morning, Sunday, to the Chancellor by Pechlin.[1] I implore you to speak of it to Maltzahn.[2] Further, the King, your Master, as Elector of Hanover, would perhaps rather have the Bishop of Lübeck, a younger son of the House of Gottorp, as neighbour for his Duchy of Lauenburg, than the son of the King of Denmark, who buys with immediate possession the Duchy of Plœn, to enlarge that son's portion, thus giving him a stretch of country from the Elbe to the Trave. Finally, remember, if all this seems trifling to you, that all my efforts about the exchange will be useless, unless you can remove this stumbling-block for me ; and, when all is said and done, it is approaching me in the wrong way to desire to reduce my uncles to beggary. Let Maltzahn write, or even send an express ; the matter is urgent. The news comes from Kiel by express. Thank you for your yesterday's letter ; I have not had the time to answer it yet.

From Sir Charles Hanbury-Williams

Monday, 11 *o'clock* [*August* 26.]

Thank you, Monsieur, for your letter written on Friday afternoon. And thank you still more for your just appreciation of my devotion to you. After you have had the kindness to tell me that you did have some regard for me, and that it had existed for a long time independent of any other tie, I very willingly concede to your honesty all secondary causes which you may think fit to add. But in the case which you quote, I can have no special merit in your eyes, since my friendship for your friendship is five years earlier than my acquaintance with you. Your good feeling towards me always credits me with qualities which I do not possess : for what special merit can I find in your eyes for loving a person, whose friend I was five years before I knew you.

[1] The Grand-Duke's Minister of Holstein. He died in the spring of 1757.
[2] The Danish Minister in Russia, who died a few months later.

I think that the Grand Chancellor may have become jealous of me. I think he is so still; for yesterday he sent word by Wolff to implore me to write him a note, in which I was to say that all I had done on your behalf had been entirely done at his request. Apparently he wished to send you this note. But Wolff had already answered that he knew me too well to dare to make me such a suggestion. But he is mistaken, for, provided that the Chancellor undertakes to return me my letter, I am ready to write anything that will please him. I shall see him this afternoon, and you shall know everything.

It is better that our interchange of letters should remain a secret between us two. The means of corresponding by Naruishkin and Swallov is so easy and so secret that no one can discover it; and as for suspicions, I laugh at them. You wish to comfort me by telling me how many friends I have at the council. But take it from me, that last Friday the whole council wanted to accept the £100,000 sterling, and Peter Schuvalov alone opposed it and prevented them from accepting it.

You do not mention whether Bernardi handed you a letter from me received from Stockholm. I have become a violent supporter of the King of Sweden. I receive no letter from any part of Europe which does not speak with great astonishment and some scorn of Russia's conduct towards Sweden, particularly that she should allow the uncle of the Grand-Duke to be insulted by a French Ambassador and sixteen ragamuffins. But it appears to me that your court has been solely occupied for nearly a year with the means of obtaining the privilege from the court of Versailles of seeing its Ambassador here.

The English returned from Oranienbaum singing the praises of the gracious Grand-Duke and the charming Grand-Duchess. They all came to see me, and I was pleased with their gratitude. I like Naruishkin. I should much like to have him living in my house for six months: he has a good heart and a quick understanding, and I should be able to make a lot of him. When the good times arrive, I will sometimes give him lessons. You will allow I am good at that, for you have known one of my pupils who has not turned out so badly. It is true, however, that the cloth must be good to make so fine a coat.

As I am about to finish this letter, I receive yours, without date, on the Lübeck affair. I will think it over at once. I will do all that time allows. Hanover and Berlin shall work for you, or I shall work no more for them.

I have thought for an hour. This is what I shall do. I shall go at once to the Great Chancellor; apparently he knows all about the matter. I will speak to him of the Danish business; he will tell me the story of Lübeck. I shall offer him my services, and I am ready to send a courier immediately to Berlin and Hanover, to pledge both courts to use all their influence in the chapter to prevent the election of the Prince of Denmark. The King is very displeased with His Danish Majesty, and I shall take care to embitter their relations.

In any case write at once (at this very moment) to the Chancellor. Tell him to send for me, and to beg me on your behalf to do all that you point out to him, for it may be that you may not yet have told him this story or that he has not spoken to me about it; and you know that there is no time to lose. I will not fail to speak of it to Maltzahn. I would prefer, however, that the Chancellor should ask me to do it, the better to hide my game. It seems to me that His Danish Majesty has become so pro-French, that he follows their example—makes use of tricks and springs surprises. Make haste to reply. This touches you and the Grand-Duke closely; and if I am always in a hurry to serve you, take note that this letter even is written in haste.

From THE GRAND-DUCHESS

Tuesday, after dinner [August 27].

I received yesterday your letter of Monday, and as Bernardi happened to be here, I wrote without delay a second letter to the Chancellor about the Lübeck affair (the first having been conveyed to him on Sunday by Pechlin). I send you copies of both.[1] But

[1] " I told Bernardi what you wished to know in your first letter. I raise no objection to the inclusion of the second considering the unquestionable necessity for it, as I am certain that the personal welfare of the Grand-Duke and the interests of Russia demand it. I will do my best. My obligations to you increase every day. After paying you and Baron Wolff, I wish the remainder to be placed in the hands of the English Ambassador, for I do not wish or intend to touch it except at a moment of

that everything should be done in order, I shall commence by answering your letter of Friday and Saturday. Forgive me, if the extreme dissipation in which we live here, has prevented me from doing so until now. I shall only pay Bernardi when I am able to do so comfortably, or if he is in urgent need. He did not even speak to me again to-day of money, either in the name of his patron or in his own. I am much annoyed that the former confides matters, which should be a complete secret, to a man like

extreme urgency. I should be ashamed to face a person whom I esteem and honour as much as I do the Ambassador, apart from any other connection, if I took all the money without dire necessity. How can the honest arguments of the Turks help us, if we do not behave as wisely as they do."

Whilst I am waiting for him to return me the first letter about the Lübeck affair, here is mine of this morning, Tuesday :—

" The shameful abandonment of my uncle, the King of Sweden, when four lines might have helped him, without thought for the contempt which recoils on the country, which can allow a French Ambassador and sixteen ragamuffins in his pay to insult a King whom the Empress of Russia has set on the throne, and whose constitution she has guaranteed—all this I think with a view to the triumph of obtaining the favour of the French court, in order that they should deign to send an Ambassador here to give laws to the great and fashions to the small—all this, I say, should disabuse me of the mistake of interceding for my relations. Nevertheless, I cannot bear to see that I am of so little repute, that His Danish Majesty should think that he can use me as his tool and dupe. I have no doubt that Monsieur Pechlin will have informed your Excellency of the meaning of all this, unless he has carried negligence to its limit in a matter so pressing. You must have received my letter, handed to his care, with the letter of the Prince Bishop of Lübeck to the Grand-Duke, which I gave orders should be communicated to you. You will see by it that they wish to deprive the younger sons of Holstein of what they have been possessed for two hundred years, and thus reduce them to beggary. His Danish Majesty, soaked with French principles, tries to imitate them : he makes use of trickery and surprises. The whole thing has been kept secret until this moment, and October 3rd is fixed for the election of a coadjutor, the younger son of His Danish Majesty. If you do not put a stop to this, you will be responsible for bringing a troop of German Princes upon my hands, who will come to beg for bread from me and bring shame and hatred upon me even in these far climes. As I believe that the interests of the King of England are bound up in this matter with those of my uncles, I beg your Excellency to send for the English Ambassador to tell him to use every means, in conjunction with your Excellency, which he thinks desirable to turn aside this fatal blow, and to avert this disgrace from a house of which the Grand-Duke and I are members, and which is already but too much decayed. The chapter of Lübeck has just elected a *dom dèchant*, named de Witzendorf, a servant of the King of England at Ratzeburg, without whose vote neither side can do anything. I suggest him to you as a useful instrument."

him; anyhow, I shall avoid indiscretions myself as much as possible.

The Chancellor, from the last letter which he wrote to me—one which I will translate for you if time permits—seems to me to be again much warmed to England.   At least he tries to inspire me with more horror of the French intrigues than I even feel already, with the desire to prevent them.   These are his proposals. He wants me to persuade the Grand-Duke (he promises to support me and to speak of it to the Grand-Duke as well as to Apraksin), to make an urgent demand to be allowed to be present at all conferences which are held, " for," says the Chancellor, " all these people will be frightened, and will never dare to back up propositions of which they know that the Grand-Duke dis- approves." This is the result of twelve thousand roubles; I shall certainly never abuse this confidence, and he shall never guess that I know his secret.   I owe you this, and shall not depart from it.   Posterity could never receive better information than yours, if you gave yourself the trouble to hand down all you know. I pride myself that I should not lose by it, after the reiterated assurances of friendship which you give me.   Persevere in your offers, and let not the oft-repeated refusal of the £100,000 sterling surprise you.   They will accept it in the end : self-interest guides everyone.   And when the moment comes that Ivan Ivanovitch is short of money, he will make them accept, in order to get his share :   and they will then borrow them from the College of Foreign Affairs, for amongst other things you must know that the cabinet borrows money from all the Colleges, and that it owes several millions which have been frittered away.

Your letters are never too long.   When I have finished reading the longest of them, I regret that I have no more to read ; they equally amuse and instruct me.   Your simplicity is wit.   You are right to write them off-hand : other people's most studied compositions do not equal yours.   The point to which you have reduced the Vice-Chancellor in three days scarcely agrees with the documents which the Chancellor has sent me by Bernardi. The whole thing is the negotiation of Douglas with Douglas.   I send you the translations of the records ; if I can do it, you shall have an extract of the whole, or, in any case, of any paper which you point out.   Alas ! he is a very poor fellow, if you can make so sure of him in three days.   I am full of obligations to Baron Wolff for his devotion.   I would like to feel fear, but I cannot ;   the invisible hand which has led me for thirteen years along a very rough road will never allow me to give way, of that I am very firmly and perhaps foolishly convinced.   If you knew all the precipices and misfortunes which have threatened me, and which I have overcome, you would place more confidence in conclusions which are too hollow for those who think as deeply as you.   Bernardi brought me the account of what I owe Wolff and the Chancellor, but said not one word.   I took it in like manner. You have spoken and acted well throughout.   You have my approval.   I am very glad that my translation of the Turkish document pleased you ;   it was translated word for word.   Peter Schuvalov has not yet appeared.

I saw some years ago the original treaty signed by Elizabeth, which that Queen concluded with Ivan Basilevitch.   It is in the Archives at Moscow.   That Prince, tyrant though he was, was a great man ;   and as I shall try, as far as my natural weakness will allow me, to imitate the great men of this country, I shall also hope to adorn your Archives one day with my name, and shall be very proud to go astray in the footprints of Peter the Great.

" My lights which act from knowledge of circumstance, and my firmness which follows from them " are very much indebted to you for the fine description with which you honour them :   my modesty pales at it, while my presumption blushes.   Naruishkin wishes to increase his titles by that of the sixth finger of my hand. I understand and approve of all your arrangements regarding my money.   Ought not something to be done for Count Poniatowski at this early stage ?

Your opinion of Roman Voronzov is very fair, and would strengthen mine, were I not also already fully convinced.   Your castles in the air are entirely in keeping with mine.   One of the pleasures which I should hope for most, would be to profit more often by your conversation.   I grant your requests beforehand, and give you a free hand in all the honours, distinctions, etc., etc., that you may desire.   They will always be less than you deserve. As far as she can do so, the Empress will repay Catherine's obligations and her own.

So much the better, if God has limited the courage of the wicked in the performance of their wicked deeds.

I returned the Grand-Duke his letter ; both Swallov and the valet were drunk. We do not know whose fault it was, as one said it was the other's. You are not often mistaken, but you were never more so than when you thought that you were giving me good news, when you informed me that your letter was finished. I must tell you that I felt worried at writing the bond for the money, on account of the risk of it falling into strange hands : try to keep it in your possession. May God preserve the King, your Master, but he is only human, and he is old, and after him, etc., etc.

You have special merit in my eyes, in spite of all you say, for your affection for Count Poniatowski. How can one feel ill-will to those who wish him happiness ? You have made him what he is ; *the cloth was good, you say.* There ! I am obliged to you for this praise which you give him : it delights me. I hope that the request which I am going to make will not bother you. I know that sometimes you have amused yourself with making portraits. Send me one of him ; it will give me great pleasure.

Peter Schuvalov, it seems to me, might be won over by Apraksin to accept the £100,000 sterling. It is the Chancellor's business. Bernardi handed me your letter from Stockholm the other evening ; I dare not think of the condition of that unhappy King. The Chancellor sent me yesterday some extracts from Panin's statements,[1] in which all that your letter contains is reported, with this addition, that the supposed letter from Count Brahé, found after his death and only credited as genuine by the ruling faction, contains accusations against the Queen of criminal connection between her and Count Hardt, and also with Count Brahé ; that they talk publicly of making this a pretext for divorcing her, for they say that as long as she, Count Hardt and Baron Wrangel are all alive, it is impossible to say that the conspiracy is at an end. I have made use of many of your

---

[1] Count Panin (1718-83), Russian Ambassador in Sweden from 1748 until 1760.

expressions in my letter to the Chancellor. I hope that you will not be annoyed at this. The greatest happiness which Naruishkin could have would be to be with you; he realizes it perfectly himself. He adores you. Thank you for the promptness with which you act and which you advise me to employ in the Lübeck affair.

There is a rumour here that the King of Prussia has thrashed the armies of the Empress-Queen in Moravia. The news comes from Tsarkoïe Selo.

Since seven in the morning until this moment, seven in the evening, omitting the hours for dinner, I have done nothing but write and read documents. Might it not be said of me that I am a Minister of State?

From SIR CHARLES HANBURY-WILLIAMS

Wednesday [*August* 28.]

Monsieur, Last night I had a very long conversation with the Great Chancellor. It lasted two full hours. I asked him, when I left, if he was satisfied with me. He answered: " Very satisfied, more than satisfied."

I soon brought the conversation round to Lübeck, and I found Beichling (Pechlin) at his house. I pointed out forcibly to him, how hard it was for the Grand-Duke to see his family and his States so totally neglected by this court. I spoke of Sweden and of this Lübeck affair, and also of the figure and the part which those, who would one day be his subjects, were obliging him to play here. I also made him understand that if the King of Denmark dealt him a blow of this kind, any satisfactory arrangement to exchange Holstein would become impracticable. He seemed struck by what I said, but at the same time did not know that the election of the coadjutor was taking place so soon. He had told me that it would not be held till the month of December. In the end, he told me that he would send Beichling (Pechlin) to my house to talk the matter over with me, and to see what could be done about it.

I have waited for him all the morning, and he has not come.

The Chancellor also told me that he was going to advise the Grand-Duke to demand a permanent seat at the conference;

otherwise in future he would sign no *doklade*. This is good advice, of which I strongly approve.

He begged me very much to trust Bernardi. He believes him to have more talent than he has, and to be better at business than he is. But, when all is said and done, we have no one but him to keep up communication between us. I asked him whether Bernardi knew of your correspondence with my friend; he swore to me that he did not. But that is not true. And when I showed some doubts on the subject, he told me that he thought that he (Bernardi) suspected it. To this I replied, that at all events he should never know anything of it from me, but that, as he wishes it, he should have my confidence on all other matters. This pleased the Chancellor. He added at once, " As *you wish* to employ him, I beg you very earnestly to do something for him; he is poor and needy." I answered, " You are his employer, but I refuse my friends nothing. I do everything for you; you do nothing for me nor for my Master." He replied that he did everything that was in his power, and that he would do more in the future. Upon that he asked for a big sum for Bernardi. I promised it to him, and shall keep my word.

Then he spoke much of you. He told me that he had sent you all the negotiations with France, from which I hope and flatter myself that I shall have some extracts. In the end he touched on Poniatowski, and told me a tale which I knew already, but which I did not want to tell you for fear of disquieting you.

The Vice-Chancellor was the person who sent an officer after Poniatowski with the snuff-box which the Empress gave him. This officer, on his return, related that as soon as Poniatowski heard at Riga that an officer was asking to see him from the Empress, he was panic-stricken, and trembled all over when the officer entered his room, but that he recovered himself when he heard what the officer had to say to him and had received the snuff-box.

This is the report of a rogue, to whom Poniatowski gave a gold watch and a hundred ducats. The story was repeated to the Empress, and has given much cause for thought to account for the reason for Poniatowski's fear.

Without entering into the above matter with the Chancellor, I said to him firmly, " Ambassador though I am, if I left here, and a Russian officer was sent after me from the Empress, I would not answer for my courage when his arrival was announced to me, for the story of La Chétardie remains fresh in everyone's memory."[1]

Upon that, he told me that you ought to be informed of it, but that he did not wish the tale to come from him. So he begged me to write him a letter containing this story, and then he would send my letter on to you.

I answered that I would think it over ; and, if you do not disapprove, I shall do it, because in your reply you can insist that it is necessary for Poniatowski's safety for him to return here as Minister from Poland, which is the one thing in the world that he desires most.

How many things did he not ask me for himself ! But in the end I am myself satisfied that we are on perfectly good terms, and that is what I wanted ; and it is to you that I owe it. But, Monsieur, the greatest trouble which I took was to discover upon what footing he really stands with the Schuvalov, and I find that he does everything that he can to be well with them, that he is really on good terms with Peter Schuvalov, but not so well with Ivan, and that he wants you to wheedle them. I was sorry to hear from him that Peter Schuvalov would not be going to Oranienbaum, because I am very sure that if you had an hour's conversation with him, you would get to know all you want. His vanity would stand little chance against your good sense. I imagine that the Vice-Chancellor's words about young Ivan are the secret which Glebov wants to tell you. The Grand Chancellor told me that if Peter Schuvalov had not prevented it, or if the Grand-Duke had been present at the council last Friday, there would have been good news to send to England.

It appears to me that the Grand Chancellor has not a suspicion of our correspondence ; so much the better.

You must press with all your strength for Poniatowski's return as Minister ; he (the Chancellor) promised me that he would bring it about. I want him to write again to Gross[2] by my next

[1] La Chétardie's letters to his court were intercepted and deciphered, and he, in consequence, was arrested and banished in June, 1744.
[2] Russian Minister in Saxony and Poland.

courier, to insist that the business should be done in the way we desire.

I shall give you very exact information of all that I say to Bernardi when I give him his money.   I want him to act promptly with me.   I have suffered too much from Funcke's[1] tricks, to place myself again in a similar position.   Bernardi is just back from Oranienbaum.   He dined here, and told me that he has handed you the papers about the negotiations with France : that it was true that the Chancellor had ordered him to bring them back with him, but that you wished to keep them, and would return them to him when you came to town.   I am delighted with all this, because I count on having some extracts.

I had very bad rheumatism last night in my arm, which still bothers me.   No news of my friend, and I do not expect that I shall have any until after his arrival at Warsaw, on September 8, n.s.

The Chancellor told me that the House of Brunswick was taking a great interest in the election of the Prince of Denmark. Had I known of this affair sooner, I could have prevented all the intrigues of that House, and I answer for it that my Master would have been delighted to prove his real affection for the Grand-Duke on this occasion.

I am very sure that I am, and that I shall be all my life, your slave : and I am certain that you believe me to be your friend. Henry the Great began his letters to Sully, *Mon ami*.   I shall feel very proud if you will do the same.

From THE GRAND-DUCHESS

Thursday morning [August 29].

I arrived very late yesterday,[2] and brought my Tuesday's packet here in my pocket, having no one to send with it to you. I received your last letter yesterday morning.   Thank you for the friendship towards me which you express in it, *mon ami*— since that is the title which you yourself suggest for me to use ; for as to the fact I am completely convinced, and I have no time to say more.   Here is an unfinished copy, not an extract, of the

---

[1] Saxon Minister in St Petersburg until May, 1756.
[2] On her return from the country.

Douglas business. I thought that these excellent documents would lose their charm and value if I made extracts from them ; and what means are there of extracting anything from matters which contain no substance ?   So I should only want to employ *an abundance of words to such an end.*

The Empress remained at the conference yesterday till six in the evening.

I am very distressed to hear that you are ill.   I am afraid that all these documents may tire you ; rather than that, do not read them, for the greater part are only rubbish.

I had heard the story of Count Poniatowski's fears from Bernardi.   I will again put pressure on the Chancellor about him. Good-bye, Monsieur, *mon bon ami*.   Good health to you, and if possible do not let these documents worry you, for they are mostly **very** badly written.

From SIR CHARLES HANBURY-WILLIAMS

Friday [*August* 30.]

Monsieur, I received from Naruishkin this afternoon your two letters of Tuesday and Thursday, with all the papers enclosed. Thank you, with all my heart, for your kindness, and for your trouble in copying and making extracts from negotiations worthy of those who planned them and full of shame for Russia.   France has held out her hand to you, and you have kissed her feet. But before I answer your letters, I must tell you all my news. They have at last determined to send an express to Copenhagen, to pass through Hamburg, in order to command Saltikov[1] to go at once to Lübeck to oppose the measures of the King of Denmark ; and I have been asked to write to our Minister at Copenhagen to support your interests.

I will do so ; but it is too late.   Maltzahn was here this morning. I told him what I thought very brusquely, and I explained to him very clearly that the King, his Master, must give up one or other, the exchange of the Duchies or the Bishopric.   He replied that it was too late.   I answered that if the matter was settled, the

---

[1] Serge Saltikov, Catherine's former lover, and Russian Minister at Hamburg.

young Prince must at once give up his coadjutorship ; for until he had taken that step, it would be impossible to propose the exchange to his Imperial Highness. When he heard me speak in that tone, he frankly owned that he had written to his court by the last post practically everything that I had just said. According to my ideas, that is where the Grand-Duke should take his stand. No negotiations on the exchange, until the Bishopric is in the hands of his Imperial Highness's family. As for the English business, I shall have my answer Saturday or Monday.

Now we must speak of that of Prussia. His Prussian Majesty, contrary to his usual custom, has made a false step, for he has declared to the court of Vienna, that this court and the Empress-Queen had concluded an offensive treaty against him in the month of January last, which had not been carried into effect this year because the Russian army had not yet got all its recruits.[1] He demanded assurances from the Empress-Queen that she would not attack him this year or the next. To all this the court of Vienna very properly replied that there was no foundation for what the King of Prussia alleged, and that no such treaty existed between the two courts ; and this is quite true. I cannot imagine who can have given such information to His Prussian Majesty.

My letters of to-day announce that, on receipt of this answer, the King of Prussia sent another courier to Vienna to demand a categorical answer whether they would attack him or not : but at the same time I am begged to make known to this court that, if the least overtures are made, the King of Prussia would be ready to send a Minister here at once, and that the Empress's mediation would be very acceptable to him. I received this news at noon, and wished to communicate it this afternoon to the Great Chancellor, but he begged me in the first instance to communicate it to the Vice-Chancellor. I did so ; and the Vice-Chancellor tells me that the Empress was extremely offended with the King of Prussia for putting forward a suggestion that she had entered into a treaty of which she had never thought ; and that he did not understand what necessity there could be for mediation, before

[1] This was quite incorrect, as Sir Charles hastened to reply to Andrew Mitchell (See *Frederick Polit. Corres.*, xiii. 469).

G

there was war. To that I replied, that the whole proposal was a glorious one for the Empress, that with one word she could prevent the outbreak of a war, which would soon become general, and for the success of which no one could answer ; but that it was necessary to decide at once what part was to be taken, for I could assure her (and it is true) that the King of Prussia had left Berlin to place himself at the head of his army. He told me that he would not fail to-morrow to consult the Great Chancellor about all that I had told him. *Mon Dieu* ! If only you were in your place, what a part you might play !

Another very bad piece of news. The Hetman's enemies will certainly drive him from hence. The Empress told his brother yesterday evening, that the times required that he should go to the Ukraine to take charge of that country. The Hetman told me that he was much afraid that his enemies were all united to ruin him. I found him very melancholy. Send me word all you know about this, and for the love of this honest man give him all your support. They are taking from you a servant who is attached to you heart and soul, and who at the right time and at the right place will be able to do you good service. The Great Chancellor finds it convenient to be ill to-day, but he sent to tell me that he would be at court to-morrow. There ends my gazette.

As for your letters—you tell me in the first, that you have sent me two letters from the Chancellor. I only found one.

As for your money—I shall send you the account as soon as I get it from Wolff, and that will be on Monday. I warn you that on Tuesday or Wednesday I shall send off a courier, so you have only to begin a letter to Poniatowski, and it will reach him by a safe hand.

I am delighted that the Chancellor, on his own account, has persuaded the Grand-Duke to insist upon his seat at the council. He will do good, and Peter Schuvalov's cackle will grow less.

As for the praise which you award to my letters, you would be wiser to say nothing : for you will make me so vain, that I shall begin to think that I write well, and in order not to lose my reputation, I shall only run after wit, I shall try to polish my phrases, I shall hunt for bons mots, and all that in a language of which I do not know the spelling. True it is that I find some very astonishing things in Russia, amongst them the Vice-Chancellor. But he does not change, he is Prussian at heart. The Great Chancellor confesses that he is no longer pro-French. As to his negotiations with Douglas, I count on having them printed as a supplement to the *Lettres d'Estrades*. But they are worth a letter to themselves, and you shall have it on the first day possible. All famous authors have their commentators ; and I wish to be the Amelot of this great d'Ossat.[1]

I add my wishes and prayers to yours, that your lucky star, which has led you thus far in safety, may protect you to the last moment of your life. Prudence alone can insure happiness; and those who are unhappy (for the most part) have only themselves to thank for it. Yet I am wrong in what I say, for, on my honour, I have done all that prudence can dictate in my present negotia-tion ; nevertheless my negotiation has been very unfortunate, and if in the end I derive some good from it, it will only be from the influence of your star. I am sorry Peter Schuvalov has not been to see you. You would have got something out of him.

I agree with you that Ivan Basilevitch was a very great prince, and Peter the Great said so too. Do you know that during a rising against him he asked Elizabeth for refuge in England ? And Elizabeth was at least as great a tyrant as he was.

I hope some day that Naruishkin will be a right arm. But for the present he must be content to be your very little finger. I am delighted that my castle in the air is to your liking. I shall be content with a hovel, so long as it is near you. You ask me for a portrait. I could do it. But I paint from nature. Take care not to repeat that request ; I am sure that I should be foolish enough to obey you.

As for affairs at Stockholm, I am almost certain that that paper of Brahé will do all that the ruling party require. I admit that I have never heard that the Queen of Sweden was fast, but then I know no gossip from that country.

Never have I read a more sensible letter, and one more full of strength and argument, than yours to the Chancellor. If you

---

[1] Amelot de la Houssaye (1634-1706) edited the letters of Cardinal d'Ossat.

have made use of some of my words and expressions, they are so neatly placed that I did not recognize them.

I told Naruishkin to-day that he must one day (God grant that that day may come soon) come to me to take lessons, and I am delighted to learn from you that he likes me.

Allow me to keep the Douglas papers for two days longer; I have had no time to read them. I am very well, and hope to have the honour of seeing you this evening. I made a stupid remark at the beginning of this letter that I had only received from you one of the Chancellor's letters. It is perfectly true that I have two, which I now return to you. Good-bye, my patron. Always I am all that you wish me to be.

From THE GRAND-DUCHESS

Sunday [Friday], August 30.

Here, *mon ami*, are the scraps of the splendid and honourable negotiations with Douglas. Had he made his first appearance at my house with a letter about the wines of Burgundy and similar balderdash, I should have had him passed out by the window instead of by the door. This was exactly what I expected from you, and the reason why the loss of the coadjutorship worried me so little. Renunciation must be the preliminary to any negotiation, unless this election can still be prevented in time. The Grand-Duke and I are quite agreed on that point. Nothing pleases me more than when great intellects trip. If I was in the position where you wish me to be, I would try to profit by the mistakes of His Prussian Majesty; and no one unless they had lost their senses would hesitate to consider these proposals. Is it not an act of folly to hand himself over to our mediation? Or is not the law of citizenship, which calls for impartiality in any mediator, in existence amongst the great?

The Grand-Duke will speak to the Hetman to-day, and is quite ready to help him. My ten days' absence has upset my news-mongers. I know nothing but what you have just sent me.

I was not able to send you my first letter to the Chancellor on the Lübeck affair. He still has it. I will send you a letter for Count Poniatowski. If you are my friend, send me his portrait.

This will go some way to dispel the loneliness of the sad prospect of five months' absence, which is still before me. The description which you give of the ambition which my praise kindles in you is the most pleasing that I have had for a long time. I shall not give in about it ; you write well, and certain it is that your letters give me much pleasure.

It seems to me from what you tell me about the Vice-Chancellor, that what is immediately before his eyes has much power over him ; and I conclude from his whole conduct that he is even a much poorer fellow than anyone thinks.

These comments will resemble Dr Matanasius and his *Chef-d'Œuvre d'un Inconnu*.

If my star does not belie itself, it is perfectly clear that your cause will not suffer in that quarter. I will speak to Peter Schuvalov to-night ; he waited for me yesterday in an ante-room where we exchanged civil speeches, and to-day he has sent me a large basket of fruit. He has taken under his wing an artillery officer whom I recommended to him. I shall never ask for shelter from the King, your Master, for I am resolved, as you know, to perish or to reign. I had forgotten the story of Ivan Basilevitz, but remembered it when I read your letter. Tell me the truth. Have you noticed any indication of blundering in Naruishkin, or did I misunderstand the meaning of your letter ?

God preserve me from seeing you in that hovel ; it would be a bad look-out for me. I am looking forward with pleasure to seeing you this evening. The health of a certain person continues to fail. With me you will always be in the place where you should be.

From THE GRAND-DUCHESS

Saturday [*August* 31].

The Grand-Duke's new penchant for a Greek girl, who is in my service, causes his frequent presence in my apartments, and prevents me from being as free as usual. That is the reason why I have not yet satisfied your curiosity about my conversation with Peter Schuvalov the day before yesterday. I opened the subject in the manner suggested by Apraksin, saying that I had learnt from the latter that he had shown more friendly feeling than I had understood. On the strength of this he began to speak loudly of his loyalty ; and this lasted for some minutes. I begged him to show me some proof of it at once. " I have heard something," said I, " explain to me what it is." He replied, " Perhaps there are people who, judging by their words and thoughts, are not on the right track." " Who are these people ? " " The Vice-Chancellor." " What does he say and do ? "

He told me that he had heard that when the signature was missing the Vice-Chancellor gave vent to rather strong language before the whole council. " What did he say ? "

" I am afraid," he answered, " to understate or overstate anything, for I was not present. I shall find out the truth, and in a short time I shall tell you this, and many other things too which will prove my loyalty and my desire to serve you."

He wished to proceed to flattery, but I escaped this by saying, " I know you have talent, and for that reason I would rather have to do with you than with others."

He answered me, " I swear that every time I knew you were displeased with my brother,[1] I avoided him and felt as much annoyed with him as you did yourself : for I exhort him, and have always exhorted him, to try to please you in everything."

I replied, "I do not wish to speak of, nor look back to, the past, but I am going to date everything from to-day."

He said to me, " To-day, then, is perhaps the most fortunate day of my existence, nor do I flatter you in what I say. This conversation gives me new life."

" I believe it," was my reply ; " but remember that my favour is not kept alive by words, but that to bestow my friendship I require definite results. In return, too, I give loyal assistance, when I so wish, to those who deserve it : and if your intentions are to be my friend, as you assure me, you will not repent it in so far at least as it depends on me. " The first proof of that," said I, " is that I do not wish your brother to be taken from us."

He replied with very many thanks.

I asked him, " Was your brother present when the Vice-Chancellor was speaking ? "

[1] Alexander Schuvalov.

He said, " I do not know, but it will not be from him, but from Apraksin, that I shall obtain the information which I have promised you."

He seemed to wish to make excuses for the Vice-Chancellor, saying, " He took the refusal of the Grand-Duke's signature as a personal reproach, because he had put the whole matter through " : and added, " They sent it to us completed."

" He was right," I said, " in this case. For him the objections of the Grand-Duke were overwhelming. When your brother begged me to speak to the Grand-Duke and to persuade him to sign, the latter gave me his reasons, which were, that he did not sign because it would be against his conscience and unbecoming to an honest man to sign what he considered to be bad and pernicious : that a French Ambassador would only be one intriguer the more, and a dangerous intriguer : that the example of La Chétardie, ungrateful as he was, though loaded with kindness, was an omen for the future : that France had never tried to do anything but lower and diminish the renown and might of Russia, and that we had no need of her."

He replied, " She might help us under certain conditions, and we could make use of her as circumstances arose."

" In what way ? " said I. " Would it be with money ? "

" Oh, no," he said. " With armies ? " " No," was his reply.

" These negotiations are uniformly unfavourable to us. Tell me then, in what way ? "

He did not know what to answer, with all his chatter, and said, " You are right. Really the Grand-Duke's views were good."

We then parted, with many assurances of zeal and great liveliness on his part. To-day, Sunday, Buturlin sent to offer me his vote at the councils, adding that, provided he knew what line I desired him to take, he would follow it blindly. I leave this point to your decision, and I think that, in spite of his weakness and knavery, we can perhaps make some use of him.

Here is my letter for Count Poniatowski. Send him a thousand silver ducats out of the money which you hold.

From Sir Charles Hanbury-Williams

Saturday [*August* 31].

Monsieur, I have received yours of yesterday. I thank you for it with all my heart, and for the enclosure. With arms like these one can fight, with a text like this one can make comment. I will do so, but not yet, because you command me to draw some portraits. I shall draw one for you because you wish it, I shall draw another for my own amusement ; but remember that I am a Dutch painter, who would consider it just as great a crime to hide a blemish as a thing of beauty. You will be pleased with the truths that I shall tell, because in my two pictures beauty comes out to the best advantage.

A conference was held to-day. I hope the Grand-Duke will have been present. It was to discuss Prussian affairs, but I do not know the upshot.

I have no news to send you, except that the King of Prussia has entered Saxony with his army, and that he has published a declaration to excuse himself for this conduct towards the King of Poland.[1]

I assure you, Monsieur, that I know of no blunders made by Naruishkin : and I must have badly expressed myself on the subject, or you must have misunderstood the sense of my letter.

Michel[2] has arrived from Paris. He went straight to Ivan Ivanovitch, and was closeted with him for an hour.

I do not yet know the reason why the Empress did not appear at the ball on Friday.

I return you your papers, and beg of you to wait patiently for my portraits and my comments; you shall have them both. I hope the Grand-Duke will have given the Hetman some comfort, for he was very worried the other night, and was afraid of his

---

[1] See *Frederick Polit. Corres.*, xiii. 279, 320, etc. The King of Poland, who was also Elector of Saxony, had granted King Frederick's request (August 29th) to be allowed to march troops across Saxony into Bohemia, on condition that the inhabitants should not be molested. Frederick's troops did not respect this promise.

[2] Evidently Michel de Rouen. He was reported at Dantzig on September 3rd, n.s., accompanied by two ladies. (*Receuil etc.* Russie, ii. 28).

enemies' designs against him. The Empress has told the Grand Master of the Hunt[1] that the Hetman must go to the Ukraine.

From SIR CHARLES HANBURY-WILLIAMS.

Monday [*September* 2].

I hoped to have finished one portrait to-day, but it is impossible, and I find that there is much to touch up.

I implore you, Monsieur, to tell me something of the decisions taken here, and whether they are really determined to go to war.

The King of Prussia has published a manifesto on his entrance into Saxony, and has at the same time sent a courier to Vienna to say that if the Empress-Queen will assure him that she will not attack him this year or next, he will return home with the greatest pleasure at the head of his army. I sent this declaration to the Great Chancellor yesterday morning, and at the same time I repeated the offer for the mediation of Her Imperial Majesty. I return you all your papers with a thousand thanks. The Great Chancellor has just sent me the King of Prussia's declaration, so you have it.

I am just the same as I have always been, and as I shall always be, towards you.

From SIR CHARLES HANBURY-WILLIAMS

Tuesday evening [*September* 3].

I am fond of the Hetman. I feel convinced that he is friendly to me, and I am pained when I see my friends in distress. They have finally decided to send him to the Ukraine ; the resolution, from what he tells me, is already signed by the whole council. He asks for your support, and I ask it for him. I ask it in this case for your own sake, for his absence does you harm. His devotion to you is most sincere, and he commands a regiment of Guards. Think over, therefore, all possible means for giving him a helping hand in this present situation. Write at least one more strong letter to the Chancellor on his behalf ; for I shall never

[1] Alexei Rasumowski.

understand his devotion to you, if he does not oppose the banishment of your best friends.

The Hetman proposes to become reconciled at once to Ivan Ivanovitch ; and, as the principal motive of the Schuvalov for being on good terms with the Hetman is that, through him, they hope to be on better terms with you, he wishes you to become rather more distant to them, at all events during the time when he is arranging his reconciliation with Ivan Ivanovitch. He believes that it is Apraksin who does him all the harm. But, Monsieur, your honour is involved in backing him up with the Chancellor. I am told the Empress is furious with me. She has been told that I have been inspiring the Grand-Duke and the Grand-Duchess with ideas which are contrary to the present policy of this court. I cannot guard against calumnies and lies, or even suspicions, but I shall continue to act in a manner that can give no one a hold over me, and I am very delighted that the Great Chancellor knows nothing of our correspondence.

The Empress is very sorry that she sent the snuff-box to Poniatowski, and said that he would have been only too glad to leave the country quietly without any present. You must begin to prepare the way with the Great Chancellor for his return, and you cannot too soon set on foot this negotiation with him.

Thank you for the story of your conversation with Peter Schuvalov. You spoke well, as you always do. But all he said is no more than whipped cream. Ivan Ivanovitch has the influence, not Peter Schuvalov. Through him, if you can win him, you could do all you want.

I will obey all your orders about Poniatowski very faithfully and accurately. I am surprised that I have no letters from him.

A conversation which I had yesterday with the Vice-Chancellor shows me clearly that the Ministry here has got into a mess in the negotiation with France, and would to be clear of it. The Vice-Chancellor said to me ; " You may be very sure, Monsieur, that all our arrangements with France amount to nothing, and that in future we shall settle nothing with the court of Versailles. You have been too much alarmed about it." I answered him that a negotiation between Russia and France, at the moment when England was making a treaty with the Empress, especially a negotiation conducted by a Scotch rebel, could not fail to alarm all the friends of Great Britain. He made me sorry for him when he spoke of public affairs and the present condition of Europe ; and I gave him in consequence a little lecture, by which he was so much impressed that he nearly acknowledged to me that they were in need of light here. It appears to me necessary, in order to keep you informed, to send you some original papers which have passed between my court and that of Vienna, and then to give you my views on the present state of affairs.

I told the two Chancellors yesterday that, if they did not conclude matters at once with me, our treaty would be broken without the King being able to prevent it, and that if I did not send him good news from hence before the opening of Parliament, which takes place about the 20th of next month, Parliament, finding the King abandoned by all his allies, would advise him to shut himself up in his island and to have nothing more to do on the Continent. This speech impressed and worried them, and will, if I am not mistaken, produce good fruits, for the Great Chancellor said at once ; " Rely on it, the whole of your business will be settled this week."

I am at work on my comments upon the important negotiations of Bekteïev, but even more on a certain two portraits : the one of the man makes great progress. Yesterday I saw marvellous sights, the masterpiece of the artillery. I saw them shoot blank cartridges from the guns. I saw a house, built of wood and plastered over with combustible matter, catch fire the moment that a red-hot bullet touched it. I saw bombs burst and mines explode. And as I understand nothing at all of these matters, I thought it very fine. All the spectators were more than pleased, and vied with one another in praise of the General.[1] I soon think of becoming a soldier, for I like professions which one can learn in a moment. I am told that it is certain that the progress in it made by Peter Schuvalov is so great, that to reward such distinguished merit they are resolved at once to make him President of the War Council. What will the Grand-Duke have to say to this ?[2]

[1] Peter Schuvalov was Master-General of the Ordnance, though he had had no military training at all.

[2] The Grand-Duke had asked for this office for himself, and had been refused.

From THE GRAND-DUCHESS

Wednesday [*September* 4].

I am very fond of the Hetman and recognize his devotion to me. He spoke to me last Sunday; and the very next day I sent to the Chancellor to complain that he was lending a hand to, and even urging on, the departure of one of my most faithful friends. This I said with some show of temper. His answer was that it was not him—but that the exigencies of the moment required the presence of the Hetman in the Ukraine : that it was not yet decided to send a minister there, and that he did not think that it would be done. My answer was to make further requests that he should remain. At this very moment, I am going to write again to ask an explanation of the pretexts which call for the presence of the Hetman in his country, and the meaning of this departure, which has been spoken of for two years.

The Chancellor sent me word this morning of everything which you tell me about Count Poniatowski and about yourself, adding that the Empress complained of the Grand-Duke, of his views which conflicted with all that was being done here and which were anti-Russian, and that she said that it was those cursed Holsteiners who inspired him with these sentiments. She said all this to the Chancellor herself on Sunday, and never went out at all, although fully dressed, as she was so cross.

I received a letter from Count Poniatowski by the Chancellor, in which he tells me that he was elected nonce of Livonia, with every formality and with all the customary routine. My letter is of August 25. Two days later he was to leave Dunaburg for Vilna in order to see Flemming[1] (who, he says, has done wonders), and from thence to go to Warsaw, where he expected to be at the latest on September 8. He sends me most affectionate messages for you. I wrote this morning to the Chancellor on the subject of his return in a little note, which I will follow up with a few lines in the letter to help the Hetman.

---

[1] Count George Flemming, Great Treasurer of Lithuania, nephew of the celebrated Minister of Augustus II. of Saxony : a man of great importance in Poland in the pro-Russian party.

I thought it well to make some show of bad temper to Bernardi, for I have remarked that, after a scene like this, people get very heated. He told me that I might question everyone's devotion, but not the Chancellor's ; and I replied, " I am not speaking of him " : but I continued to give vent to general complaints, which might in detail apply to him.

I have reason to think, from what Michel told Naruishkin, that the complaints against Poniatowski are prompted by Douglas and himself.

The Chancellor has again sent me word that though war was not finally resolved upon, it was none the less certain : and that this anger against you was the result of your proposals of mediation without orders from your court.

The Grand-Duke says that if the *doklade* for the departure of the Hetman is brought to him for his signature, he will not sign it. Thank you for the trouble which you are taking for me about the portraits and the comments. I think that what has given rise to the idea that Peter Schuvalov may become President of the College of War is, that, at Apraksin's departure, he will perhaps fill his place : but then, according to the laws of Peter the Great, good-bye to his seat in the Senate. I was sorry to have at once repeated these rumours to the Grand-Duke, for he was in such a rage that he spoke of nothing but fighting Peter Schuvalov. At all events that will help the Hetman, as the Grand-Duke will cold-shoulder the Schuvalov for some days ; and I shall let it be known that it is because they are sending away the first-named : and then we shall hook Peter Schuvalov on account of overtures made by him to Ivan Ivanovitch. I sent word to the Chancellor that I shall no longer be able to speak to Peter Schuvalov as on the previous occasion, without destroying my reputation with the public. He has only to repeat this to his friend Apraksin, who arranged this conversation. I added that I shall repent of that meeting, because nothing but vapouring had come of it.

Here is something better. The Grand-Duke begins to make a great change in his anti-Russian opinions, and has become very reasonable about many things. I think that your advice does him no harm.

From THE GRAND-DUCHESS

Friday [*September* 6].

Apraksin spoke to me yesterday of his departure. I said to him : " I do not like war. There is nothing so good as peace." He answered, " If the King of Prussia attacks me, I shall fight. If not, I remain quiet." He appeared to me to let this slip out, for he corrected himself, and tried to efface these words by a flood of other talk.

Here is something to raise a laugh. The person, on whose cough you were counting yesterday, does nothing but talk in the privacy of her chamber of going to command the army in person. One of her women said to her the other day, " How can you ? You are a woman." She replied, " My father went ; do you believe that I am stupider than he ? " The other answered, " He was a man, and you are not." She began to get angry, and persisted in saying that she wished to go to the war herself. They add that the good lady, far from being able to perform such a feat, cannot climb her own stairs without losing her breath. The lifts which have been made everywhere are convincing proofs. The habitual flattery to which they treat her is to the effect that she surpasses her father in activity, deeds and merit. And she believes it so well, that she begins to say the same thing herself. The fatigues of yesterday brought on terrible abdominal pains, accompanied by the old troubles. She told me so herself, as she left the room, and my news of to-day is confirmed. The Hetman will tell you still more. I leave it to him. Rumour has it, amongst other things, that Peter Schuvalov has changed his love.

From SIR CHARLES HANBURY-WILLIAMS

Friday morning [*September* 6].

I am much obliged to you, Monsieur, for your letter of Wednesday, and am delighted to see how well you back up your friends. I entirely approve of all you have done about the Hetman, as well as of your future policy towards the Schuvalov.

It is not true that the Empress is angry with me for offering mediation to this court. The Vice-Chancellor told me that this offer had been well received, and that something will even be said to me about it at the conference which I am to have to-morrow. But the Empress has said that I was plying the Grand-Duke with bad advice, that I sent it through Poniatowski to the Hetman, and that he passed it on to the Grand-Duke. One must have more than a master-mind to see through such plots. Continue to press the Great Chancellor for Poniatowski's return ; by that means you will see whether he is your friend. I have grave doubts about it.

Friday evening.

I have this moment returned from the Great Chancellor, and I am pained to feel that my duty obliges me to give you a faithful account of our interview, because I am sure that you will feel it very much.

I have suspected for some time past that the Great Chancellor was jealous of Poniatowski's favour with you, and even of mine, and that he could not bear anyone to share it with him. Instead of beginning on public affairs, he said, in rather a cringing manner, that the Empress had grave suspicions of me, that she laid at my door the Grand-Duke's conduct on present affairs, and that you encouraged him to act in the way he does at my suggestion. I answered that he knew better than anyone that I never interfered. He replied that the Empress was very angry with me, and that, as he was my true friend, he advised me to set my own house in order by the next courier. I begged him to explain himself. He said that I should do well to ask for my recall. I was a little taken aback by this advice. But, pulling myself together at once, I told him that I would do nothing of the sort, that I was innocent, and no coward, and would not run away : that they might hold as many suspicions as they liked, but that I defied the whole world to prove the least thing against me. Finally, I told him that I would not hear a further word on this subject. After that, he began to tell me that Poniatowski could not return here, that it was too dangerous, and that he begged me to tell him so. I answered that after what he had just told me, I was firmly resolved to have nothing more to do with this affair. On that he handed me a letter which you had sent him for Poniatowski, saying that I must get it conveyed to him. I replied that he had safe means of sending letters, whereas I had none. " Cannot you give it," said he, " to your courier, who will soon be leaving ? " " No," I said, " for he does not go to Warsaw." " But he passes through by Dantzig, and from thence (he said) it can be sent to him." " I know no one at Dantzig whom I can trust, and I will take no risk. Rely on it that, from devotion to her and love of myself, I shall take care from henceforth to be very much on my guard." He then said to me, " But you correspond with her." " That is not true," I said to him. " I have no correspondence with her except through you. The Poniatowski affair came about without my knowledge. They have put confidence in me though I never asked for it, and I will die rather than betray it. Thank God, I am an Ambassador, and responsible only to my Master. And if it were not that I thought it would please my enemies, I would ask for my recall to-morrow."

Can you imagine, Monsieur, that after all this he made me the greatest protestations of friendship, which I received coldly ; and even after that begged me to write him the letter which I had promised him, in which I was to say that it was by his desire that I had procured money for you, and in which I was to tell him the story of Poniatowski's fears at Riga. To that I replied, " I told you I would have nothing more to do with these matters, and I shall keep my word. Let us speak of other things. I shall get annoyed, and we must change the subject or I leave your house." Then he began to speak of the conference which I am to have with him and the Vice-Chancellor to-morrow. He carped at me, and vexed me as much as he could. In the end I said to him, " Your bad temper will not persuade me to ask for my recall, and to-morrow I shall hope to find you in a less carping and more sensible mood."

There, Monsieur, is a very interesting tale for you. Your two friends are unjustly treated and persecuted by a third, whom you look upon as your greatest support. For myself, I do not care, but I am enraged about you and my friend, and am in the depths of despair. They want me to go and Poniatowski not to return.

All that is clear. I had almost forgotten to tell you that, as I left, he begged me very earnestly never to speak of our conversation, and asked me to give him my word to that effect. I gave it, and I glory in breaking it.

I am in no condition at present to give you advice. My brain is too heated. What horrible design had he in view, when he asked me for the letter in which I was to speak of your money and Poniatowski's fears ? Answer me this riddle. I dare not answer it myself.

I know also on good authority that he has told people whom he should not have told, that I boasted of having your confidence and that of the Grand-Duke. Why say such a thing, when it is not true ? Well, his jealousy and his ambition have made him determined to vex and persecute me, and to debar Poniatowski from any hope of returning here.

I return you the note which you made out for the King. Let the Chancellor know in a few days that you will send a similar one to Wolff, payable to Wolff. But never mention the one which you have sent me.

I would prefer your money to remain in Wolff's hands. I will let you know the cost of this business, and you may send me the amount by Swallov, for I do not want the Chancellor to know even this. The money due to you will be (as I told you) over 42,000 roubles. You see my position. Arrange for me to be in a position to help you. Poor Poniatowski !

Midnight has struck. I am off to bed. But I feel certain beforehand that I shall not get much sleep ; in any case I shall offer up prayers for your present safety and future triumph.

Forgive this scrawl ; it is horrible. You see that I make no comments. I have related the facts to you in a most accurate manner.

From THE GRAND-DUCHESS

Saturday, towards evening [September 7].

The overwhelming news contained in your letter of Friday had the usual effect of similar news upon me. It has only fortified my courage. Far from despairing of success, I am daring

H

enough to expect that the Chancellor, from the inner conviction of his bad conscience, will agree to my requests and importunities.

After three hours of despondency, to the great regret of Naruishkin who knew nothing of the reason, I sent for Bernardi, and asked him on his entrance for the answer to my letters. He told me that he had none as yet. I replied, " I am sorry that you are so stupid to-day (I call him stupid when he comes empty-handed) ; for being unwell and in a very dismal mood, I am waiting for some comfort from the Chancellor." He replied, " The Empress's remarks seem to be troubling you." " No," said I, " I don't care a rap. The Chancellor knows the cause of my annoyance, for he has not kept his promise to put me in a position to despise all these bad reports." He asked me what they were. But I told him definitely that he should know nothing until I was sure that what I wanted was done. " One hand washes the other. Nothing is done for me ; I shall do nothing for the others." I packed him off immediately. I shall send every day, even twice a day, to press for the return of Count Poniatowski.

The end of your conversation with the Chancellor shows repentance and indecision on his part. What do I not owe to your friendship and skill in reducing him to that point ? My letter which he wished to persuade you to send was my second reply to Poniatowski. He had, I think, sent the first. But perhaps he did not know how to send the second. I feel really vexed and annoyed at his conduct towards you. I am silent about his trickery and low cunning. An honest Chancellor would be a marvel. Be assured that I will push him to such a degree that I will either quarrel with or get the better of him. Your integrity and behaviour towards me find me with no words to express my gratitude. My pain is great at causing you pain : but I am somewhat consoled by the thought that Count Poniatowski knows nothing of this caprice. I judge by my situation what he would have felt. I hope that he will only hear it from my lips, and when the impression will no longer cause him pain. Some town gossip has just reached me that the Queen of Sweden has made her escape to Denmark, and that the King will be held responsible for her flight.

From Sir Charles Hanbury-Williams

Sunday [September 8].

Monsieur, I am delighted to find that you are not cast down by my bad news. I am so, on your account. All you say on the matter is very sensible. Follow up your scheme, for the Great Chancellor to show you a scheme to secure Count Poniatowski's return. Be firm but kind. I have decided, if he speaks of it to me, to beg him at once to change the subject : for I will not enter into this affair in any manner with the Chancellor. He lays snares for me every day in all sorts of ways. I shall know how to avoid them. He only considers himself : and all my kindnesses are already forgotten. But thank God ! I have still something to distribute.[1] I have already shown it to him in the distance ; and he has the eye of an eagle for such matters. I think you will do well to let out nothing to Bernardi which could lead him to suspect any intercourse between us. Continue to press the Chancellor for Poniatowski's return, because without him the affair will be impossible. If I am to believe all I hear, the Chancellor was himself responsible for the suspicions.

I shall never raise your hopes : and I tell you that Poniatowski's return must be arranged through the Chancellor ; otherwise there is no security for him in this country. He would then throw all the blame on me, and though I am ready to risk all for you, I do not wish to risk anything for him, and henceforth I will not move in these intrigues except by your orders. For you I will do anything. But prudence must guide us, for treachery threatens. Above all, I persist that our correspondence must remain an impenetrable secret.

Let us speak of other things. Without knowing the why or the wherefore, I have become a sort of favourite and confidant of the King of Prussia. He sends me word that he recognizes me to be an honest man, and that he would like to believe that I am one of his friends : that he well knows that I had been his

---

[1] See *Frederick Polit. Corres.* xiii. 328. Frederick wrote to Andrew Mitchell on September 2nd, n.s., authorizing him to tell Sir Charles to offer Bestuzhev 100,000 crowns, as the price of his support.

mortal enemy, and that I have done him harm : but that he wishes to make advances to me, and that he knows that I can be won more easily by confidence than by money. Nevertheless, he has put a very considerable sum at my disposal to make use of at this court. You think me large-hearted. I tell you that the present which was intended for me was returned by the courier who brought me the remainder. If I can help him I shall do so, and shall prevent Russia from fighting without generals or officers. The Chancellor has already told me that he was no longer the same as he used to be, that he was in favour of Prussia against France : and to pay you back for the news which you gave me about Apraksin, I will tell you a few words that the Chancellor (who is still completely Austrian at heart) let drop to me :—" To what does this King of Prussia aspire ? Does he want to fight the whole world ? It is true that he has chosen the moment to attack the Empress-Queen when we are not in a condition to defend her at once." Instead of commenting on this remark, I showed him the big gilded pill still closer. He said that he did not understand me. But he said that the King of Prussia was a great king, that his armies were in very good order, and that he feared for the Austrians.

In short, the King of Prussia is in Bohemia at this moment with a hundred thousand men, and the Empress-Queen has no more than seventy thousand in the two camps of Kollin and Moravia. The King of Prussia is determined to strike a great blow, and to make peace at once, as he did in Saxony in the year 1745.

I send you Poniatowski's letter. The part written in another handwriting is from the Great Treasurer Flemming. You also receive the letter from the King of Poland, and the very singular answer from His Prussian Majesty ; you will see how he censures Count Brühl.[1]

I had my conference yesterday ; but they were so convinced of the injustice which is being done to us here, that, of their own accord, they desired to speak again to the Empress, in order to

---

[1] Of Brühl Frederick wrote : " His bad intentions are but too well-known to me, and his evil plots I could prove in black and white." See also *Frederick Polit. Corres.* xiii. 346.

persuade her to accept the hundred thousand pounds sterling.[1]
Continue to protect me, for I am entirely yours.

From THE GRAND-DUCHESS

Sunday.   8 o'clock in the evening [September 8].

It is some sort of consolation to me in my deep distress to be
able to write to you.   In answer to my yesterday's commission,
the Chancellor returned me both my letters to Count Poniatowski,
adding that he had no one whom he could send with them : that
he had asked you to take charge of them, but you had refused
to accept them, saying that even if Count Poniatowski should
return here, you would no longer have him in your house, and
that you had shown much feeling against the Count.   I pretended
to be astonished, and replied that I hoped your impressions were
only passing ones, and that my confidence in him left me no doubt
that he would keep his word to me about the Count's return, and
that I repeated my most pressing entreaties that he should work
for it.   Bernardi told me that the Chancellor had spoken to the
Vice-Chancellor about Count Poniatowski's brother being pro-
moted to the post of Little General in the event of the death of the
Great General Branicki,[2] but that he had answered that matters
must be allowed to remain dormant for some time, because the
Empress's feelings were unfavourable to them.   I sent a reply,
saying that I desired him to press the matter just as much as the
Count's return, for it could certainly be done if he wished it :
and that I would listen to no more excuses.   But after Bernardi
had gone out, I discovered in his packet a little note in German,
which to be intelligible required an interpreter : but, notwithstanding its diffuseness, I made out that he wished my letters to
reach their destination through your agency, though he never

---

[1] Sir Charles wrote the same to Lord Holdernesse (September 18th, n.s.,
Record Office.)   He added that he thought it clear, that the court did not
wish to break with England, but was resolved to get everything out of
her that was possible.   Catherine's confidence in the Chancellor had
the effect of counteracting Sir Charles's estimate of how far he was to be
trusted.

[2] See *ante*, p. 37.

mentioned your name. I wrote in German, also in the package, that I asked him what had become of the messenger sent expressly with Count Poniatowski's letter from Mitau, and why my letters had not been sent to him when that opportunity offered; for when anyone was master of a situation and wished to do something, difficulties did not arise : that if I had not entire confidence in his assurances, I should be in despair, that I therefore begged him very earnestly to fulfil them, and that he could by one word set at rest the minds of those who had chosen him for their support.

Without a moment's delay I sent to call Bernardi back, and heatedly told him how astonished I was at the return of my two letters, and at the defective note, " which," said I, " I do not at all understand. I too know all about Ivan Schuvalov's remarks, though I do not speak about them." I repeated to him all my strongest reasons, and sent him off, intimating that any delay in answering would arouse my suspicions. He made a great point of knowing about these remarks of Ivan Schuvalov, but I did not tell him what they were, adding, " It is enough that I am afraid of being deceived by everyone. Consequently I shall make my plans as soon as I receive a decided answer from the Chancellor. Will he really help me or not in what I ask ? "

These were Ivan Schuvalov's remarks. He announced that it was the Chancellor who was doing you harm with the Empress, and that by putting the French Embassy, to which he himself had brought the Empress to agree, on the shoulders of the Schuvalov and the Vice-Chancellor, he raised himself in your eyes. This may perhaps help to turn him to my purpose. A further weapon in reserve is, that I shall let loose my tongue against Funcke, on the grounds that his lack of resolution perchance emanated from him. His affection for Funcke may help me to reduce him to sincerity.

In God's name give me your advice, for my head reels. Abandon me not in my present distress, and help me to make some profit out of this man whom I fear to recognize as a traitor.

He sent me word about the Hetman, that it was a feather in his cap to go to the Ukraine, but that it would be a pleasure to help him notwithstanding.

Scold me frankly, if I have done the wrong thing, and set me on the right road. I ask for nothing better.

Here are the two notes, of which I spoke to you before.

From SIR CHARLES HANBURY-WILLIAMS

[Sunday, September 8.]

I am busier than I have ever been in my life, and have no time to go into anything but one matter which closely affects you. Bring things to a head with the Chancellor as quickly as possible. Make sure whether he is your friend, that is to say, whether he will help you in what you have at heart ; for if he will not, you must make a complete change, and I have already made out a plan.

I implore you, Monsieur, to write a further letter to Poniatowski to inform him of his position at this court. You are afraid of causing him anxiety ; but he would be far more surprised, if, on arriving at Riga, he was not allowed to pass further. It is almost your duty, therefore, to inform him of what is going on, assuring him at the same time that we are both working for his return. You know from Bernardi that all your money is at your disposal. I have nothing more to do with it ; and you must send me the thousand ducats for Poniatowski to-morrow night at latest. I have received your letter with the enclosure for Poniatowski. If I can, I will write to you again to-night.

From SIR CHARLES HANBURY-WILLIAMS

Sunday [September 8.]

It is for me to ask your pardon, not for you to make excuses to me. Never make them. I am yours heart and soul.

I fear that it must have cost you a great deal to write your last letter to Poniatowski, but your love and my friendship for him demanded it from you. I am sorry for you, and enter into all your distress. I will tell you all my thoughts on it, and will give you new advice in a few days. But meanwhile be assured that I am as anxious for the return of Poniatowski as you are, and that I shall be in a position to work for it with the Great Chancellor ; and I give you my word that if he does not do it, I shall find some pretext to quarrel with him. He shall never have a penny of his pension. He is poor at present. But he shall help you, or I will not assist him any more. I shall write everything to Poniatowski, but in such a way as to allow him to feel that his return is quite feasible. I shall assure him of your constancy and of my perseverance in his service. I send you one of his letters ; it will at least give you a quarter of an hour's comfort.

I wanted to write at greater length, but I am interrupted, and I do not want to keep you a moment from reading the enclosed. Continue to press the Great Chancellor ; take no excuse. He can do what you ask, if he pleases.

From Sir Charles Hanbury-Williams

Monday [*September* 9.]

Monsieur, I intended to write you a long letter this morning, but yours of yesterday has required too much thought to enable me to offer you my advice at once. I shall take till to-morrow.

It is true that I told the Chancellor that I would not have Poniatowski in my house. But this is how I came to say it, when he had pointed out to me the dangerous position in which Poniatowski would be placed upon his return here, and that suspicion against him was so strong that he would be everywhere under observation. " What would that matter, if he was a Minister ? " And then, to lay stress on that point, which I have always thought most essential, I added, " For as things are now, he can no longer remain in my house."

It is also true that I showed a lot of temper.

Good-bye, Monsieur, till to-morrow. I am not well, the result of an accident which happened to me on my way home yesterday, and of which I will tell you another day. Do not be anxious. Do not let both of us be ill. Let me be the only one.

From THE GRAND-DUCHESS

Monday [*September* 9.]

Thank you for the balm which you have just sent me. Things most difficult become easy for me when you advise on them—witness the letter yesterday for the Count. Here is one which I beg of you to send through to him if you can. I am sorry that troublesome people have prevented me from receiving a longer letter. Remember, when you have time, you have promised me thousands of things. Here is one of them, which will give me an opening ; it seems to me certain that firmness will carry it through for us. Bernardi arrived to-day quite out of breath, to bring me the money which I am sending you for Count Poniatowski. He tells me that the Chancellor is very ill, and that the annoyance which I am causing him by my suspicions was making him worse. I told him that it depended entirely on him to put an end to them. He swore by Heaven and Hell that he would do it, but tried afterwards to suggest patience and delay, since, as the King of Poland was virtually a prisoner, it was difficult to send anything to reach him. Upon that, I pretended to be angry, and said to Bernardi that if the Chancellor forbade Brühl to eat, I was fully convinced that he would obey : and that if he came to me again with pretences instead of a definite answer, not only would I forbid him to enter my room, but I would also take it to mean that no answer was a definite one. I became rather violent with him. I saw a moment when he was ready to fall on his knees to plead the cause of his patron. He was very disturbed ; for he had never seen me in a state like I was in at that moment.

What do I not owe you for the assurances which you give me, that you take as much interest as I do in the return of Count Poniatowski ! You will understand my gratitude better than I can express it. The Count sends you word that he has received your letter of August 21 with the greatest pleasure in the world. He tells me to ask you for the story about the diabolical laziness of the Palatine of Russia.[1]

[1] Prince Augustus Czartoryski, Poniatowski's uncle.

From Sir Charles Hanbury-Williams

Monday evening [September 9.]

I am going to confess to you, Monsieur. My promised devotion will show itself. I will speak openly, I will speak truthfully. The Chancellor wishes to have you in his power for the present, because that is the reason why the Schuvalov are afraid of him and court him. Their fears of the future bring about this result. If the Empress dies, you already know all his expectations. His expectations are vast, and it is from you he wishes to secure them.

But what treatment does he merit at your hands for the past, the present or the future ?

For the past I must ask you for the information. I do not know. For the present he makes use of you in order to govern the Grand-Duke ; and for the future his safety entirely depends on you.

How does he repay you his present debts or his future expectations ? You only ask him to do things that are easy. It costs him nothing to dispatch a courier to his cousin at Mitau ; we pay for the rest. It was to secure Poniatowski's return that I was induced to reveal the secret to him ; you thought yourself sure enough of him to believe that he would help you readily enough in this matter. But you must know that he is afraid of Poniatowski and his enterprising spirit. When he told him that he had been five times to Oranienbaum, the Chancellor said to me, "He is devilishly bold." But Poniatowski said that without my approval, for to the Chancellor he should have appeared gentleness itself—a man who would not dare to undertake anything that was not done under his auspices.

I again repeat to you that the Chancellor cannot tolerate anyone who shares your favour with him. He tells you that it is a feather in the Hetman's cap for him to go to the Ukraine. He advises me, as my best friend, to ask for my recall ; and he not only opposes Poniatowski's return but even refuses to send him one of your letters. What can one do then with such a man ? He thinks only of himself. He asks for everything, and does nothing. I have known for some time of his treachery to me ;

he is England's greatest enemy at this court. He only thinks (with regard to you) of high favour in your reign : he does nothing to deserve it, neither from you nor from the Grand-Duke Sweden is my proof of this.

Your answer to all this will be, " What shall I do ? " Very well, Monsieur, you ask me for my advice. Here it is. Always remember that the minister who finds fault without offering a remedy is an idiot. Yet even the ablest physicians cannot always make a cure.

My devotion to you (which becomes greater every day), my friendship for another, and my own personal character, oblige me to speak as follows.

Poniatowski's return can only be secured by the Chancellor. I own that I am very much afraid that it is the latter who has provoked the Empress against him—a horrible thought, but, as he has it in his power to assist us, we must not quarrel with him. I am ready to offer myself as the sacrifice. Send Bernardi to tell the Chancellor that you wish me to send the two letters to Poniatowski, and that, if he agrees, you will acquaint me by Bernardi or by him. Add that you will not expose him to anything dangerous. But continue to insist upon him paving the way for the return. I shall haughtily refuse to mix myself in this affair, and therefore, if he does not wish to quarrel absolutely with you, he must send your letters and arrange for Poniatowski's return ; and if you appear to be angry with me, so much the better, because he will think from that that I have lost my credit with you, and that when he has Poniatowski to himself, it will be easier for him to govern him. That will also remove any suspicion of our secret correspondence. Implore him to take a strong line with me, to threaten me with the loss of your favour ; and when he sees that I stand out, he will believe me ruined with you, and that at least he has floored a rival. When he perceives that your anger is real, and that there is no one but him to help you, he will do it, for fear that you might put yourself into the hands of other Russians. That is my advice.

Certainly, the first thing I must think of as your servant and friend is the return of Poniatowski. Without some change in the Chancellor and (both through him and his friends) in the Empress, his return is impossible. He would come here as a suspect, he would be treated accordingly. I should be unable to protect him ; and a situation too calamitous for me to contemplate with composure might follow. Speak to Bernardi with firmness but without passion. Base your connection with the Chancellor on the service which he will render you in this affair. Say that you want to play a sure game, and that friends will not fail you. Above all put no faith in anything which you are told comes from me : I do not intend to explain myself to anyone but to you. You have a right to speak to me. Always remember that the secret of our correspondence must be absolutely sacred.

Bernardi has been here this evening. He talked to me of your affair ; he told me that it was the cause of your illness, that you were pushing the Chancellor into a corner, and that I must interfere. I replied, " What do you mean ? I have already been told that I am so much under suspicion here that I must leave, and do they now wish to draw me again into interference in matters as delicate as these ? I refuse to have anything to do with them. I have said so before, and I repeat it." " But you will anger your friend and protector," was the answer I received. " She does not get angry without good reason " (I replied), " and she would not ask me to do things which would do me harm." I long for Poniatowski's return. I will do all that is in my power to obtain it, but cannot quiet the suspicions of the Empress. That is the business of the Chancellor and his friends. Yet I own that when I see him refusing to send a letter to Mitau, I despair of everything. Bernardi had spoken to me about sending your letters. I will send them without their knowledge. In the end, Bernardi talked to me so much that I was obliged to say to him, " The Chancellor advised me to be on my guard, and I shall follow his advice." Good-bye, you will make me speak and act in everything that you wish ; but when I see trouble for you and the fact that passion no longer listens to reason, I shall oppose your desires with a firmness equal to the eagerness which I shall always feel in obeying you in all that can be of use, or even of pleasure, to you.

Tuesday [September 10.]

Here is more advice. I spoke to the Hetman to-night, and I am very pleased with him ; his devotion to you is steadfast. He believes that he is sure of being able to re-establish himself with Ivan Ivanovitch, and I shall be delighted if he can. All that you tell me, and all that I know from elsewhere, convinces me of the great use which you are to the Chancellor, and of his dishonesty towards you and me. I think that his connection with the Schuvalov is only founded, on their side, upon their belief in his great influence with you, and on the promises which he has possibly made to them of your protection in the future. It is the only reason which I can see for their union with him. It is always in your power, therefore, to attach them to you by means of any person who is recognized to possess your confidence. If my reasoning is right, no one will know better how to make use of it than you ; and, if I know the Chancellor, he will tremble at the first word which shows signs of coldness on your part, and will not be able to put up with the slightest threat of a change of your friends. Rely on it, Monsieur, your support is even now his mainstay. There is no necessity, therefore, to stage the future.

I tell you all this, in order to make you realize your full power, and to point out to you that it is your fault if he does not grant all you demand from him

Remember that on every occasion when the Grand-Duke has not blindly obeyed the wishes of those who are in power, the Schuvalov have always descended upon the Chancellor, to bring him back to the path by your help. They even accuse him to the Empress of being the author of the measures which his Imperial Highness adopts. He takes credit for this with you, and says that he is sacrificed to your interests. But, on the other hand, the more they suspect him, the more he is feared ; and if it could be proved that the Grand-Duke was actually following the advice of the Chancellor, the Schuvalov would pay their court to him more than ever, and his influence would be considerably increased.

That is the reason why he wishes to reign alone in your good graces. That is the reason why he would be delighted if I departed to England, and the Hetman to the Ukraine, and if Poniatowski should never return to Petersburg. By the laws of friendship and by those of gratitude, he should employ in your service a portion of the influence which you secure for him ; and I own to you that I am shocked to see that he will not send a letter from here to Mitau when you order it. And so, Monsieur, he must assist you in this affair : he can, if he will. I have never doubted for one moment that any Russian would not believe that his greatest happiness lay in possessing your confidence ; their interest demands it, and that is all there is to be said.

Carry out your scheme about the Great Chancellor with firmness and without heat, but end thus, " Will you pledge yourself that Poniatowski shall be back here by Christmas ; for his return by your solicitation is the price which I place on my present friendship and future protection ? "

Ivan Ivanovitch speaks the truth. The Chancellor does me harm with the Empress, and the House of Austria has bought him. Apraksin does even worse ; but neither I nor my affairs should count for anything. I think only of you. Your position occupies me for eighteen hours out of the twenty-four. I esteem you, I honour you, I pity you.

Bernardi was here last night, and spoke to me of your letters. I told him that I had quite made up my mind to have nothing more to do with your affairs. He spoke to me for the first time of Count Poniatowski. I said little to him in reply, and beg you to look on anything which he tells you comes from me as rubbish. I find nothing to cavil at in all you do : I promise to scold you when I think that you are doing wrong. For the present, follow the plan which I have indicated to you ; and if in the end the Chancellor will not help you, you must take another line. I advise you to think it out in time, and I shall do the same. My arm, my heart, my head, are yours.

Wednesday [*September* 11.]

Bernardi was here yesterday morning. He brought me great assurances from the Chancellor that Count Poniatowski's return was certain, and that he would send my letters in a few days— that he was seeking a safe opportunity. He added that the Chancellor had stamped his foot on reading my German note; and that the one in the same language, which I had taken as intended for me, was addressed to Count Poniatowski among my letters which were to be sent to him by you. I did actually read it again, and this is possible. Bernardi is to bring me this morning a letter from the Chancellor, which, he says, will relieve all my doubts, for they seem rather anxious about them—more proof, it seems to me, of their bad conscience. Our correspondence is a secret from them and will remain so, have no doubts on that score. Thank you very much indeed for your confession : I fully believe all you say. This has all the semblance of truth ; but man is an incomprehensible animal. The truth of the reasons which you give me for making the Chancellor fear both you and Count Poniatowski, does not prevent me from hoping that my frequent remonstrances and all the manœuvres which I shall employ will force him to bring back the Count (Bernardi's remark that I was pushing the Chancellor into a corner is worthy of notice). I sent to tell him that I shall go to his house to ask if he is not restoring him to me. And if this method was not the only one left for me, I should have great hopes of it ; for although I know full well that he only cares for himself, I still believe that I am myself, money always excepted, one of the things which make most impression with him or on him.

The one line in your letter, " I am ready to be the sacrifice," prevents me from following your advice about sending the letters. Everything you tell me is very clever and very good, but it would be cruel for me to do this at the cost of the best and most faithful friend I have ; and unless you tell me that it will be advantageous to you that the Chancellor should believe you to have quarrelled with me, I shall not follow your advice.

The Chancellor has just written to me. Here is my answer, which I shall not send without your approval.[1] You will form an opinion of the contents of his letter by my own ; my position is precarious, but I flatter myself, nevertheless, that I shall pull through. I will send you the two letters for Count Poniatowski with a third, and if the Chancellor asks for them back, I will send him others. I do not know what I am saying, or what I am doing. I can truly say that it is the first time in my life that I feel like this.

The confidence which the King of Prussia places in you flatters my discernment. Bernardi spoke to me the other day of preparations for war. I replied : " Hard words break no bones ! "[2] He answered, " In God's name, don't talk like that."

---

[1] THE GRAND-DUCHESS TO THE GREAT CHANCELLOR.

Tuesday, September 11.

The letter which your Excellency (has written me) very far from re-assuring me about my fears, has only increased them. In it you give me assurances of friendship. But you tell me nothing about the essential point of my anxiety—the return of Count Poniatowski. You do more: after exhausting yourself in protestations and vows of help for everyone and against everyone, you discover a difficulty and a risk in sending a letter to Mitau. You again insinuate at the end of your note that patience is necessary, and you try to make me understand that dangerous and delicate situations are the cause of your delays. You are clever, I know that well. But this caution, very far from making me believe that you can base these arguments on idle words (very contemptible, but said to originate with you), only causes me more alarm than ever about your intentions. I have no doubt also that certain persons, whom you like and who do not see their interest in this, will make use of all their wicked wits to frustrate my demands. But allow me to tell you that I shall insist on being given the preference, and have a right to it. Without breaking your vows of service and devotion, you can in no way excuse yourself from giving me proofs of them on this occasion. This is the only one, and perhaps the easiest, with which I should supply you, if I wished to stand on all my rights. I could represent that, omitting my great desire (which I think deserves consideration) for Ct P.'s return, the return for the sacred friendship which I bear you and our mutual obligations to one another ought to weigh with you in support of my cause. This, without boring you further, you may be absolutely certain that I shall press to a finish with all the firmness with which nature has endowed me. Count Poniatowski's return is in your hands alone. Will you undertake then that Count Poniatowski will be here by Christmas ? For his return, under your special care, is the price which I place on my present friendship and my future protection. An answer, if you please, to this last sentence.

[2] " L'on ne tuera avec tous les bruits que des poules."

Count Poniatowski's letter gave me a happy quarter of an hour, each time I re-read it. I am very glad that their affairs go on well; Flemming's behaviour does honour to you. I return the correspondence of the Kings of Poland and Prussia. The last bears the stamp of His Prussian Majesty; the cuts at Count Brühl are good.

I have this moment received your Tuesday's letter, which fills me with gratitude. I cannot find words to express to you all I owe you. Since our strength is so great, let us use it for so worthy a cause. I shall spare no effort, pray do the same with your advice. The reconciliation which has almost been arranged between the Hetman and the Schuvalov delights me. Why do you not say a word about your health? You well know how it interests me. You also promised to tell the story of your accident on Sunday, which was inconveniencing you.

From Sir Charles Hanbury-Williams

Wednesday [September 11].

Your letter only reached me quite late. It is my fault, for I only returned home at midnight. But as I think it necessary that your answer to the Chancellor should reach him as soon as possible, I shall not go to bed till I have given my entire approval of all that you say in that reply. The last paragraph is full of vigour, and will show him that you will not allow yourself to be laughed at. In it you speak in a manner which is worthy of you; and there is no more to be said.

I have already pointed out to you the actual power which you have over him; and you snatch the right moment to make use of it. I have proved the one to you, and your good sense has dictated the other.

That is all I shall say to you now. I shall answer your letter to-morrow; therefore I do not return it to you. But set in motion the one to the Chancellor as soon as you like. No! it is better to return to you your two letters. So here is the other one as well.

I

From Sir Charles Hanbury-Williams

Wednesday [*September* 11].

I could not send off my courier till after midnight. I wrote over sixty pages yesterday with my own hand, twelve of which were to Count Poniatowski. I painted for him all our troubles and difficulties. But at the same time I unfolded to him my plan for getting over them. When I spoke to him of the Empress's anger, I assured him of your affection, constancy, and determination to bring him back. When I alluded to the Chancellor's treachery, I promised him to oppose strongly all that man does and to have no further consideration for him, and said that you were of the same mind, and were resolved not to continue in friendship with one who did not assist you in what you had most at heart. In order to give him complete relief, I promised to arrange again for letters to reach him in a week, and I will keep my word. For I know too well what he must suffer in the suspense, and I never wish my friends to suffer when I can help to relieve them from their anxieties. So you have only to press the Chancellor and to prepare letters for Poniatowski ; for I do not wish that the man whom we love should not receive all the comfort that we can give him at the earliest possible moment. Your four letters to Poniatowski have gone by my courier, and the money with them.

Why are you always badly served ? Instead of ducats you have sent him imperials, which are worth nothing in Poland. Follow my advice, and order Bernardi to go to Wolff and settle your account with him, and give orders that your balance in ducats and imperials should be brought to you.

Personally, I have nothing more to do here. Your court loves Austria and Saxony too well to think of England ; and in the answer which the two Chancellors have at last given me, there is not a word about the defence of Hanover, after all the promises which they have made both to you and to me : and the hundred thousand pounds sterling has neither been accepted nor refused. What say you, Monsieur, of the good faith of your court ?

Bernardi tells me that the Chancellor is in despair ; so much the better. He begged me, on his behalf, to write you a letter to calm your transports. I replied that I would not write, that the Chancellor had told me that I was already suspected at court, and that I shall be very careful not to give proofs against myself : but that, to please him, though he deserved no favour nor even indulgence from me, I would speak to you on Friday.

I am going to take up the Poniatowski matter with him upon other lines. Something happened last night which put the idea into my head. Bernardi had told me that the Chancellor would be delighted to see me, if I would go to his house. I went there yesterday at five o'clock. I was told that he was asleep. I went in to see his wife,[1] and in a quarter of an hour, his son came to pay me the following compliment, " General Apraksin has just gone in to see my father : he may stay an hour or two. But if you will wait here till he goes, my father will be delighted to see you ! " I replied that I had things to do, and off I went. But while I was with Madame la Chancelière, our conversation turned on Poniatowski, and she related to me in great confidence everything that the Empress had said, all of which the Great Chancellor had already told me about Poniatowski. I answered haughtily that it was not Poniatowski who was suspected, but that it was me, and that all this talk was only an indirect blow aimed at me : that if it was true that Poniatowski had been frightened by the arrival of an officer sent by the Empress, no one should be astonished, that this Government was formidable, and that the most innocent people show alarm when they cannot act in their own defence : and that the examples which had taken place in this country justify fear. I believed myself (said I) that all that wretched, ungrateful officer had said to be false, but that I had made up my mind to have this story cleared up, in order to vindicate and maintain the character of my absent friend : and that I knew full well how to do it, notwithstanding the threats or

---

[1] Poniatowski in his *Mémoires*, speaks of Madame Bestuzhev, who had always been extremely kind to him, as the one person in the world to whom the Chancellor was always pleasant and patient, even under the great provocation of her fits of temper. He adds that their son was a monster steeped in vice of every description, a fact which was fully realized by his parents.

flatteries of those who pretended to be my friends, and who, if they had any feelings of gratitude, should be so. Believe me, Monsieur, she was quite as frightened at my words as ever Poniatowski was at Riga, and begged me to tell no one that she had spoken to me of this affair, to which I replied, " I promise, provided you will give me another promise—to tell your husband, and the whole world if so you wish, all that I have just said to you."

This will all amuse you, because it affects you. Continue to press the Chancellor ; he is a very slippery eel. Write him letters in the tone which you have employed hitherto, and write often. Threaten Bernardi. Do not get angry, but tell him firmly in a few days, that it is quite plain to you that the Chancellor will drive you to find other friends, and that you have a large choice who are in a better position to help you than he is.

This is my advice. I do not want you to be taken in ; and it is time that you should give up the part of friend, and take up that of heir, to Russia.

Believe me, Monsieur, you have no need to spur me on, when the interests of my friends are at stake. The Hetman is the first martyr to your favour. Your generous heart will one day repay him his present sufferings. After his departure you must find means of information elsewhere. Troubetskoï is better known to you than to me ; and I always leave the choice of your Russian friends to you. You may be certain that I spoke warmly of your heart in my letter to Poniatowski. I tried to make him recognize his troubles without instilling despair, and I promise you that when he has read my letter three times, he will be as relieved as any absent lover can be. Do not tell me that I make pleasant speeches to you. I only tell you the truth. Trust me ; I repeat that you are endowed by nature and by your diligence to make the first figure in the world. Flattery only speaks ; I wish to convince you by my actions of my way of thinking of you. The Great Chancellor is telling you through Bernardi that he wishes to help you, but at the same time he begs you to have patience. He has preached the same doctrine to me for a whole year, and has notwithstanding deceived me in the end.

I must explain to you shortly the plan which I have proposed to Poniatowski. As the jealousy of the Great Chancellor has produced this storm, it is for him in the first place to lull it to rest. It is therefore necessary for you to make use of all your influence with him to make him do so ; after that you must threaten him with the loss of your friendship in the present and of your protection in the future; and, in the end, if he will not lend himself to your wishes, you must break with him and look for other friends. Ivan Ivanovitch is the only one who can bring about what you wish, and I believe that he would readily lend himself to do it, Monsieur, if you promise him your friendship and confidence. That is where you will be driven in the end.

One thing I promise you. The Chancellor will never have a penny of his pension until Poniatowski returns. I shall quarrel with him, I shall make my court quarrel with him. I shall do everything for you and my friend.

When Bernardi comes to me to complain of your conduct, I pay no heed and laugh in his face.

Good-bye, Monsieur, my pen falls from my hand. I am tired out and none too well, but yours always.

Politics I leave for another time.

From Sir Charles Hanbury-Williams

Friday [*September* 13].

I was an hour last night with the Great Chancellor, and he would have detained me longer, if I would have stayed. He was like the land of Canaan, all milk and honey.

I began by communicating to him some letters I had just received from Berlin. He begged me to bring them to the conference to be held at his house to-morrow, and told me that at it they were to give me the thanks of the Empress for the manner in which I had demeaned myself here with regard to the King of Prussia.

We also talked a great deal about the King of Prussia. He began by abusing him, storming at all he had done. He told me that he had acted in the cruellest manner towards the Queen of Poland, that he had seized her closet and her privy purse, and that she and the greater part of the royal family at Dresden were almost treated as prisoners of war. To all this I made no answer, or rather I showed little interest in the whole matter. Finally, he became less aggressive, and began to speak of money, and asked me to repeat what I told him the other day. I did so, but less cordially, saying that it was true that I was charged with very important commissions and was even in a position to make him great offers,[1] but that I saw he was set against the King of Prussia and therefore should remain silent in future. On that, he asked me if my Master knew of all this. I replied that I never acted without orders, but that the most important orders I had were from a great banker at Amsterdam. " Ah," he said, " that is another matter. Though I do not like the King of Prussia, I will do anything for the King of England." I answered that I no longer saw what he could do. " Oh," said he, " We must await events, which will come fast enough, and then we will take counsel together." Instead of answering these suggestions, I replied that he could trust me, that the amount was very large, and that it was actually in my hands. At this his mouth watered, his eyes glistened, he shook my hand. " We will do great things," he said. And I am sure that he thought so much about that money, that he never slept at all that night. At the end, he came to your affairs. He wanted me to do everything ; the despatch of the letters, the advice to Poniatowski not to return, were all to come from me. The Chancellor's position and the suspicions which they hold of me at court ought to alarm me ; and finally I ought to persuade you to adopt his views.

My answer was, " I will send no letters, I will not interfere in this affair of Poniatowski : I am not in correspondence with the Grand-Duchess, and I do not wish to be. If I have helped her, it was at your entreaty that I did so, and I do not wish to mix myself up in any new intrigues. I am not in the least alarmed about

---

[1] The instructions from London were those of August 31, n.s. (Record Office), that Sir Charles might inform the Chancellor under a pledge of complete secrecy that Peter Schuvalov was actually said to have a private agreement with Mr Hop, of Amsterdam, to furnish the French with naval stores. We have seen also that Sir Charles had recently received Mitchell's letter of September 4, n.s., intimating that the King of Prussia authorized Sir Charles to buy Bestuzhev's friendship, if it could be had, for 100,000 crowns.

your position at court (which I consider very good), nor at the suspicions about me. No one has proofs against me, and I, from my reputation, am above all calumny and lies. I do not despise the favour of sovereigns, but, if I have it not, I shall not die of grief. In fact, in the present state of affairs, I wish to live quietly at home: and since after the next conference I shall have very little to do here, you will be less troubled by my visits, and I have even made up my mind not to carry out certain new instructions which I have received to-day from London and Berlin."

His curiosity is very enormous, and my last words excited him. He replied that at the moment my position at court was no longer so bad, that I could come to him when I wished, that he recognized the extent of my friendship for him, and that if I had something new to propose he would give me all the assistance in his power. I replied that our affairs were in such a state of disorder here than another scheme must be thought out: that I was actually now engaged in drawing up one to send to my court, but that it would take time to consider, correct, and carry it out, and that when I received the King's instructions, I would not fail to speak to him about it.

He appeared to me to be rather surprised, and with more humility than I had ever known in him, said to me, " At all events, if you will not confide your secret to me, be assured that I will assist you and the King, your Master, in everything. But," he added, " you must assist me with the Grand-Duchess."

I answered, " I am ready to do so, provided that you show me the means. But I will neither take any active step nor write."

" Write for me the letter which you promised," said he.

" I should have already done so," I said ; " it was written and Bernardi saw it ; but as you tell me that I am under suspicion, I have changed my mind, and am resolved not to do it."

Upon this I got up to go. He ran after me, embraced me, and assured me a thousand times of his friendship. I then left. From this conversation I discovered a secret, from which I have laid down the maxim, that in order not to be on bad terms with the Great Chancellor, one must never try to be in favour with him.

The reason why I refused him my help with you is clear. It

would have been (in appearance at least) to furnish him with weapons. And perhaps in the end he would throw the blame for his own bad conduct on to me.

One word from you is my most sacred law. When I think of you, my duty to my Master grows less. I am ready to carry out all the orders you can give me, provided they are not dangerous to you ; for in that case I shall disobey with a firmness equal to the obedience with which I would carry out all others.

Your letter to the Chancellor was excellent ; and I wait with impatience to know what effect it has produced and what answer you have received.

I am so busy that I have not been able to see the Hetman for some days. I will send you the news of Europe to-morrow. I am yours, yours only, and all yours. I esteem you, I honour you, I adore you. I shall die convinced that there was never a sweetness, a soundness, a face, a heart, a head, to equal yours.

From THE GRAND-DUCHESS

Saturday, 3 hours after dinner [September 14].

I sent a rude letter to the Chancellor on Thursday. Bernardi was not at his lodging, though my man returned there three times, so I suppose the Chancellor will not have received it at the earliest until Friday morning. I have no answer yet. I am going to adopt your maxim, never to be on very good terms with him when I want anything. His greed for money, resembling that of a Pasha, suggests to me the thought of offering him a part of the money which owing to your care is with Wolff, if Count Poniatowski is here for Christmas. I am overdone with his knavish tricks ; never has my annoyance been so acute as that which I feel on this occasion. I cannot conceive what makes him act so badly towards me, or what causes his hatred for Poniatowski. I think I perceive in it the hand of Funcke ; it is a sudden change of conduct. I thank you for your behaviour, and for all that you have said and done. I implore you to neglect nothing which might hasten Poniatowski's return. You will oblige me in a very tender spot. I shall follow your counsel blindly ; my heart and my head, notwithstanding the praise which it has pleased you to shower on them, are quite dejected.

The Chancellor has sent me word that he will send me the Marquis de l'Hôpital's[1] instructions. The Hetman, to my very great regret, told me this morning that he had to-day received the order to leave as soon as possible. I have thoughts of establishing a closer connection with Prince Troubetskoï, and I shall make no difficulty about writing to him. I am trying to unearth some sure method ; for the departure of the Hetman will upset our plans very much. I think that my friend Adadurov[2] will be able to help you ; I shall sound the ford, and shall notify you of everything. My head is splendid, when it has one like yours to think for it. You have, I think, received the *Memoirs of Madame de Maintenon* by Swallov. They come to me from a French comedian, and as there are only three copies, of which Count Esterhazy has one, keep them rather out of sight, for fear M. Douglas should suspect communication between us. I am suspicious of all Frenchmen !

The Empress still talks of going to command the army. She wants to take the Grand-Duke with her and to leave me here with my son—a plan to which the Grand-Duke will not readily consent. He will distribute his order on the 20th to the oldest Generals who have not received it. *This idea originated with me.* You will give me great pleasure by relating, when you have time, details of the King of Prussia's conduct to the royal family of Poland. Will you kindly get the Hetman to ask Prince Troubetskoï what is written on the enclosed paper. When I receive the answer, I will write to you why I want this information. My gratitude follows your friendship step by step, that is to say, it increases every day.

Here is the packet for Count Poniatowski. I have said nothing about the Chancellor's stupidities, because I hope that it is transient and think it very contemptible.

[1] The new French Ambassador. He was Inspector-General of French cavalry, and was Ambassador in Naples from 1740 till 1751.

[2] Catherine's former instructor in the Russian language, at this time Master of the Heralds.

From THE GRAND-DUCHESS

Tuesday, after dinner [September 17].

Bernardi was here this morning. He brought me back my letters from the Chancellor, who, he says, is in mortal anxiety. He again sent me assurances that he would do everything to secure the Count's return, but Bernardi made me suspicious of their sincerity, by saying, " If you really insist, he will be able to return as Saxon Minister." I said to him, " No, I want it to be as it was promised ; this is only an excuse on your part." I read him a lecture on all he said, founded on your principles, and I venture to say that he remained throughout abashed and quite downcast. I found a reason to write again to the Chancellor. My letters have made some impression on him. I enclose the bond for Wolff. If you are our friend, continue to advise me, and do not abandon me to the intense anxiety which grows on me more and more. I feel inclined to go and plead my own cause with the Chancellor. I feel certain that I should win him over from all these other considerations. No, say I, do what you will, he is as fond of me as the man can be fond of anyone. To turn from our gloomy picture, I am going to tell you what I did this morning. The Grand-Duke came to tell me that Sampçoi[1] had come to show him some portraits, that he had afterwards point-blank, as they say, made complaints that Douglas wished to do him harm, and then that he added, " It is said in the town that your Imperial Highness is very annoyed about the French Ambassador, and that you are afraid that the man who comes will intrigue against the succession." The Grand-Duke contented himself with saying : " Mind your own business, Monsieur, or you will never enter my room again."

Thereupon, I found a pretext to send for Sampçoi. After he had shown me what I wanted to see, and, finding that he did not make similar remarks to me, I said to him, " What are these remarks which you have been making to the Grand-Duke ? " Trembling, he began to repeat them to me. I answered him,

---

[1] A French miniature painter.

" Do you know the laws of the country in which you are meddling with matters of this kind ? " He said, " No." " Well," said I, " you should know them. Whoever speaks of things like these, or even mentions them, is sent to the Fortress " ; and added, " Tell those who approve of what you are doing or who send you to make such remarks, that their messengers will one day be thrown out of the window." This is the second emissary from Douglas whom I have discovered this week, but I will teach them to chatter : and if I catch another, upon my honour, I will hand them over to Alexander Schuvalov.

Peter Schuvalov also sent me two emissaries ; and Apraksin has proposed to Ismaïlov that he should be go-between with Peter Schuvalov, as he was between Apraksin and me. He came to tell me this, and to ask my advice. I told him that I would think over it, solely to enable me to ask for your opinion. My head is a blank. I swear to you that I neither think nor act except by instinct or by your advice. Pity my situation. Bernardi said to me this morning, " You are in deep distress "

From Sir Charles Hanbury-Williams

[Thursday, September 19.]

Bernardi happened to be here when the post arrived, so, after reading Poniatowski's letter, I told him that I had received one from him ; and as he said that he was going to you at once, I agreed to his request to send it to you. But the truth was that I had sent for Swallov and found that he was not at home, so I did not wish to deprive you for a moment of the pleasure of reading his letter.

You know that the name of the Countess of Essex[1] always signifies your own.

I received your letter of yesterday, with the one which you had written to the Chancellor. We shall have leisure to talk to-morrow at supper ; so take no step until I have spoken to you. You show a lot of temper before Bernardi, and that might make

---

[1] Sir Charles's eldest daughter. Sir Charles was here alluding to their secret code.

the Chancellor imagine that this fit will pass. Speak to him gently, coldly and firmly. But not with temper ; you will do your health harm, and that is too precious for me not to beg you on my knees to be careful of it. I am not well. My head is very bad ; I have difficulty in writing, and I worked so hard last Tuesday that I lost my appetite.[1] I beg you therefore to allow me a few days to send you the outline of a scheme for your affairs. It appears to me from Poniatowski's letter, that the King, his Master, will come to Poland. Then all will go well ; and if peace is made between Prussia and Saxony, he will certainly come. Poniatowski says positively that the two Kings have agreed. How could you believe, even for one moment, that I would desert you ? I have sworn devotion, and my services are at your command. I shall never break my word to anyone. I am ready to run all risks, all dangers, where your service is concerned, and I would fain flatter myself that my letter of yesterday will have convinced you of it. I have only written you this letter to explain my reason for sending Poniatowski's letter by Bernardi. I will answer yours to-morrow, and will return it at the same time. When I desert you, may God desert me.

From THE GRAND-DUCHESS

Saturday [September 21].

I hope with all my heart that you have recovered from the fatigue of yesterday, and from the indisposition which too much overwork has caused you. Since you told me that you had hopes of Count Poniatowski's return, I feel much relieved. The letter which you sent me by Bernardi raised those hopes, but I needed your confirmation to satisfy them. I am delighted to see that my obligations have a right to increase every moment. The details of your conversation with the Chancellor suggest that idea. I am getting a letter ready for the Count. Thank you for having mentioned him several times to me yesterday, and for having so carefully worded your letter so as to cause him less anxiety. I

[1] His post day. Four long letters from him to Holdernesse of that date, on various subjects, are in the Record Office.

am very nervous all the same about his health after he receives it ; anxiety does him harm. I am going to ask Bernardi very sweetly for my money, and I shall show a better face to him in accordance with your wish, and in order to prevent him from bothering you three times a day. I am ashamed of the conduct of our court towards your own ; I shall try one day to make amends for it.

'Tis fine talking indeed (forgive the expression), when you say to me, " You show too much temper to Bernardi " ; this is more easily said than done. I shall try, however, to follow your advice.

I never doubted that you would fulfil your promises of friendship ; what I said to you on the subject was prompted by affliction and not by distrust, for I am fully convinced of the sincerity of your friendship. Forgive this scrawl ; I write this all in a hurry and without thought. I was forgetting to tell you that the Vice-Chancellor made great protestations to me, with a very contrite air. Peter Schuvalov yesterday let out to me the rest of what he had not told me on St Alexander's day, but which I knew. Apraksin rather kept away from me. Buturlin complained to me of the Grand-Duke, wishing to put the blame on me for his scolding for a real piece of impertinence which he was guilty of to the Grand-Duke. I politely gave him a piece of my mind. The day before yesterday they scolded you, and yesterday they praised me. Reconcile these differences if you can. How did the performance of *La nuit chargée d'étoiles* please you ? I thought I was looking at a prologue of the German comedy. I forgot to tell you that at supper. You did not tell me whether you liked my friend Adadurov ; at least, I will answer for it, that he is a very trustworthy man.

From SIR CHARLES HANBURY-WILLIAMS

Sunday [September 22].

I am sure that you will be sorry to hear that I am not at all well, and that my illness causes me such pain in my head that I have much difficulty in writing to you, and that I cannot be present at court to-night.

Wednesday's letters will go far to clear up the conditions of Count Poniatowski's return. I am awaiting them with impatience; and before they arrive and we know whether the King of Poland goes to Warsaw this year, it is impossible to form any plan : because in the event of the Diet being held, Poniatowski will certainly return here as Minister, and all will go well. But if the King of Poland remains in Saxony, his return will be more difficult ; but even in that case, if the Chancellor acts in good earnest, this should only delay the matter for a month or six weeks.

This is the comfort which common sense allows me to offer you. You reproach me for my outspokenness. Forgive me if I tell you that it is to your advantage that your adviser should always be as frank as possible, that he should take a calm view of affairs, and that he should always speak to you with cool judgment. I do not expect temper to do all that I point out, but it will do something, and that is all to the good. Always remember that my advice has but one object in view, your advantage and your happiness. To show you that in your circumstances I think it necessary that you should show some temper, I advise you never to send Bernardi away without some strong message to the Chancellor, for he must certainly not imagine that you are becoming less determined in this matter. Humour the Vice-Chancellor, if only to prevent him from doing you harm.

The Hetman told me that the Empress had been in a very bad humour with me. But he was in a very bad humour himself. Certainly Her Imperial Majesty has never received me so well, all the time I have been at Petersburg, as she did on the last court day. And when she spoke to Esterhazy a second time, she ordered Ivan Ivanovitch to come and talk to me, which he did.

The Chancellor has promised you papers about M. de l'Hôpital. If you could get a sight of the instructions here given to Count Bestuzhev,[1] you would delight me. It is true that the lady, the other evening, had all the appearance of the Goddess of Night, but she lacked a full moon on the front of her skirt ; with that,

---

[1] Count Michael Bestuzhev, the newly-appointed Russian Ambassador to the court of Versailles.

the costume would have been perfect and well worthy of the theatre.

I was not pleased with Poniatowski's letter. It was the first which I had received from him since he arrived at Warsaw, and it is written in haste.[1] I do not like that, but I am very fond of him.

[1] STANISLAS PONIATOWSKI TO SIR C. HANBURY-WILLIAMS.

Warsaw, September 20, n.s. 1756.

Although I shall have a safe opportunity of writing to you within the next few days, I cannot delay so long without writing to tell you that I love you as my second father. It is a name which I owe you for so many reasons that I shall never change it. You can judge better than I can ever express to you how touched I am by all that you tell me of the *Countess of Essex* (Catherine) in your letter of August 21. May God bless her, and make her as happy as she deserves to be. And may she always win at *l'Ombre* (Poniatowski) since she likes that game.

All who love you here are almost in tears that you are not here. I give you no details to-day, for I write in haste from the house of the Marshal,[a] who also greets you. Almost the whole of my family and the Primate are assembled here, awaiting the result of the strange scene which is taking place in Saxony.

The mail no longer reaches us from the court. Certain special letters come through from Dresden, but these give us no certain or reliable intelligence, for the Prussian army is between Dresden and the Saxon camp pitched in a pretty strong position. The King is there in person ; the Queen remains in Dresden. One day we are told that the King of Prussia has induced our King to accede to the treaty which he made with yours last winter, and that even the six thousand Saxons will be employed for the defence of Hanover, on which condition the King of Prussia will withdraw his troops for Saxony, and compensate for any damage that they have done. Another day we were told that the two camps were watching one another, that the French were promising our King all kind of assistance and that the Austrians were assembling troops on the frontiers of Saxony. In fact, contradiction follows contradiction.

As far as we are concerned, we want to have our King here. The Grand Chancellor Malachowski has gone by his orders into Saxony ; and it is imagined that this is to draw up statements to inform the Polish nation of the reasons which have caused the failure of the Diet.

It is also true that the last messenger, who arrived a week ago from our King, brought the Marshal a positive assurance that by some means or other the King will be here for the Diet. It is said that the King of Prussia declares that he will open a road for him across Silesia. It remains to be seen if he will take that route. If the din in Saxony continues, and the King does not come to Poland, I shall go wherever he goes, in order to hand to him the Empress's letter.

They have just come to tell us that the arrangements are concluded

---

[a] Flemming, who was Marshal of the Tribunal of Lithuania at this time.

I was told yesterday that the difficulties about the march of your troops will increase from day to day, and that the Chancellor begins to entertain more peaceful ideas.

From THE GRAND-DUCHESS

Monday morning [September 23].

I hasten to write, to enquire after the state of your health and how you have passed the night.[1] Here is a letter which savours of a barbarian. I have just written it to the Chancellor.[2] In

between our King and the King of Prussia. I cannot refrain from saying *Thank God!*

Adieu, my dear friend. Love him who is devoted to you heart and soul, and to all that belongs to you. You well realize that among that number the *Countess of Essex* (Catherine) comes first.

Adieu, my dear, dear friend. God bless all I love.[a] I hope you have received a long letter from Vilna.

[1] An unfinished copy of this sentence, on a separate sheet, crossed out in pencil, was found with the letters. (This helps to prove what we supposed, that Williams had copies made of Catherine's letters before returning them, and that in this way the collection has been handed down to us.—G.)

[2] THE GRAND-DUCHESS TO THE GREAT CHANCELLOR.

As your Excellency is ill, I am sorry that you should have had the trouble of writing two full pages without giving me the clear answer for which I asked you, and without which neither my mind nor heart can find rest. On the contrary they provide fresh food for my anxiety. On the subject of the impertinent article in the Cologne *Gazette*, you sent me word that, as MM. Esterhazy and Douglas had received their plenary powers, the Ministry would not accede to the Treaty of Versailles unless the guarantee about Hanover was made the first article. I much doubt whether England will desire it under such conditions, and whether the guarantee about Hanover, inserted there, could ever efface the treachery shown to her by our court, a thought as harmful to our honour as to our interest. Your Excellency is in a position to prevent similar false steps. I am sure that you will find a desire at the conferences to support you upon this matter ; and Peter Schuvalov, whose vote is at your disposal, will not oppose it. By that you will smother the conflagration which will certainly break out, for the Grand-Duke will never consent to place his signature to a mean act of treachery, and will look upon whoever gives a lead to it as an enemy of Russia and of himself ; and what earthly good can we look for in Russia from these confounded French to make us so partial towards them. Or must it be, because the Empress-Queen commits a folly, that her example should be a law to us and involve us. Nothing could

[a] This sentence in English.

reading it, I hope that the epithets will not frighten you.   The noblest sentiments in the world, expressed in the noblest language, would meet with less consideration with him than hard words. The letter, to which this is an answer, is full of protestations, of oaths, of loyalty, of tenderness ; but, on the other hand, not one word of what I have asked him.   No Petersburg gazette announces the impossibility of sending anything to Saxony in safety ; and I would bet that he had had this article printed himself, with the intention of convincing me, for it is entirely in his style.   I do not wish to take advantage of your patience.   I hope to hear you are better.   Here is a letter for Count Poniatowski.

From Sir Charles Hanbury-Williams

Monday evening [September 23].

Monsieur, Your kindness to me is very great.   You are always doing me good.   Your letter has done so, and I have great need of it.

An illness, with which I am afflicted for the first time in my life, plagues me a great deal.   Besides the pain and discomfort, I have such terrible headaches that I write these few lines with difficulty. I was attacked by fever yesterday evening ; Foussatier[1] took nearly sixteen ounces of blood from me, and that relieved me a little.   My illness is the same which so often plagues the Chancellor.

Your letter to the Chancellor is excellent, with the exception that it would be better not to mention the court of Vienna.   The Hetman told me that the Great Chancellor was more in favour than ever, and that he was very much afraid that he was making his court to the Empress at your expense.   He told me that they were abusing me, but he could not say for what.

Forgive this short letter.   You would not have received it at

be more ridiculous.   I give you facts, and you will repay me in words ; my ideas are nevertheless all drawn from the system which you have fathered.

[1] French surgeon to Empress Elizabeth, and later to Catherine.   He was first appointed in 1756.

K

all, if your kindness had not made me feel that my health was of interest to you.

Ever since I made it up between you and Bernardi, he comes no more to my house. I return you your letter to the Chancellor : the others I will return you all together.

From THE GRAND-DUCHESS

Tuesday afternoon [*September* 24].

I do not like your notes when they are an effort to you. I am afraid of them making you worse. Rather dictate them to someone. Your condition pains me extremely, but you should realize that your illness gives you a promise of at least a hundred years of life. I sent for Bernardi after dinner to-day, and, though very pleased that it gave me time to correct the paragraph which you did not like in my letter to the Chancellor, I scolded him for not having come yesterday to fetch my answer. He brought me the copy of a letter from the Chancellor to Brühl, written in German, which is to go by an express from the Saxon *chargé-d'affaires*. The following is the translation :—

" As I have received no news from Count Poniatowski, Stolnik of Lithuania, in person, nor from anyone else of his arrival at your court, I do myself the honour of sending you copies of the letters of recommendation which Her Imperial Majesty's approval of his conduct have procured for him. At the same time, I am bound to tell you that, considering the present critical and delicate position of affairs, I find it all the more necessary that an Envoy-Extraordinary should be sent here without delay from the Kingdom of Poland, whose presence would draw closer the ties of friendship between the two courts ; and as I have found no one who can be more pleasing to my court than Count Poniatowski, I suggest him to you. As he has won Her Imperial Majesty's favour and the goodwill of her whole court, and by this happy combination is in a better position than anyone else to serve his King and Country, I recommend him to your Excellency in the strongest and highest terms."

What do you say to that ? It seems to me fairly satisfactory !

The copies for Brühl are the only things that displease me. I did not open these letters in Bernardi's presence. He was evidently very anxious that I should do so, though he said that he did not know their contents. I told him that, as I did not wish it, I had no doubt that there would soon be a treaty or an accession to the treaty concluded with France. He replied, " Surely the Chancellor will only do as you wish." My answer was that I saw no sign of it, but that very likely he was making his court at my expense. He runs after me like the devil. May God grant you good health, happiness, and all the blessings imaginable.

From Sir Charles Hanbury-Williams

Wednesday [*September* 25]. *Dictated.*

I feel just a little better, but my head pains me all the while. A certain Count Massio has arrived here ; he is a native of Piedmont, and is very well recommended to me. I only saw him for a quarter of an hour ; he is not good-looking, but has talent.

Your letter will go the day after to-morrow, and I shall not fail to give my friend all details of your resolute conduct.

When one of the principal servants is ill, the state of his health is reported to his master ; and that is why this letter is written, for the servant is not yet in a fit state to write a letter. I still have one of yours, which I hope soon to answer.

From Sir Charles Hanbury-Williams

[*Thursday, September* 26.] *Dictated.*

Monsieur, Everything that you have written to the Chancellor, on public as well as on personal matters, is certainly well put ; and its effect has shown it. The letter which he has written to Brühl will settle the matter ; but there is one weak spot. The King of Poland cannot send a Minister from the Republic without the consent of the Senate. But from Dresden he can send a nobleman entrusted with his Polish business. Forgive me if I am critical on a subject in which you are so closely interested ; but at the same time I own that the Chancellor is acting well in what he has done.

On all that concerns Europe, I send you the two last papers which passed between the courts of Vienna and Berlin, and the statement of the King of Prussia.[1] I am told that His Prussian Majesty found enough in the closet at Dresden to justify all that he has done in Saxony ; he has said so himself to our Minister, Lord Stormont. After speaking to this Minister of the position of England in relation to Austria and Russia, he ended by saying, " Believe me, my Lord, the King, your Master, has only one ally left ; but that ally is a good one."

Indeed, Monsieur, I do not know what to say of your court. *Mon Dieu !* Why did they refuse so glorious an opportunity for mediation ? What do they want to do ? The following are the consequences of an alliance with France. I bring them to your notice, for I believe them to be true ; otherwise I should not put them before you.

As soon as it is known in London that Russia has acceded to the Treaty of Versailles, my country will look upon the Empress as worse than an enemy, as a treacherous friend, who has betrayed us by prevarications, false assurances and delays, and who, after ratifying a treaty guaranteed by her own signature and under the Great Seal of her Empire, has construed it in a manner that nullifies all the promised defence.

Austria is already looked upon as a monster of ingratitude, and she is seen in her true light ; for at this very moment the King writes to me as follows, facts to which you will have difficulty in giving credence :—" I have the best information that the House of Austria never ceases to press France to make a descent on my realms."

As for France, she is a formidable enemy, but an open one, who never pretends to be our friend, and who cannot and will not forgive us for having often prevented her from becoming the mistress of Europe.

[1] Compare *Frederick Polit. Corres.*, xiii. 224. Andrew Mitchell sent Sir Charles a copy of this declaration of Frederick's reasons for entering Saxony.

This is how things will be viewed at home, and this will be the result. Forsaken by Russia, betrayed and driven to extremities by the ingratitude of the House of Austria, we have no other resource left but to make a close alliance with the King of Prussia, to give him our money, and to furnish him at once with fifty thousand men. Your allies it is, who are bringing about this alliance ; and with forces as great as these His Prussian Majesty will face the world. In the meantime, he attacks the Empress-Queen purely because she will give him no assurance of peace. He is in Bohemia ; he will eagerly seek out the Imperial army. He is superior in strength and will overwhelm them. After that, he will force them to a peace : or he will go straight to Vienna and will at once put the Austrian States out of condition to help their sovereign. If he makes peace, Russia will not be included (Austria has never thought of her allies, as was proved by the last peace with the Turks). And if, at that time, your troops happen to be outside the limit of your Empire, you will be in a bad way.

Let us examine for a moment the consequences of the war which you are about to commence, even if it should prove successful. If the King of Prussia is conquered, the union between France and Austria will become closer, and once the House of Brandenburg is beaten down, there will no longer be any power on the Continent which will be capable of resisting that union, and which will not be forced to bow down to their will. Russia, being no longer of any use to them, will be set aside, and will have nothing further to say in the affairs of Europe. I am afraid, too, of another result, the universal establishment of the Catholic religion, and am afraid of it with good reason. What I tell you is not a day-dream, it is a scheme which is already prepared.

The intentions of Russia in entering into this war may be generous and good. They wish to help an ally who is attacked ; yet the enclosed papers prove that that ally drew this attack upon herself, and the statement of the King of Prussia shows that he who attacks is not always the aggressor. But the designs of Austria and of France are neither good nor generous ; and without knowing it, Russia will support them until she finds herself powerless to prevent or stop them, and then she will find herself at the mercy of these two ambitious powers, who, taking off the mask, will dictate to her the part she is to play in Europe. Like Saxony, who in the last war assisted the King of Prussia to beat Austria, and then, when the Empress-Queen became much weakened, the King of Poland, wishing, too late, to help her, was himself overwhelmed.

The Empress is at present passionately eager for the war. It is the sovereign in every court who sets the tune, and one would say, from hearing certain people speak here, that a war is now as necessary at present for Russia as blood-letting is for a pleurisy. But are your troops trained and up to strength? Are your officers brave and experienced? Have your Field-Marshals ever commanded, have they ever seen an hostile army? Are your coffers so full that a war will necessitate no new taxes nor cause danger to this Empire?

The maxim of your Ministry, that no one could attack this Empire without danger to themselves nor with hope of being able to harm Russia, is absolutely false, and I am going to prove it to you. The state of this Empire is no longer what it was during the wars of Peter the Great. Moscow was then the capital, and is, from its isolation and the nature of the surrounding country, almost inaccessible to a large foreign army. You had neither Carelia, nor Ingria, nor Esthonia, nor Livonia (without mentioning Courland). The good port of Riga was not yours, and there were nothing but woods and bogs where Petersburg has sprung up. Your large trade of to-day was then confined to a few ships which came to Archangel, and the Baltic knew no Russian vessels. All these new acquisitions are open to attack, and in very close proximity to the King of Prussia. Riga alone, in his hands, would pay him for the expense of a long war.

A further consideration. You have seen, Monsieur, that the Turks have declared that the moment Russia joins with France and Austria, they would make a treaty with the King of Prussia. They will do so, for it is in their interest to do it; and perhaps Russia will force England to repudiate that treaty. If, in consequence of that treaty, they attack the Empress-Queen in Hungary, it is at once a victory for the King of Prussia and a defeat for Russia; for again in that case His Prussian Majesty would be free to turn the force of his arms against you and oblige you to send half of your army against the Turks. Always avoid war with the Ottomans, for campaigns against them, although victorious like those of Münich,[1] can cost you a hundred thousand men, without a pitched battle.

On what is this desperate resolve founded, this desire to march troops to defend and avenge the Empress-Queen, who could, as you see, have maintained peace by saying four words ? Always remember that you are going to fight for a court incapable of friendship or gratitude ; for if all the obligations which she owes to England could not produce these, I fail to see how any other nation, which has not lost its head, can ever expect to receive marks of them. May not a great King attempt an understanding with that proud Empress-Queen ? Dare one not ask for assurances of peace, when one is suspicious of being attacked ? If she had designed to attack the King of Prussia, her secret was badly kept. If she had no such design, for love of the peace of Europe she might have told him so. But since the discovery of her sinister plot against England, she may well be suspected of even more sinister designs.

England will decide upon her line of conduct with regret, but she will decide on it ; and Russia's desertion and Austria's treachery will give the fatal blow to the whole ancient system. The Chancellor, as you said, fathered it. Does he wish, for no reason at all, to smother his own child ?

If the French unite with the Austrians in entering Germany, we shall join with the King of Prussia to prevent their entry, as we are bound to do by our last treaty with His Prussian Majesty. These are steps which tend to an intermission of our friendship, or perhaps to a rupture between England and Russia. Now this is the one thing in the world that I, and you also, would avoid.

My letters of to-day say that the greater part of the Prussian army has already entered Bohemia, and that the Saxon army, being destitute of provisions, will be obliged to surrender to the King of Prussia at the first opportunity. You may be sure that the King of Prussia has found in the closet at Dresden material to justify all that he said in his Statement and all that he has done

[1] In 1737 and 1738.

in Saxony. You will be much surprised to hear that M. Durand,[1] the French Minister at Warsaw, paid a formal visit to the Primate of Poland, to declare to him that France, ever mindful of the welfare of the Republic, could not but feel very uneasy should the present rumour that a Russian army-corps was to pass through Poland to succour the Empress-Queen prove correct, and that he desired in consequence that all possible opposition should be made to their passage.[2]

There is a report in the town that Esterhazy has received a courier, announcing that the Prussians had beaten the Saxons, but that the King of Prussia had lost ten thousand men. I do not believe a word of it ; for the last letters from Berlin are of the 25th of this month, n.s. (nothing later is possible), and then the King of Prussia had no intention of attacking them, feeling certain of forcing the Saxons to surrender, as he had already cut off all their means of provisioning themselves.

I have just this moment received some letters from Poland, which I will send you this afternoon. I am also sending you a letter from Sweden : and I can tell you, to please the Grand-Duke and yourself, Monsieur, that the King, my Master, has made friends again with the King of Sweden.

From SIR CHARLES HANBURY-WILLIAMS

Friday afternoon [*September 27*].

After the long letter which you should have received this morning, I shall make this one as short as possible, out of pity for you. You see that it has taken me some time to decipher the names for you in Poniatowski's letter, and that is the reason why I have not been able to send it sooner. You are also receiving letters from his father, his mother, and his two uncles the Princes

---

[1] François-Marie Durand, *chargé d'affaires* in London in 1749 and in Holland in 1751. He arrived in Poland in July, 1751.

[2] Durand seems to have been acting on his own initiative, as we shall see later. His action was disavowed from Versailles.

SIR CHARLES HANBURY-WILLIAMS

Czartoryski.[1]   Perhaps I find in these letters the wherewithal to
flatter my vanity; and it pleases me to feel that you should know
that in other countries at any rate I was loved and esteemed by
very estimable people.

[1] STANISLAS PONIATOWSKI TO SIR C. HANBURY-WILLIAMS.

Warsaw, September 26, n.s. 1756.

Mon cher et respectable Ami!

My second Father! O dulce decus meum! There is no name known
to tenderness by which my heart does not know you, and which it does
not owe you. My gratitude to you becomes one of the first duties of my
life, and it will always be with the most lively satisfaction that I shall
repay it.

To begin by giving you an account of all that concerns me since our
separation, I will tell you, first of all, that I wrote to you on August 9 and
12, September 2 and 20, and to our humble friend the 12th, 14th, and
25th of August, and the 13th and 23rd of September. Have all these letters
reached you? I have only received hers of August 2, and yours of August
21. . . .

My letter from Vilna of September 2 will have informed you that I
am nonce, and that our Treasurer Flemming speaks, acts, and writes
in a manner worthy of a monument in Westminster Abbey with an in-
scription from your pen. After this, I passed through Bialystok[a] where
le maître (Lieven) began by trying to intimidate me by telling me that
they were displeased with me at our court, but when he saw by my answers
and demeanour that I was far from feeling any alarm, he changed his
tone, began by speaking horribly ill of our court, and finished by asking
me what they thought of him in Russia, and when I answered that they
would be very pleased to see him on the Russian side, he said to me,
" Well, what do they know? " He arrives at Warsaw to-morrow.

Brutus (his father) and *Clélie* (his mother) received me more warmly
than ever. Brutus is just what I should wish him to be, and earnestly
begs that *Bonneau* (Sir Charles) should ask *l'ami* (his father) that *Collom-
bine* (Poniatowski) should go to *Faiblesse* (Russia), so as to hasten and
decide the everlasting deliberations of *la Vertu* (his mother), who, however,
made *le Damoiseau* (Poniatowski) thoroughly understand that she guessed
everything, and even gave him advice in the presence of *la Legèreté*
(Count Czartoryski, Palatine of Russia), whose too close questions he had
hitherto avoided.

The Primate, my two uncles, the Straznik my cousin, are here, the two
Vice-Chancellors, my brother the Grand Chamberlain, the good and the
bad Rzewuski,[b] the Bishop of Livonia, the eldest Solkov, several Potockis,
Bishop Soltyk, the eldest Pocieyc, Sosnowski, and many other senators,
nonces, friends and enemies, whose numbers increase every day, as October
4, the day for deciding the opening of the Diet, approaches. All the Polish
public (notwithstanding the extreme annoyance which reigned in their minds

[a] The home of his brother-in-law, Count Branicki, Great General of Poland.

[b] From the code, " the good " Rzewuski seems to have been Count Francis Rzewuski, Great Notary of
the court.

The most interesting passage in Poniatowski's letter is where he begs me to write to his father and urge his return. His mother loves him ; she has good sense, but is very bigoted. However, I have more influence with her than anyone else, and I shall make full use of it on this occasion.

a month ago) is kept inactive, awaiting the development of the scene in Saxony. The uncertainty of all that we know leaves me nothing to tell you, except that our King was on the 19th inst. in his camp, composed of 15,000 or 16,000 men, situated on the banks of the Elbe between Koenigstein, Sonnenstein and Pirna, and covered on the other flank by a small rivulet : that the King of Prussia had an army of 40,000 men camped between Dresden and the Saxon camp, and had cut off all communication between Dresden and the camp ; that Prince Ferdinand of Brunswick was with 20,000 men between the Saxon camp and Bohemia. To-day, August 27, we learn that an army corps of 25,000 Prussians are marching into Bohemia from the direction of Egra, and that Marshal Schwerin, also with 20,000 men, has already passed Glatz, the last Prussian fortress in Silesia.

Our Grand Chancellor Malachowski was to leave Dresden on the 22nd, after seeing our King in his camp on the 20th and 21st ; therefore we may expect him here at any moment, and, should he arrive before the messenger leaves, I shall add anything new that he may have to say at the end of my letter.

Meanwhile, I will tell you the very singular conduct of the French Ministers here. De Broglie said to Monsieur Gross, apparently believing that Russia had acceded to the Treaty of Versailles, that he (Broglie) was writing to the Great Generals telling them to facilitate the passage of the Russian troops through Poland (this little tone of authority was flattering for that nation !) ; and yesterday Monsieur Durand came to beg the Primate to prevent the Russian troops from entering Poland. The former replied it was only the States in Session who had the power formally to grant or to refuse such a request, but that our experience of the last passage of Russian troops encouraged us to believe that we had nothing to fear. To that Durand answered : " *That he would write this to Douglas and to the Grand Seigneur, to represent to them how serious was the presence of a Russian Army in Poland.*" The Primate recounted this to Monsieur Weimarn[a] and Rzewuski, who reported it to their courts. I cannot praise this Weimarn enough ; we owe him to General Lieven. He is one of those men of the world whose perception is very quick and ready. Gross had sent to his court the answer which the court of Saxony had given to the strong remonstrances made by the Russian Minister in Saxony in the month of March or April, and in this answer Brühl defended himself, and brought accusations against us in a thousand lies, which Weimarn entirely explained away ; and on the arrival of that messenger at Petersburg the Russian Ministry will be exactly informed of our true position, and of the rights and needs of our party. To be able to stand against the intrigues and the money which France employs and lavishes here, we shall require a hundred thousand crowns the first year, decreasing to

[a] Hans Weimarn, a Russian general, sent to Poland during the summer of 1756 on a diplomatic mission.

You see that although Poniatowski writes me a long letter, he again writes in haste ; and on that most important point, Durand's declaration, his uncle is more accurate than he is. He will receive a reprimand for this. Do I flatter you, when I tell you that I want to scold him ?

What do you say to this action of Durand ? What will your

twenty thousand for future ones ; for the impression of superiority which our success has given us in the two or three first tribunals will make things easier from year to year. If the King does not arrive for the first day of the Diet, probably he will not come at all. I think that the majority of the nonces who are of our party will subscribe to a manifesto, stating that, being unable to fulfil their functions as nonces, they beg the Primate to write to the King that these said nonces complain of all the different grievances set out in the manifesto. On that the Primate will write a letter to the King, in which the principal point will be, that, in order to begin to redress all the harm which has been done, he should give an order quashing the commission at Dubno* ; and I think that, if all this takes place, I shall be the bearer of this letter from the Primate.

We have just had news that the Grand Chancellor Malachowski will only arrive in two days ; consequently I can tell you nothing with any certainty of what has taken place in Saxony. I feel very angry that I cannot reach *le Poisson* (Gross) and *l'Aimant* (Brühl). Everyone has tried to persuade me here that *le Poisson* has been bought by *l'Aimant*. I always said I would *not write anything about it*, but that his conduct did not astonish me, and that I would wager it would change if *l'Etourdie* (Poniatowski) could see him.

Patience ! Providence has done too much not to do the rest. I must further add that there begins to be some slight indication of collusion between Monsieur Durand and ————[?]. It is being spread about here, and————[?] does not deny it, that the King of Prussia wishes to publish the proofs, which he says are in his possession, that the court of Saxony has announced in Russia and at Vienna that in the early stages she would affect a complete neutrality, but that when the King of Prussia found himself attacked on all sides, Saxony would deal him the *coup-de-grâce*. And so, on this account, the King of Prussia, they say, will ask the King of Poland to dismiss Brühl from his person and from his council, or to hand over to him his army, his revenues, and Koenigstein: (he will ask) that the Saxons should swear allegiance to the King of Prussia, and that the latter will then give the King of Poland an escort of 1,500 men to conduct him to his kingdom. Monsieur ————[?] begins to court us strongly. *Le Damoiseau* (Poniatowski) cannot imagine why he hears no word of what *Mari* (the Great Chancellor) promised him from *l'homme* (Catherine). I feel persuaded that this is the fault of the latter, but the latter must clear this matter up with *Mari*, and he must urge on what means so much to *l'Etourdie* (Poniatowski) and *le Tier* (Catherine).

I am enchanted with all you tell me concerning the *Countess of Essex* (Catherine). May Heaven protect her ! Thank you for having informed

---

a **A** reference to the Ostrog question, see p. 212.

court say ? What will the ungrateful House of Austria say ? Here is an opportunity for the Great Chancellor even to break with France, if he was really inclined to do so.

Bernardi told me that your last letter made a great impression

me of so many interesting details about her. I very much like her love for *l'Ombre* (Poniatowski).

I appreciate your kindness about the questions which you ask me about my brother, the Abbé. I have every reason to believe we shall be satisfied with him.

My brother, the Grand Chamberlain, has just come in, and takes my pen to tell you himself how devoted he is to you. There is a vile gazette which annoys me, in which it is said that you are recalled, and that my Lord Stormont is to replace you.

I have again forgotten to tell you that the Austrian army was in no position to hold its own against the King of Prussia a fortnight ago. Since then we have had no reliable news. I retract all I said to you in my letter of the 20th about the settlement between our King and that of Prussia, which was then spoken of as a certainty.

Adieu. They are hurrying me ; for the messenger is leaving. Notwithstanding the length of this letter, I still have a thousand things to say to you, which I must swallow. I am at present like the Hebrews, who turn four times a day in the direction of the Sacred City, and four times address mental prayers to it, however far they may be away. Once more, Adieu. Would that I could speak to you instead of writing !

STANISLAS PONIATOWSKI.

Warsaw, 28 *September*, 1756.

It is a cursed thing to be parted from those one loves.

COUNT PONIATOWSKI, CASTELLAN OF CRACOW,[a] TO SIR C. HANBURY-WILLIAMS.

26 *September*, 1756.

Mon cher Seigneur,

I am too happy to learn from such flattering testimony as yours, that my son has, partly at least, known how to repay you for what I owe you, and to respond to the care which you have been good enough to show in his training.

I beg you will receive most sincere thanks which I offer you from the depths of my heart, with the assurance that my devotion to you is and will be as great and as constant as is your due.

The strange scene now taking place in Saxony keeps us in sad uncertainty. We do not know if, or when, we shall see our King in Poland. We do not yet know if the King of Prussia has allowed the Grand Chancellor of the Crown, Count Malachowski, to see his master. Every day we are informed by public report of one new proposal more unexpected than the next. And so affairs in Germany must take some stable turn before it can be possible to arrive at any decision here where the daily

---

[a] Stanislas's father.

on him. Follow up your blow. We shall reap good results from it. I am sure that peace can still be made, if the Great Chancellor wishes it. I will speak forcibly to him on the first opportunity. But I dare not go out, and I am still unwell.

expectancy of some great event holds our minds in the grip of an inaction of which there was little appearance a month ago. My best wishes, my very dear Chevalier, are that your health should be good, and that you should retain for us that friendship which we cherish above all things in this world.

PONIATOWSKI.

P.S.—The Stolnik relates to you our position in further detail.

FROM COUNTESS PONIATOWSKA TO SIR C. HANBURY-WILLIAMS.

My heart feels deeply, my dear Chevalier, the obligations which I owe to you on the Stolnik's account. It is also not very easy to find words in which to express myself. If the sincere gratitude which I feel could pay my debt to you, I should surely not be far behindhand. Accept it, I beg you. I shall be too happy, if time and opportunity should offer me the means of giving you proof of the sincere esteem, tender affection and perfect regard, with which I am, Monsieur,

Your very humble, and very obedient servant,

PONIATOWSKA C. C.[a]

FROM PRINCE CZARTORYSKI, PALATINE OF RUSSIA, TO SIR C. HANBURY-WILLIAMS.

Warsaw, 26 September, 1756.

I have seen my nephew again with delight, and I am delighted to find in the letter which he has handed to me from you the sentiments which you express concerning him. He authorizes me to confess to you that I think that he deserves them. My nephew told me all that is of general and personal interest to us. I always felt the truth and the extent of your affection, but now I am more convinced of it than ever. What can I say to you in return? I know what I owe you. The same devotion which I once promised you will now become even deeper and more intense, and will be assured for the rest of my life.

You know that the catastrophe in Saxony must keep all our minds in suspense, and of necessity delay all resolutions and arrangements. Consequently, the date for the return of my nephew to St Petersburg becomes more uncertain; but at least it will not be my fault if it is not hastened as much as possible, should it be only for your own satisfaction.

You will probably hear it from other sources, but I am none the less glad to be able to tell you this singular fact. Monsieur Durand, in a conference held to-day with the Primate, said to him, that France was

---

[a] Castellane of Cracow.

To explain Poniatowski's letter still further, you should know that I always called Prince Adam,[1] either the *First of Men* or *Brighello*, and that I am fonder of Rzewuski, next to Poniatowski, than of any man in Poland.

I hope that my long letter of this morning will not have wearied you. It contains my real views, and I add that the true alliance for Russia is the Maritime Powers[2] and Prussia. I am ready to prove it to you when you so wish. I will partly do so in two words. Prussia, if you are allied with France, is your most dangerous enemy: if allied with England, your most useful friend. Ostermann used to say so, and he was a very great man.

From THE GRAND-DUCHESS

Saturday morning [September 28].

Do you think that you are writing me something new, when you tell me that you have won the esteem and friendship of people of merit wherever you have been ? I am so certain of it, that I cannot understand how anyone could feel otherwise, unless bereft of their senses. The gratitude which I now owe you would no

very mindful of the welfare of the Republic, and could but feel very anxious, if a rumour which is current should be true that a Russian army-corps would pass through Poland to the assistance of the Empress-Queen ; and that he consequently wished that all possible opposition would be made to it. This is the outline of M. Durand's discourse ; while we know, without any possible doubt, that M. de Broglie shortly before informed the appointed Great Generals that it would be well to put no difficulties in the way of the passage of the Russian troops ; for you know that the French speak to their partisans here as M. d'Havrincour does in Sweden.

The man who is taking your horses sent me word from Mitau, that on finding no arrangements made, he had decided to go on to Petersburg. I much hope that he will arrive safely with his horses. I renew my thanks to you for the carriage, which will be a great comfort to me against our badly paved roads.

My wife is very touched by the honour you do her in remembering her. She begs me to send you many nice messages. Relying upon what my nephew says, I begin this letter, and finish it, without ceremony.

[1] Prince Adam Casimir Czartoryski (1734-1823), son of Prince Augustus Czartoryski, Palatine of Russia.

[2] England and Holland.

longer inspire me, when I grow tired of singing your praises, even to the point of inflaming the jealousy of the Chancellor—the one thing, I think, which injures you with him. Well, I swear that all these people together who have written to you, do not love you, would not know how to love you and reverence you as much as I do. Besides, what is there that you are not doing for me ? You are my friend, my counsellor ; indeed I feel deeply what I owe you. After you, the conduct of the King, your Master, delights me. His reconciliation with my uncle, the King of Sweden, and the little turn which you give to it, fills me with the desire to be able to pay my score to him, to your nation, and more particularly to you, my good and faithful friend. I shall do everything in my power with the Chancellor and with others to prevent foolish action. As such I count everything which departs from the ancient system.

When the news which Count Poniatowski and his uncle have sent you of the conference between Durand and the Primate is known here, it will have an effect and will begin to beget suspicions in men's minds. Have no fear, I will get Weimarn's despatch out of the Chancellor, to see what it is worth. Thank you for all those letters. I do not know if I told you that Prince Troubetskoï assured me on Sunday last that they had heard nothing as yet at the conferences of the accession, or even of plenary powers, and on that he promised me his assistance : but his spirit was shaken by the performances of the King of Prussia.

Beyond all doubt you do not propitiate me when you upbraid Count Poniatowski ; but his crime is not very great. He tells you nearly the same story as his uncle. It remains to be seen who is mistaken.

If Brühl sees that the Chancellor sincerely desires Count Poniatowski's return, it is to be believed that he will think of that expedient, if the other proves impossible. I shall continue to point it out to the Chancellor. I am very glad that you thought him more sincere than he would have been without you.

Forgive the confusion in this letter ; I write as things come into my mind. Here are your letters, except the big despatch which I want to read over again, and the printed paper which I thought would please the Grand-Duke. He will hold his tongue about it, and does not know that it comes from you. I will return it to you at the first opportunity.

I end by thanking you for all the trouble which you are taking on my behalf. So much writing, with a headache, must have tired you out.

I forgot to tell you that this Hening Gyllenborg is the one I knew,[1] and that I am delighted to see that he is with the King; but his lack of courage, notwithstanding his spirit and talents, has made a sad hole in his reputation, ever since the last Diet, of which he was Marshal. They were forced to do battle, and he said he was ill. So he was, but from fear.

How is your health? The invasion of England, urged on by Austria, is the blackest crime that one can conceive. It has a taste of Philip II. and his branch. It makes every honourable man shudder.

From SIR CHARLES HANBURY-WILLIAMS

Sunday [September 29].

Monsieur, This is all that has reached me by the last post from Berlin, of the 2nd inst., n.s. The Saxons are entirely surrounded, and it is expected every day that they will surrender. Marshal Schwerin has actually prevented the juncture of the Moravian army with that of Bohemia; and two regiments of Prussian Hussars have had considerably the best of an affair with five regiments of Austrian Hussars whom they attacked near Königgratz. The greater part of the Prussian army is camped near Aussig, under the command of Field-Marshal Keith and Prince Edward of Brunswick; while the army of the Field-Marshal Brown is at Budin, only four miles from one another. We can, therefore, at any moment, expect news of the greatest importance. The only news I have from Sweden is that the Diet will end on the 15th of this month.

---

[1] Catherine had first met Count Hening Adolf Gyllenborg as a child in Hamburg, when he was on a mission, and saw him later on her arrival in St Petersburg, where he had been sent from Sweden to announce the Crown Prince's marriage to Princess Louise of Prussia.

From THE GRAND DUCHESS

Monday afternoon [*September* 30].

The Empress did not go out yesterday, because she finds difficulty in lacing her dress from the pains in her body. She has similar pains in her legs, and her cough is worse again. She drags herself to meals, nevertheless, so that it may be said that she has been seen, but she must in reality be very ill. No one speaks nor hears anything at the council so far of the accession or of an alliance with France, but they follow the old system—those are Troubetskoï's own words yesterday. I sounded and re-sounded Apraksin yesterday in different ways. He told me that his orders had been with the Empress for eight days, and that they were not signed yet. He was waiting for them, he said, and for money to start on his journey. I asked him, " Will you attack Memel ? " " No," he said, " What could one do with that little hole. It will be ours, when we want it ; and when we have won more useful victories, the swamps which it defends are not worth the trouble spent on them." " Your route then lies through Poland ? " I said. " Yes," was his answer, " if needs be." " But do you think," I answered, " that the King of Prussia is waiting for you ? Everything will be done and finished before you arrive, and you will return as you went, without seeing the enemy." " You think then," he replied, " that he will come to terms with the others in order to fight us alone ? " " No," said I, " I feel very sure and certain that he does not intend to go as far as war with us."

It appeared to me that he seemed overjoyed at these words. He answered me, " My regiments have already advanced into Courland further than they were, but they have not yet got all their stores."

" Yes," said I, " and those stores in Courland will soon be exhausted, for an addition of 80,000 men is a big one."

" Lithuania will bring us some if we pay for them," he added.

" You will go and take them," I said, " you forget what you are saying." He burst out laughing ; and I concluded that he

L

did not know what his objective was, and that all the preparations which are being made were nothing but bluff, that there is nothing yet settled, and that many things are needed before they can be in a position to undertake anything.

The mediation which was suggested has been refused, because they were afraid of being taken in by empty words. I am very curious to know what you have gleaned from my good friend the Chancellor when he was drunk. Allowing for some bad faith and treachery, I still believe him to be my friend. I take great care not to confuse a friendship like yours with that of the common herd. I implore Heaven to bless you.

From Sir Charles Hanbury-Williams

Tuesday evening [*October* 1].

I have just received your letter, and thank you a thousand times. Continue to judge my gratitude by your favours.

My conversation with the Great Chancellor, last Sunday, which you want to know about, was very confused. He was drunk and in a very bad temper. I wished to flatter him. I wished to frighten him, but he did not understand me, and all his remarks ended in, " Remember to speak for me to the Grand-Duchess." I answered him every time, " I never have the opportunity." They say that wine brings out the truth; if that is so, he is violently pro-Austrian and even more pro-Saxon. The next time I go to his house, I shall go before dinner.

I see that my dear Naruishkin is very dissatisfied with Ismaïlov, and even jealous of his favour with you. I am very fond of Naruishkin; and I implore you by any influence that I have with you to set him at his ease. I know that he is one of my friends, and I beg you to give him your support. I am delighted that Troubetskoï speaks openly to you; you will make good use of it. Have you any channel by which to convey your wishes to him ?

I beg of you to finish off the business with Wolff, because I want to be clear of any matter which is known to the Chancellor.

Then after that I will tell you the amount which I paid to our Treasury for the payment of the sum. Will you have the kindness to send it to me ?

You speak to me of my friendship for you ; in truth, it is a devotion which has no limit. I know your worth ; and it is my life's glory to have been able, by my truthfulness, my honesty and my devotion, to win your protection.

Wednesday.

I am grieved not to have seen you at the *intermezzo* last night, and the Empress in your place (I wish you were installed in hers). She sent us some grapes from Astrakhan, which were excellent ; but they gave me the colic.

I have always forgotten to sing you Adadurov's praises. I have seen no product of this country more dependable than him. He has talent, experience and good manners. In truth, he is a Russian who has taken pains with himself !

I have just learnt that Esterhazy has learnt, by an express of which he does not say one word, that a great body of Prussian hussars and dragoons have surprised a great body of Austrian cavalry under the command of Prince Piccolomini, and has cut them to pieces and taken many prisoners. You shall to-morrow have everything that I learn by the post.

I beg you to send me word of everything that you hear in these critical times.

From SIR CHARLES HANBURY-WILLIAMS

[October 2(?), 1756.]¹

I think you might show the enclosed to the Grand-Duke, and even say that it comes from me ; but insist upon the communica-

---

¹ This letter, which appears in M. Goriaïnov's text as A.78. [Undated. November, 1756] must be misplaced, and should belong to the first days of October. It can only refer to the first news of the battle of Lobositz, fought on October 1, n.s. The battle was in reality indecisive. Each side lost about 3,000 men.

tion being kept secret. It is news that will make our enemies tremble ; and I imagine that I shall give you pleasure, when I tell you that the moderation of the King of Prussia is as great as his victory, and that he places peace once more in my hands and in those of Russia. I am going to speak to the Great Chancellor about it. Adieu, give me always your support ; no one adores you like I do. You are the second person in this town who has heard this news.

From Sir Charles Hanbury-Williams

Thursday [October 3].

I have such a terrible headache that I could not answer your yesterday's letter, and must be content for the present to thank you for it. I send you the Berlin gazette for the Grand-Duke He may feel certain, as you may too, that the Austrians have received an all but mortal blow, and that they have lost between seven and eight thousand men, and the King of Prussia only two thousand.

I saw the letter from Field-Marshal Brown to the Empress-Queen, and after reading it one understands nothing of what had happened. He insists that Prince Ferdinand of Brunswick has been killed, but, unhappily for Brown, the Prince is perfectly well.

Friday [October 4].

I could not finish this letter yesterday, and I shall not write much to-day. I had sent some tea to the Duchess of Brunswick by Mme Munchausen, wife of the King's First Minister at Hanover, and in my letter to her I sent my compliments to the Duchess and to Princess Caroline, her daughter, who will be Princess of Wales.[1] I had also begged Mme Munchausen to send me some

[1] During one of his visits to Hanover, King George received the Duchess of Brunswick-Wolfenbuttel and her two daughters. So taken was he with the latter that he subsequently set his heart upon a match between the eldest, Caroline, and his grandson, Prince George of Wales. Indeed, he went so far as to say that he regretted that old age made it impossible

hams and sausages. All this is to throw some light on the enclosures addressed to Madame Munchausen, which I send to amuse you, and to show you that, one day, perhaps, I shall be in favour with Princess Caroline.

Naruishkin has been to my house ; but there were people there, and I will soon arrange a more convenient time for him. He is extremely anxious, and repeated to me some remarks which Ismaïlov has made about him—very cutting. But all I implore you is to treat him well until after our interview, and then I will send you my opinion in greater detail.

I am not at all well. I am very busy, and obliged to work hard in spite of myself.

From THE GRAND-DUCHESS

Friday [*October* 4].

As I always await your letters with impatience, the one which I received after dinner gave me the pleasure which I expected from it. The Chancellor tried to be sulky with me on Sunday, standing behind the Grand-Duke's chair at cards and talking to him with Apraksin two feet away from me. I wished to turn round and speak to him, but as soon as he saw my intention he moved away. He was very drunk.

Your dear Naruishkin has an excellent heart, but is a man of very small intellect, who, at his first appearance in the world, fell into the hands of a very proud and suspicious man, M. de Saltikov,[1] whose faults he copied, but they have been somewhat counteracted by his daily intercourse with Count Poniatowski over a period of ten months. But the praise which the goodness of his heart has won for him, he attributes too readily to talent. This sometimes gives him an insupportable self-conceit and all

for him to marry her himself. But Princess Augusta had other views for her son, and set her face against the marriage. Prince George was well primed with lies about the young lady and with aspersions on her character ; so the scheme came to naught.

The letters which Sir Charles mentions are in the Phillipps collection, but are of no special interest here.

[1] Serge Saltikov.

the jealousy natural to a mind like his. He feels certain that whenever Ismaïlov speaks to me, it can only be to tell me something against him (*which in point of fact has never occurred*). " For," says he, " you cannot trust him at all, indeed you should rather mistrust him." Naruishkin does not understand that use can be made of a tool without confiding in him. To make him happy, I shall never speak to the other in his presence. Troubetskoï talks to me quite openly and frankly, but does not wish for an intermediary, from fear of being betrayed : not even Adadurov, whom I suggested to him myself and of whom I am as sure as of myself. Patience ! It will come.

A week ago I wrote to you to say that the Chancellor had sent to ask me for a bond similar to the one for Wolff. " The Ambassador," he said, " will send it by his messenger." I made it out ; but some days ago Bernardi brought it back to me saying that the last words must be erased. Here it is. I told him to get the 21,000 which were left, and to bring them to me. He came the next day to tell me that Wolff had sent some gold coins to the Mint to make imperials, and that they would be ready in four days. Yesterday he told me that the Empress had taken Wolff's imperials and all the money which they were coining, that I must wait some days to give them time to make more, but that if I wanted roubles, the sum was ready. Imagine the inconvenience of such money ; how was it to be brought or locked up ? I do not want ducats either, for Bernardi would make a profit on them. So I shall wait ; perhaps he is lying. I answered him, " There are always difficulties about everything which passes through your hands." I am very cold to him, and received in the same manner his announcement of the visit of Peter Schuvalov to the Chancellor. I reminded him about M. de l'Hôpital's instructions, and asked for those of his brother. Peter Schuvalov is sending his son to the Austrian army. He took leave of us yesterday ; it is a sudden resolution. Did he think that *Don Miguel's*[1] departure was preceded by the accomplishment of your wishes ?

The profit which I obtain from your friendship is more real

[1] Michael Bestuzhev, a code word.

than the credit which you think mine brings you. I must tell you the truth. Adadurov had asked for a private interview of at least an hour. I could find no better time than on Tuesday during the *intermezzo*. I was also very much afraid that I might grow cold. He was with me from nine o'clock till eleven. He brought me advice, words, assertions, re-assertions, indeed everything. Our conversation almost resembled the general confessions of Catholics. My regard for him is strengthened by your approval. Some former indiscretions about me of the Master of the Horse[1] (a most imprudent man, but one capable of looking anyone boldly in the face) had partly led to this visit.

The news which you send me is true, and Schuvalov told me about it ; but they make so little of this encounter, that they make out that it is not worth a mention. I wanted to arrive at more details, but how could he give them when that was all he knew ?

Since you want something new, let me tell you that a comet was seen the day before yesterday and yesterday in broad daylight : that in addition to this comet, the sudden death of Baron Stroganov, deeply lamented by all for the goodness of his heart, so terrified the Empress that she has had an increase of breathlessness ; that the pains in the lower part of her belly, added to the constant ailments of which you know, have given rise to the fear of a cancer, and that her legs are no less swollen and dropsy is certain. Her cough was so bad after Tuesday, that she did not get up next day, but yesterday restlessness made her resolve to drive about the town.

The Grand-Duke has been in bed since yesterday with diarrhœa, but that is better. I hope that your colic is over. You have a singular antipathy to the lady of the grapes ; everything that comes from her seems to do you harm. I have a sick headache nearly every day. You know what gives it to me. I have just heard that a *ukase* has been published, to assemble 30,000 recruits under the sole direction and command of Peter Schuvalov, to be called the Reserve Corps ; and people argue and differ about it,

[1] Peter Sumarokov (1709-80).

but all call him a second Godunov. As a result I have received a great number of new promises of service. *Friday, 8 o'clock at night.*

From THE GRAND-DUCHESS

Saturday, at 3 o'clock [October 5].

I sent you word yesterday that Peter Schuvalov's son was starting. He is not going, for this reason. After he had taken his leave of the Empress, she began to scold his mother, because, after telling her that he was going with Count Bestuzhev,[1] she had changed her mind. The latter tried to defend herself ; and the Empress then told her that she and her husband deceived her, robbed her, and caused her to be hated, and finally repeated with great vehemence all that is laid at their door; the consequence of which was that they again decided to send the boy with Count Bestuzhev. There is a report in the town that Count Poniatowski is under arrest in Poland, but my heart and common sense tell me that it is false. They do not make arrests like this in that country. I beg you to speak of all the false stories about him to Ivan Ivanovitch, if the opportunity occurs : I think it would have good effect and serve to silence his enemies, when it is known that you take his part. I also wish to send to ask the Chancellor the reason for what the Empress said about him, calling him a spy of the King of Prussia. I shall ask for the papers from which she gets these things, and shall make a fuss about it.

To what party does the Great Chancellor of Poland, Malachowski, belong ? Thank you for your news : I await some from Poland with impatience.

I pour out my woes to you ; comfort me.

---

[1] Michael Bestuzhev, who was going to Paris as Ambassador.

From SIR CHARLES HANBURY-WILLIAMS

Sunday [*October* 6].

Thank you very much, Monsieur, for your letter of Friday ; and at this very moment I have just received yesterday's. I look upon what you are doing for Naruishkin as done at my request, and consequently I shall make him come to my house to give him some advice, which I see that he needs. Since you have had such a long conversation with Adadurov, I would like very much to speak to him again, and I shall beg him to come to my house on the first dark night.

As so much difficulty is being made about your money, give orders that 5,000 roubles in gold should be brought to you at a time ; that is not difficult. All money leaving our Treasury pays about 6 per cent. to the officials, which is repaid when the money is returned. Therefore, on the 44,000 roubles, there is about 2,600 to be paid, which will be refunded to you. I have already paid it in London, and I shall be obliged if you will send it to me at your convenience.

From SIR CHARLES HANBURY-WILLIAMS

Monday [*October* 7].

Thank you for what you wish to do for Naruishkin. I add it to my account with you. But I must speak to him myself, to give him some advice, of which I see he is in great need.

On Friday evening I had a conversation of two hours with the Great Chancellor. He was in a very good temper. He spoke a great deal about you, detailing all the services which he had rendered you, and saying that at his age he could look for nothing, that he had enough to live on and that was enough for him ; but nevertheless he showed clearly that he is more afraid of the loss of your favour than of anything else, as he begged me a hundred times over to persuade you that he was doing all he could for Poniatowski's return. To this I replied that you were resolved to test his friendship in that way, that you were quite convinced that Poniatowski would return if he really wished it, and that it was not in my power to make you think differently : that I knew that it was what you had most at heart, and that I advised him as a true friend not to play with the matter, for, as you had set your mind on his return, I was sure that, if he did not bring it about, you would try every other method of obtaining the accomplishment of what you so ardently desired. He seemed moved by my words, and said to me, " I am doing all I can ; if it does not succeed, she cannot blame me." I answered that this was not an affair of State nor of reason, but of passion, and that it was for him to consider well what the consequences would be if it failed, and that as far as I was concerned, ever since he had told me that I was under suspicion at court, I would have nothing more to do with it. To this he replied that the Empress had spoken well of me the other day.

I replied, " I shall try then, by my conduct, to deserve the continuation of her goodwill. I am determined to have nothing more to do with the matter." I told him that Poniatowski's immediate return was his only means of securing the continuation of the great influence which he had with you. I assure you that these last words made an impression on him. But I am more alarmed, Monsieur, at another piece of news, to which it seems to me that you pay too little heed. You tell me that they are to raise thirty thousand men, and that they will all be under the command of Peter Schuvalov. It is an army in the hands of a subject. It is a Prætorian Guard, who could dispose of an empire and make the sovereign dependent on its authority. The *ukase* is already signed, and they are going to raise the men. A visit to the Chancellor is well worth while paying, to obtain such a command ; and in this instance the Chancellor is either no longer your friend, or he is taken in by Peter Schuvalov. Do not think, Monsieur, that this addition to the Russian forces has any influence on my fears about your succession. The war will probably be ended in Germany before the Russians leave their country. And you will soon see the King of Prussia in a condition to face everyone. But that the Empress's council allows one subject to have 30,000 men at his disposal is the blackest betrayal of the

Empire and the succession imaginable. If you remember a long letter which I wrote to you last week, and which you told me that you read over twice, you will see that my prophecies are already almost fulfilled. To beat seventy thousand men, the flower of the Austrian army, with forty thousand, is a victory unprecedented. The victor knows well how to profit by it. But rely upon it, his moderation, of which I hold proof in my hand, is as great as his valour. *Mon Dieu!* what a scheme I could draw up in two hours to secure everlasting glory for Russia! *Mon Dieu!* if you were in your place! But it is in vain, as David says, to charm the deaf adder: or to show the finest paintings to the blind.

Notwithstanding all that has happened since I have been in this country, my heart still inclines towards Russia; that is to say, she is dear to me, because one day you will reign there; and it infuriates me to see the condition in which you will find this Empire on your accession. Remember that it is zeal, affection, devotion, adoration, which speak. I recognize the long-standing and natural alliance between our two courts, and the mutual utility which we can be to one another. I see it on the point of being wrecked by a dandy, and by a Minister who believes himself to be greater and more indispensable in times of trouble: and to the taste of the one and the ambition of the other, I see the Empress and the Russian Empire sacrificed.

It is sorrow, not anger, which causes these reflections. It is to you alone, who deign to accept my confidence, that I open my secret thoughts. Ask the Chancellor what they intend to do after the news of this victory, and whether Russia in her turn wishes to draw upon her the King of Prussia, who is far from wishing to become your enemy, but would stand up against you without fear.

You may be certain of the truth of all that follows. The King of Prussia will soon have more than two hundred thousand men on foot, his troops all trained for war, and all well commanded. For him England will open her treasure chests, which Russia has refused. You may look upon the House of Austria as in no position to act and her peace made with his Prussian Majesty, and then you will see these two hundred thousand men turned against France and Russia. A single defeat will take Courland and Livonia from you ; and probably he will advance still further, so that the peace, which will be forced upon you, will be anything but an honourable one.

Let us change the subject. How ridiculous to say that Poniatowski is arrested in Poland ; no one is arrested in that country, certainly no one of his name. *Mon Dieu!* how I long for his return for my own comfort. A friend so faithful, a confidant so brilliant and reliable, is invaluable. What an assistance he would be to me at this moment—he who shares my sorrows and my joys, who loves me without self-interest, who is devoted to me without ulterior motives and respects me just because he knows me ! It is true that I feel a father's tenderness for him. He is mine elect, my adopted child ; and I congratulate myself when I feel every day that you and my own good sense equally approve of my choice. I shall soon send you his portrait, on a large scale and on a small. But I have a terrible amount to do ; and I conclude both out of regard for you and for myself.

From SIR CHARLES HANBURY-WILLIAMS

October.

Overwhelmed with business owing to the arrival of my post yesterday, I have only time to send you the enclosed.[1] I had

---

[1] FROM STANISLAS PONIATOWSKI TO SIR CHARLES HANBURY-WILLIAMS.

Au Cabinet, October 17, n.s. [1756].

Mon cher et respectable Ami,

I have received your letter of September 17th. I have copied it. I have burnt the original, and now I answer it. I will not endeavour to describe to you all the divers emotions which so deeply moved me when I read your letter and the six enclosures. You know my feelings, you know to what excess I love *Collette* (Catherine) : so you can judge of my condition. But the question is to grapple with adversity, and not to weep over it. I come to the main point. It is absolutely untrue that the bearer of that snuff-box could have seen the least mark of fear in me ! For I never felt the least sign of it. I was chattering to Horn, who was in my room, and I was putting on my shirt, when they came to tell me

instructed Poniatowski to continue to make adverse comments on the King of Prussia, and he obeys.   The end of his letter refers to what he wishes me to write to his mother.

But the principal reason for this letter is to let you know that

that there was an officer who wished to speak to me.   As, a short time before, two officers, compatriots of mine, worthless fellows, had come and annoyed me, I thought it might be a third of the same kind, and I did not even much hurry myself to see him.   However, after a few minutes, I went out into the ante-room in my shirt, where I found a somewhat ill-favoured individual, not in uniform, who at once with low bows presented me with a velvet box adorned with gold lace.   Judge whether this introduction was very alarming ?   What he said to me was even less so ; so believe on my word of honour that this is no untruth.

I attribute this invention to *Accajou* (Ivan Schuvalov) who, becoming uneasy apparently at the approval which *La Prudence* (the Empress) had bestowed on my letters, and also by this gift, seems to have thought that I might again become a danger to him, and was anxious to give me a *coup-de-grâce* to prevent my return.

L Italien (Galitzin) and *L'Adroit* (Betski), inspired by *Accajou*, will have whispered to the messenger to repeat the matter to *L'Intègre* (the Vice-Chancellor), in the manner in which he again repeated it to *La Poutres* (the Empress).   For I do not believe the *Intègre* capable of being purely malevolent, especially to someone who has done him no harm ; and, besides, a plot like this is beyond him.

I entirely agree with your views about *Le Patron* (the Great Chancellor) in this affair.   He was anxious to remove the rivals whom he fears in *Collette's* (Catherine) favour, for he is supremely jealous about her, and not knowing her sufficiently, believed that absence would efface me from her mind, and from her heart ; otherwise he would not have attempted it. For this reason, I think, he exaggerates to *Collette* and to you the fears and danger of this pretended discovery, and though I am convinced that he is quite pleased with this tale of my fright, I do not believe that he has invented it, and still less that he has betrayed the secret of my heart. The most that he will have done will be to make good use of the suspicions of the politicians of your liaison with M———— (Catherine) through me and *Le Petit* (the Hetman).   After all, so long as he keeps to the politics, nothing is lost ; and we both know that the most terrible remarks made by *La Prudence* (the Empress) do not prevent her a week later, and sometimes even the following day, from contradicting herself and praising the person whom she has just abused.

As to a change of hands, I believe it to be useful for *Le Patron* (the Great Chancellor) to be afraid of it, but without it actually taking place.   It appears to me that *Collette* would lose too much by depriving herself of this man of iron, in whose heart, for all that, she has known how to inspire a true passion.   My resentment, however great, must always be subservient to the interests of *Collette*.   One can but believe that the de-cisive moment is near ; and then, if *Le Patron* should think that he has too irreconcilably offended her, he will not help her.   I reproach myself with nothing which is prescribed by your skill and tender affection for her

in three days at the latest, I shall send a courier to Dantzig, and that you can write to my friend with every safety. I have a courier always in readiness at Dantzig to go to Warsaw.

Send me news of what is being done here ; and be assured that

and for me ; but I should also reproach myself, if I did not write all my thoughts about what concerns her. If I can assure her happiness, even at the expense of my own, it must be done. I promise you both obedience and patience, because I love her and because you are our guide.

I think, however, that if I am appointed Minister, I can and should go. To justify this, I must tell you that in the uncertainty in which the blockade of the Saxon camp places us, which may end any day, and on the supposition that *Le Poisson* (Gross) would then have access to our King, I sent him by messenger the letter from *Le Patron* with yours, to which he answered as follows, of date October 9 [n.s.] :—

" I had yesterday the satisfaction of receiving your letter of the 1st nst., which appeared to me to be in good condition and not to have passed through inquisitive and indiscreet hands. I scarcely know how to express to you, Monsieur, how sensible I am of the assurances of friendship which you are good enough to renew to me, though I must add, notwithstanding all *insinuations* to the *contrary*, that I have always felt reluctant to disbelieve them. So much so, Monsieur, that assuredly I desire nothing so much as to retain the honour of your friendship and the affection of all your illustrious family. I shall try to prove this to you, by employing all my powers to second the scheme which you have had the kindness to communicate to me, and which I see is confirmed by the letter of H. Ex. the Great Chancellor. I much regret to be unable to take the matter in hand as soon as I should wish, but as you yourself feel, Monsieur, until the King has more leisure, it will be impossible to propose such a thing to His Majesty. Further, Monsieur, I have already been informed from elsewhere of the distinctions which your merit has gained for you at my court, therefore you must permit me, taking the interest in it which I do, to congratulate you with all my heart, and to wish you the continuance of uninterrupted prosperity, begging you at the same time to be entirely persuaded, etc., etc., etc.

" I await a more safe opportunity to answer our common friend, the G. Ch. Besides which I hope soon to have the opportunity of embracing you in Poland, for in one way or another it appears to me that we shall have to winter there."

What further decided me to send him my letter, without waiting to hand it to him myself, was that several repeated warnings and various indications which reached us made it evident here that Gross, believing himself to have much cause for complaint against me and all my family, and even against you, was acting and talking much to our disadvantage. I think I can see in his answer a man who is pleased to have no reason for hating us, and whose intention is to help me. We cannot sufficiently praise Rzewuski and Weimarn, especially the latter, whose intelligence entirely equals his good will.

The failure of the Diet has rendered useless to us the considerable majority which we had both in numbers and quality, of friendly nonces

my zeal, my devotion, and my affection for you increase every day.

I have not yet time to answer your last letter, so I am still keeping it.

who were armed with very stringent instructions. Flemming answers for the continuation of our success in Lithuania, provided that the French money which increases there daily, as well as in Poland, does not swamp everything in the end. Weimarn has asked the Princes for 100,000 roubles the first year, with the promise that less will be required in the following years. The manifesto of which I spoke to you in my last letter has not been published here as was intended, because it would be too long and because it would be useless to give it in detail here.

My brother-in-law[a] equally hates the Marshal of the Court[b] who has played him a thousand tricks ; and so long as the King is absent he acts as master of Poland. I am much afraid that some orders sent to him by our King to reinforce the garrison of Dantzig, which he is tempted to execute, will draw trouble on ourselves with the King of Prussia, who only requires one pretext to take a whole country under his *protection*.

I think it very superfluous to add to this letter news that will already be very well known when this reaches you, and the more so as we do not know the consequences of the sanguinary but indecisive battle of Lobositz, fought on October 1. An indistinct report reaches us that another battle has been fought between Schwerin and Piccolomini, in which the Prussians had the advantage. My brother, the captain of Grenadiers, came through the former without a scratch, although he saw eleven captains of Grenadiers killed or wounded round him.

It appears to me that you and *Collette* would do better if you made use of the New Style for your dates instead of the Old, without adding the year, or even the place, unless you put *Paris* (St Petersburg), *Versailles* (Peterhof), or *Choisi* (Oranienbaum). Tell me, both of you, what you think of my idea, whether, though *Le Patron*, from fear of ill-will, refuses to send me the answers to my two letters by his relation at Mitau, I may not still send a special messenger to his relation to convey my letters to *Collette*. I ask this all the more boldly, because some presentiment makes me hope that this confounded man will become more tractable. If you can win over *Accajou* (Ivan Ivanovitch), do so ; to this I give my entire consent. I will ratify beforehand all that you do together. When *l'Amour* (Catherine) and *La Sagesse* (Sir Charles) are in agreement, what is there that cannot be accomplished ?

I am delighted to hear that the King of Prussia does you justice. In return, I will give you this news, that I know from Prince Adam,[c] that Kaunitz is so hated by the Austrians that the day of his disgrace will be a day of fête in Vienna. The Emperor detests him. Gibson's man took seven days to come here, but I would have paid him ten. Assurances and such convincing proof of the love of *Collette*, and of your affection, are comfort indeed in the midst of the keenest anxiety. I do not thank you each individually for the *tea* (money), for what is there that I do not

[a] Count Branicki, Great General of Poland.   [b] Count Mniszek, Brühl's son-in-law.
[c] Czartoryski.

From Sir Charles Hanbury-Williams

Monday evening [October 14].[1]

I am awaiting another letter from you, before speaking to you again on the subject of my last. I have thought well over all that I have written to you, and I am more and more convinced of the following truth. Apraksin and the Chancellor intimidate

owe to you ? I am very glad she has had some. The departure of *Le Petit* (the Hetman) affects me very much. It is hard to think that an honest man should suffer for having been one of my friends ; for that is at least made the occasion for his dismissal, though it may not be the original cause. It preys on my mind to think that three friends such as *Le Petit*, *le Jou-Jou* (Apraksin), and *Le Valet* (Lieven), all three so devoted to *Collette*, and myself, will perhaps be far from her *au demain matin* (death of the Empress). But think what I feel when I read in your letter that *Collette* has been ill with anxiety about me ! I beg you to send this letter to *Collette* with the enclosed, for I have written all that has taken place in this one.

You give me sincere pleasure when you tell me that your health is better. It is one anxiety the less for me. I would gladly whip Charlotte for causing sorrow to such a father as you are, and I bless Fanny.[a]

Do not be annoyed or astonished if you find nothing in this letter to amuse you, or to make you laugh. One must feel gay to be amusing, and all I can do is not to feel despondent. I have been forced by circumstances, details of which I send to *Collette*, to tell my secret to Flemming and to the Palatine of Russia. Reassure her about the character of these two men, who, on this occasion as on all former ones, have given me the strongest assurances of honour and friendship.

My mother's love for me makes her ardently desire the same thing that I do ; while her religious scruples, which have become very strong, force her to say *non consentio*. Nevertheless, she says it with tears, and in the weakest possible manner, My Father, in despair over these contradictions, does not dare treat them harshly, but has nevertheless quite firmly resolved that I shall go when the time comes. Write to him (when the time comes), and say that you require me.

Adieu, my dear and worthy friend, my adopted Father. After *Collette* I love no one so much as you.

[1] After October 7 there is a gap in the correspondence.—G. Letter A.35 in M. Goriaïnov's text (p. 196) has been moved from its position after the letter of October 5 to precede this one. It must be some days later, as it encloses the above letter from Poniatowski, dated October 17, n.s., which corresponds to October 6, o.s.

[a] Poniatowski refers to Sir Charles's daughters, the youngest of whom was giving her father some anxiety, owing to her wish to marry a certain Mr Hobart, of whom Sir Charles disapproved as a son-in-law. She married the Hon. Robert Boyle-Walsingham two years later.

the Schuvalov by boasting that they possess your entire confidence and only use the influence which they have thereby obtained for their own personal advantage : and, by making to the Schuvalov promises regarding the future, which they have no right to make, they are securing their present advantage.

Imagine to yourself the relations between the Great Chancellor and Peter Schuvalov by what follows. He said the other day to the Empress that in the present critical times this Empire could scarcely exist without the counsel of a man like Peter Schuvalov. And to me he says that he should be hanged sky-high. But always remember that, though it is I who give the advice, it is you who must take the decision, for you know this country better than I do.

Here is splendid news. Saxony has surrendered to the King of Prussia. The King of Poland has shut himself up in the Castle of Königstein. We have not yet received the terms of the capitulation. But we know that it is arranged. I shall have them on Wednesday. The King of Prussia has again fallen on the rear guard of the Austrian army and has hacked them to pieces. They lost 1,500 men.

What a man that King is. He makes war, makes peace, and writes books, all at the same time ! Yesterday a work reached me which he has prepared for his justification, written with the greatest clearness and distinctness, very amusing and full of curious anecdotes ; and another, full of what he calls, *Pièces Justicatives*, which are for the most part letters from certain courts and ministers, which he has intercepted.[1] What pleases me most is that Russia is well spoken of throughout ; and he gives proof of and exposes all the intrigues and false intelligence by which the Empress has been influenced and irritated against him. In it the court of Vienna does not make too fine a figure, and M. Funcke plays a considerable part. The Great Chancellor is spared, perhaps out of love for me, and in order to further the present views of the King of Prussia, which, I assure you, tend only to peace. Among other lies which he exposes, that of his

[1] Mitchell sent these to Sir Charles on October 21, n.s.

M

plot with the King of Denmark to seize Holstein is cleared up, and for its falseness he calls to witness the King of Denmark.

It is certainly a charming book, and you shall have it to-morrow. Tell the Grand-Duke that you will have the work, for I want him to see it. He will be instructed and amused by it. I shall try to procure another copy ; it is a work to keep and to read over and over again.

Here is a piece of good news which I have just heard. The King of Poland has certainly left Dresden for Warsaw, and should be there by now. You can only have the King of Prussia's papers when the Great Chancellor returns them to me. I saw him to-night, but he had been drinking. Be sure, Monsieur, that England has no other friend here but you, and that the treaty with France goes ahead very fast.

Adadurov dined here last Saturday, and pleases me very much : he is your zealous servant. He has good sense and good manners. He is extremely worried about Peter Schuvalov's great command. Do you know that Peter Schuvalov is now in charge of the management of all the public treasure, and that he has taken over the pin money of the Empress from old Ivan Antonovitch Cherkassov ?

I commend myself to you always. The King of Prussia will increase his army in Bohemia by eight thousand men, for he is resolved to put an end to everything as soon as possible.

From THE GRAND-DUCHESS

Tuesday, 5 o'clock in the evening [October 15].

Although I know that you are overwhelmed with business, I must not fail to tell you all I know. Bernardi has just left me The Chancellor sent me word that at the conference yesterday there was a desire to break with England at all cost, that he had furiously opposed it, pointing out the disgrace, the ruin to commerce, and France's lack of good faith : " In a word," said he, " all that my zeal for the good cause and my duty could inspire me to do." Apraksin supported him. He adds that he has put everything straight, and that he hopes to carry it with a high hand. Afterwards, they dealt with the question of the King of Prussia, and it was reported that he intended, in the event of war being declared against him, or, if you prefer it, of being attacked, to publish a manifesto in Russia in favour of Prince Ivan. They thought proper to report this at once to the Empress, and she replied : " I shall have Prince Ivan's head cut off as soon as that manifesto appears."

Then the Chancellor begged me to write you a letter, to tell you that he was giving much attention to your affairs, that he had overcome all opposition, that your treaty would not be broken, and that to please England he would be more favourably inclined towards the King of Prussia than he had been, and that though our army might cross the frontiers it would go no farther. He asserts that a letter of this kind from me to you would be a guarantee for you, that you might write it to anyone who was interested, and that in that way things would begin to quiet down. I answered that I will not write, that I had no one by whom I could do so, and that I knew the danger of a letter to an Ambassador—the very idea terrified me. Bernardi said to me, " Then I will tell him by word of mouth, if you will allow me ? " To this I replied, " On that, you are your own master." Draw your own conclusions, therefore, my lord, and do as you think proper. I said to Bernardi, " Tell the Chancellor, in answer to the news which he has sent me, that the Empress had some sort of convulsions yesterday, that she was bled at midnight, that this is the second relapse in three days, and that when I am in her place, I shall give business the turn that I think fitting : that I no longer know what to trust nor what to stick to, that I am paid everywhere in words but see no results, and shall begin to have doubts about everything." Then Bernardi told me that the Vice-Chancellor had shown the Chancellor a letter from M. de l'Hôpital to Michel, in which the former urges the latter to arrange that less should be said about his journey to Russia ; and that this was the second one which Michel had received on the same subject from the same person. He tells me now that he has not been able to promise me M. de L'Hôpital's instructions, because he asserts that he has not got them. " But perhaps," he added, " they are like my brother's," which, he maintains, are not yet prepared and are to be sent after him by a courier. They say *Don Miguel* (Michael Bestuzhev) was just about to take leave of the Empress when she collapsed : the fingers of her hands were bent back, her feet and arms were cold as ice, her eyes sightless. They drew much blood from her : and sight and feeling returned. What do you say to that ? To-day she is being purged. She is in bed. Here is a letter for Count Poniatowski ; thank you for his. You do not doubt my friendship, do you ?

From Sir Charles Hanbury-Williams

Wednesday [October 16].

You ask me, Monsieur, for tons of advice on your present position. This is all that I have to offer you. In the event of the death, you are, thank God, on the spot. The Grand-Duke and you must show yourselves almost at once, but not until the oath to both of you has been settled and taken by the Ministers or Minister who are first admitted to your presence. No one should kiss your hands before they have taken the oath ; receive no one badly the first days, but take special notice of your protégés. Let your looks denote plenty of determination and calmness. If the Grand-Duke Paul is well, you should show him in your arms for a moment.

There is no necessity whatever for even thinking of your safety or protection. The title of the Grand-Duke is as clear as daylight; there is none better in Europe. Everyone will bow down, everyone will prostrate themselves before you, and you will ascend the throne with the same ease as I sit down to a meal.

If a will is found, and it is not altogether favourable to you, it would be best to suppress it. Lay claim to no title but the lineage of Peter the Great.

The Grand-Duke must assemble regiments of the Guards at the first opportunity, and show himself to them.

This is all that I have to say on this subject. If they will have the kindness to die, all the rest will go like clockwork.

I am greatly obliged to you for Panin's letters. His last is

good, so good that I seem to see in him a future Vice-Chancellor.[1]
I sent you the letters from Brunswick to amuse you. Alas!
That court is too small for you to give it a moment's thought.
The head of the family is devoted to you, and is your zealous
friend.

How stupid this new lie is about the King of Prussia. The
Empress's answer, however, pleases me ; it is concise and full of
dignity.

Everything that Bernardi told you from the Chancellor may
be true. But you will be able to clear that matter up for yourself at the first opportunity with Troubetskoï. I am rather
suspicious about it. He courts me, because he has not a halfpenny, and he sends every day to beg me to advance him a
half-year of his pension. But I must have other proof before
I grant his demand, after all we have seen happening. Am
I not right ?

With regard to *Don Miguel*, I must tell you a story. His
brother sent for me the other day to tell me that *Miguel* was a
very much interested party, and that he advised me to win him
over and to write to my Master and to the King of Prussia to tell
them to send some trustworthy person to meet him on the road,
and to speak to him in that manner which so successfully per-
suades almost all mankind.

Don Miguel dined at his brother's house yesterday. The party
may have been cheerful ! But if there was milk on the table, I
feel sure that it would have become sour at once at the sight of
their two faces.

I am delighted to be in agreement with de l'Hôpital about his
journey. He has only to delay it as long as he wishes. It seems
to me that Russia is more anxious to see him than he is to see
Russia.

The Hetman had promised me last night some news of the
Empress. Roman[2] was to come to his house from the court to
bring it ; but although I waited for it with great impatience

[1] Russian Minister in Sweden. Sir Charles's prophecy came true.
Catherine appointed Panin Minister for Foreign Affairs in 1763, with all
the power of a Great Chancellor.
[2] Roman Voronzov.

until two hours after midnight, I received none, and still remain between fear, joy and hope.

When I went to bed, so brilliant a scene rose up before my eyes that I never closed them all night long ; yet it was a night well-spent. I intend to put in writing my vision, which embraces the future splendour of your reign.

I shall take care of the letter for Poniatowski ; you acted like an angel with Bernardi. I have not yet seen him. No, Monsieur, I never had doubts of your protection. If I had for one moment, my misery would equal the triumph and happiness which I feel in possessing it.

From THE GRAND-DUCHESS

Thursday [October 17].

I shall follow your last advice the more readily because it appears to me better suited to present circumstances, and because too many precautions might show more weakness and too much fear. Apraksin sent to tell me this morning, that the Schuvalov could not make enough of him yesterday and the day before, and fawned upon him. He said that their fear was pitiful, that to quiet them, he swore many times to them that they had nothing to fear, that he assured them that they had everything to hope for from me, and that he, Apraksin, had no other support or protector but me. He sent to ask me whether under present circumstances I gave him orders to leave or to remain, and said that he would delay or hasten his departure according to my command. I sent him word in reply that he had spoken very wisely to the Schuvalov, and that I desired him most strongly to remain, and that it would be a mark of loyalty to me.

During yesterday she had three attacks of giddiness or fainting. She is very nervous, and terrifies herself, weeps, is frightened, and, when she is asked why, answers that she is afraid of losing her sight. There are moments when she forgets where she is and does not recognize those around her. It is said, however, that she has passed a good night, and that she will move to-day to the Winter Palace. They give her innumerable drugs ; and she takes everything very willingly. My surgeon, a man of great experience and good sense, expects an apoplectic seizure, which would certainly carry her off. Three people who never leave her room, and who do not know about one another, inform me of what is going on, and will not fail to acquaint me when the crucial moment arrives.

I have for some time past seen a future Vice-Chancellor in Panin; and I am delighted that you should think so.

I have had some little suspicions of treachery on the part of the Chancellor, so well have you taught me to know him; and you are quite right to show him the golden apple, without giving it to him until you have tasted something.

Bernardi has just left me at this very moment. He promises me 1,000 imperials to-night or to-morrow morning. I told him I would not believe it until I had them in my hand. I spoke of Count Poniatowski; he swore to me that the Chancellor was working sincerely for his return. See how they flatter me at the critical moment. The Chancellor believes that the Empress is worse than I do personally.

Bernardi takes you a note which he and the Chancellor have composed, written as though they were my words. He showed it to me, and I returned it to him without comment.

I only hope that your vision of happiness may come true, but I will tell you in confidence that I am afraid of not being able to live up to a name which has too soon become famous. If I dare to use such an expression, I have within myself great enemies to my success, which you may well know nothing about; how shall I avoid being led, how shall I act to escape being blinded? I shall say like Madame de Maintenon, " Pray God for me "; but I swear to you my vanity and my ambition tremble at the thought that I may yet have to complain of some unknown enemy.

Are you writing, or have you written to Count Poniatowski's mother, to hasten these everlasting deliberations?

From Sir Charles Hanbury-Williams

Friday [*October* 18].

The enclosed will be read before this ; it came to me by a safe hand. I send it to you at the actual moment that I receive it. He does not write a word to me. But he does not love me the less ; and if I could send you some of his letters by each post, I shall forgive him if he wrote to me but once a year.

I have just received your letter of yesterday. I could always wish that my advice would prove agreeable to you. When we both agree, I shall always be satisfied, and shall feel confident that the advice is good. If Apraksin is your friend, he will not go. It is very necessary for the Schuvalov to humour your friends : nevertheless, they would do better to make their court to you.

I look upon the illness of the Empress as likely to be fatal. The Hetman let fall a word to me yesterday which convinced me of this ; the trouble is in her womb. If that is the case, all the pains in her head come from it and will end, as your surgeon says, in apoplexy. She believes herself to be very ill, as is shown by her willingness to take drugs. I am delighted to hear that you are kept so well informed of her condition ; that is very necessary for you. I do not know whom the Chancellor fell foul of at the conference last Monday. The Vice-Chancellor was not there ; he is still ill, and I think that all this last story is an invention. Bernardi pulled out of his pocket this morning the paper which you mentioned to me. But he did not tell me that you had ordered him to speak to me about it : and afterwards he told me under the seal of secrecy that the Russian troops would not march this year. The Chancellor is rather stupid, he might have extracted good payment for this assurance.

I do not know what Poniatowski has written to you, but I am preparing the letter for his mother, which will go by a courier.

I shall answer the rest of your letter to-night or to-morrow morning, because I do not want to deprive you any longer of the pleasure of the enclosed.

From Sir Charles Hanbury-Williams

Friday evening [October 18].

My duty towards you, Monsieur, constrains me to offer you my thoughts and advice on a part of your last letter.

Apraksin sent to tell you that the Schuvalov could not make enough of him during the illness of the Empress, and that their consternation was very great : that he has given them assurances of your future protection, and that you have not revoked the assurances which he gave.

My conscience and unalterable devotion oblige me to tell you that all this answers the purpose of the Schuvalov and Apraksin very well, but that it does not enhance your credit, nor does it give you the authority which such a situation should give you By disposing of your future favours, Apraksin assumes a great power at present, which he does not use for your interest nor for your scheme. The Schuvalov, having no more fear before their eyes, will continue to reign at their pleasure, will follow up their fatal projects unchecked, and will maintain France at this court with a high hand : and all their creatures, trusting in Apraksin's influence, will look no further for support.

You it is, Monsieur, nevertheless, who are the source of their influence at the present time, and of their hopes for the future ; but I confess that I observe with regret that they only make use of your protection for themselves, without ever thinking of doing the least thing that is pleasing to you. Apraksin's offer to go or stay in accordance with your orders is no more than a compliment. You knew already that the Russian troops were not to cross the frontier this year ; it matters little therefore whether their Field-Marshal remains at Petersburg or goes to Riga.

By all this you see, Monsieur, that I do not at all approve of the orders which you have given to Apraksin to humour the Schuvalov. The vast activities of Peter Schuvalov continue and increase every day, and with encouragement from you they will overstep all bounds. Yet, notwithstanding your treatment of them, I cannot, after the most careful reflection, remember even one single mark that this family has shown you of a desire to please.

Let me also tell you that if the Schuvalov believe that you are so entirely in the hands of Apraksin and the Chancellor, the high ideal, which they have justly conceived of you, will diminish; perhaps the same thing will happen in the case of the Chancellor and Apraksin. And although I feel very certain that at a proper time and at a proper place you will convince the whole of Europe of your great talents, yet I could not for a moment bear to catch a glimpse of any decline of public belief in you without the deepest regret.

After pointing out the evil, this is what I believe to be the best remedy. Allow no one at all to be in a position to answer for your future favours to people who in no way seek to please you, and tell Apraksin, or send him word, that you quite realize the present state of affairs : that to please him and the Chancellor, up till now, you have treated the Schuvalov with kindness, but that you are tired of seeing no return from them, and finally that, if they wish to have any hope of your favours in future, they must deserve them, both by adhering to you and by carrying out your wishes at the present time ; and that without this you will change your line of conduct. If they offer to obey your orders, I will furnish you with means to prove their obedience, and to act as a test of their devotion.

It remains to be seen whether the banishment of the Hetman is the work of Apraksin and the Chancellor. That is how your friends treat your friends.

I beg you to read this letter twice over, and remember that a whole-hearted devotion dictates it.

From THE GRAND-DUCHESS

Saturday, 9 o'clock in the morning [*October* 19].

Count Poniatowski does not write to you, but he sends me thousands of messages for you, one more charming than another. He urges me to beg you, and also the Chancellor, to write to his mother, asking her to let him go. I only await your answer to commence my negotiation with the Chancellor. He says that it is the hope of their party, for it would be to their advantage that our army should enter their country as soon as possible. He adds that he takes the side of Gross and defends him, but that it is generally asserted, and especially by their Great Chancellor, who has lately returned from Saxony, that Gross is closely allied with Brühl and Mniszek.[1] To finish this extract, I must tell you that they say there that the army under Prince Piccolomini, which was opposing that of Marshal Schwerin, retired in great haste before him, and that Schwerin caught them up and defeated the rear-guard. The Count is also very pleased with Weimarn, and wishes to convey by a safe means to Gross what he is entrusted with for him.

Your intelligence about the illness of the Empress is not new to me. I have not been able to send it to you, but my surgeon certainly considers that the frequent pains, in addition to her continuous illness for two years past, may give rise to suspicions of cancer.

I beg you to inform the Hetman of what follows. I am assured that, ever since the Empress has been ill, when Ivan Ivanovitch enters, she either pretends to wish to sleep or seeks some other excuse for making him leave her room, and that she tells him sometimes three times over to go away without him doing so : but that when the Grand Master of the Hunt[2] comes, she is pleased to see him and allows him to remain. In fact, my gazette says that she cannot bear the one, while the other is appreciated and very welcome.

On her arrival here,[3] she went to bed and fell asleep shortly afterwards. That sleep lasted till midday yesterday, a drowsy sleep, according to what they say. They wake her often, but she goes to sleep again at once. She is very weak with this and with a perpetual craving for sleep ; nevertheless she gets up at intervals. I have heard nothing as yet to-day, but my tongues

---

[1] Count George Augustus Mniszek (1716-78), Brühl's son-in-law.
[2] Alexei Rasumowski, the Empress's reputed husband.
[3] At the Winter Palace. It may be again noted that the Empress did not die till 1763.

are instructed in all they have to do or observe, especially if Schuvalov writes anything, whether secretly or in her presence. But this so far has not occurred. I owe some new spies to Apraksin, who has trained two who are of great use to me. Condoïdi[1] took two oaths to the Empress before she would take his drugs, first, that he was really treating her for her illness, second, that she was in no danger. This he did. He sleeps next her room. I send you an answer for the Count, and in order not to tire your eyes, I shall not tell you how deeply I revere you.

From THE GRAND-DUCHESS

Saturday afternoon [*October* 19].

I read all your letters more than twice over : this one perplexes me. If I can speak to Apraksin to-morrow I will do so, and in the manner which you wish. I will insist that, in return for the assurances which he gave them, he should extract a promise from them that they will delay the arrival of the French Ambassador, and that he should advise them to keep quieter; for that otherwise I shall not ratify those promises.

Bernardi came to tell me to-day from you to accept ducats I answered him curtly that I did not want them ; and I conclude from your proceeding that the Chancellor has made up his mind and does not wish me to have my money. He wanted to have further speech with me, but I preserved an icy silence and sent him away. The high opinions that the Schuvalov may have of me, and which will grow less if they believe me to be in the hands of the Chancellor and Apraksin, could not be lower than those which I begin to hold about myself. The nearer I see the time approaching, the more I am afraid that my spirit will play me false, and that it will prove nothing but tinsel or counterfeit coin. Perhaps it is foolish to tell you this, but I swear to you that friendship has much to do with it. I am keeping your letter to read again, and will return it to you to-morrow.

I had already torn up this letter, because neither the beginning

---

[1] Peter Sakarovitch Condoïdi, the Empress's surgeon.

nor the end sufficiently expressed my thoughts, but I send it to you, as you must know the paragraph about Bernardi.

From SIR CHARLES HANBURY-WILLIAMS

Tuesday, after dinner [October 22].

You may rejoice, Monsieur, for it seems to me very probable that Count Poniatowski will soon be able to arrive here. It is quite natural that the King of Poland should send someone to inform the Empress of his arrival in his kingdom, and will not fail to call a session of the Senate ; he will then be able to appoint him his envoy to this court. Here is the picture which I place before you. Do you approve it ?

I have set my English merchants to work to procure me some imperials. But there is an order at each College that none are to be paid to anyone except the court and Field-Marshal Apraksin. So you will be obliged to accept ducats. Bernardi brought me two thousand which you refused ; but under the present circumstances you can do nothing else but take them. As for the matter of the receipt, I have arranged it all between myself, Wolff and Bernardi.

I beg you to try to find out what happened at the conference on Sunday night, and at the one held yesterday morning. Douglas asks for a conference to make great offers from France. I will send you the King of Prussia's writings the moment that the Chancellor returns them to me. They will amuse you, and will give you a wealth of information.

It is my post-day ; but I could not resist sending you the first paragraph of this letter.

From THE GRAND-DUCHESS

Wednesday, after dinner [October 23].

Apraksin has paid me as usual in words, assuring me that Peter Schuvalov will do all I want him to do as soon as he knows what it is. This is what I think. Through whom do you wish me to make my purpose known to him ? If through Apraksin, he will tamper with my words and alter them to suit his own views or those of the Chancellor. If I speak to him myself, he will boast of it ; it will reach the ears of the Empress and will bring down some abuse on my head, which I may never hear but which will do harm to the cause that I have at heart. If I light upon some surer channel, the Chancellor and Apraksin will be consumed with the jealousy which might be expected of them, and once that is aroused, the Chancellor, with his well-known vindictiveness, will take his revenge in schemes different from those which he has conceived for me. I should tell you further, that the Chancellor's plan is the only one which alarms me, for his alone can arrive at *results* ; other people's are only fancies like my own. Therefore it appears to me to be expedient for my personal interests at the moment, subject to your advice, to humour everyone and thus reach the summit more easily. Look, this is what I have done : if what I am arranging can be combined with my [projects], and in order that everything shall be done in due order, you must put up with some tiresome extracts of two conversations with Bernardi.

He came the day before yesterday to bring me two thousand ducats, saying that you had sent them to me. I refused them point-blank, adopting the ground that I would not be deceived, and that, since I had been promised imperials, there was nothing for it but to give them to me. Following that up, I seized the opportunity to dilate on other instances when, in the space of twenty-four hours, he had told me black was white, and where Count Poniatowski's return, the guarantee for Hanover, promised but not carried out, the Hetman's departure, etc., were not the least proofs that I had been duped by them ; that it was a rôle that I was tired of playing, and that all these things fit in very nicely with the word *ungrateful* to his Excellency, which Bernardi had had the impertinence to fling at me. I spoke firmly, and better than yesterday, on which occasion he had found means, on his arrival, to soften me immediately by making me believe that the return of Count Poniatowski was a certainty, because of the arrival of the King in Poland. This corner-stone removed, he turned out his pockets, and, finding nothing, told me that he had

forgotten a draft for a Treaty of Commerce, which you had given
to him for the Chancellor to correct.   I asked him whether it
was not more likely to be the one with France, which the whole
town said had made progress, and about which it was related that
the articles were at present being secretly drafted by the Chancellor
and Douglas : and told him that my indignation would be the
sure reward of any such proceeding, and that the Grand-Duke
would never forgive anyone, whosoever it might be, for opposing
his purpose at the very moment when he was about to ascend the
throne.   He replied he knew nothing of it, but that the Chancellor had ordered him to tell me that the three Schuvalov must
without fail be placed under arrest as soon as the Empress's
death had taken place, and that this must be done by the Grand
Master of the Hunt.   I said, " You are lying, the Chancellor
never gave you this order, for he is rendering signal service to
Peter Schuvalov with the Empress, and never tires of praising
him."   He began to weep, and declared that he had never told
me anything but what he had been ordered to say.   I replied,
" Then you justify yourself at the expense of your patron, for I
know that he backs up Peter Schuvalov in word and deed.   On
the other hand, Peter Schuvalov, with whom he has influence,
only on account of the influence which they believe him to have
with me, does not so much neglect his own interests as not to
curry favour with me on the strength of his friendship for the
Chancellor ; and I am pretty well informed of all that happens
on both sides.   Apraksin has given them his word that no
harm shall come to them.   I have no wish to go back on that.
But I add one condition, that if Peter Schuvalov does not fall
in with my views, all promises shall be null and void.   I have no
doubt that the Chancellor would approve of this last point from
every point of view.   To express my wishes clearly, they are
that all intrigues with France should be given up ; if not, so much
the worse for those who allow themselves to be drawn in."

The Grand-Duke and I await the King of Prussia's books with
equal impatience.   Bernardi has repeated to me what you said
to him about them, and begged me to be so bold as to tell you
something favourable to the Chancellor about these papers of the
King of Prussia ; to which I replied, " The Chancellor always

wishes for my influence to be useful to him, but his own actions will be of little use to him either with me or with the Ambassador, unless I am very much mistaken."

Peter Schuvalov was in a very bad humour yesterday morning. Do you know that the intention was that the 30,000 men he is raising were to have been raised by Buturlin, who refused, saying, " I am offered them *to keep me away from the court.*"

The Empress went yesterday to the Cloister of St Alexander. She is better ; but the old women say that one must await the new moon to be sure. Certain it is that her brain had been affected. Her head is weaker than all the rest of her body, although she is very weak. Just as I finish this, your note of yesterday is brought to me. I am grateful to you for the promptness with which you tell me the good news.[1] The Chancellor had already sought to win me favour with it, as you will see by the contents of this untidy scrawl ; but I did not dare to rejoice, for fear that my joy might evaporate into smoke. But as you seem to have the same news, everything appears to me to have reached a surer foundation.

The Grand-Duke after dinner to-day at last woke up to the fact about Peter Schuvalov. The 30,000 men seemed to him terrible, and Peter Schuvalov's plans apparent in all their seriousness. Somebody, I know not who, had been telling him all sorts of things about them. He came to me full of alarm; for in moments of great crisis he looks to me alone to suggest remedies. Anyhow, we agreed that he should pay more attention to the officers of the Guard than he had done up to now, and that in Church he should make ten or twelve more signs of the cross.

From Sir Charles Hanbury-Williams

Wednesday evening [*October* 23].

You will have seen, Monsieur, from the message which you sent me by Bernardi (apparently at the request of the Chancellor), how this new paper of the King of Prussia has embarrassed that

---

[1] Of Poniatowski's return.

Minister. He might well shiver at the thought of a second thunder-bolt of the same kind. I did not fail yesterday to obey your orders, and, although he lies well, from me he will only obtain everything through you.

I sent him those celebrated papers yesterday morning, and I sent three times to his house to-day to get them back, without finding him ready to return them. I am burning with impatience for you to read them. You will then be fully convinced of all the black plots and sinister designs directed against that Prince. You will see the trouble which has been taken to ruin him in the estimation of the Empress. You will see through the plot, made in June last, to get the Hetman sent away. In fact, you will be thoroughly convinced that he would have been sacrificed to his enemies, if he had not prevented and anticipated the blow which was about to annihilate him.

The whole book proves what care he has taken to show consideration for Russia, and even for the person of the Empress: and it is clear he would still gladly be reconciled here. But every ear is deaf to truth, and they will listen to nothing but passion, calumny, and lies.

I think of your position a great deal, and I remain convinced, to say the least, that your friends are in the hands of your enemies and dare not oppose their wishes to help you. Bernardi showed me a list of your complaints which he read this morning to the Chancellor. It is very well drawn up, and I fully approve of it. Really it is time that he should give you some mark of devotion, and you well deserve it from him.

I did not fail to write to Poniatowski's mother. The letter was couched in strong terms; and I made her feel that, if she thought that she was under any obligation to me, she had only to prove her gratitude by sending back her son. I made much of the use which he was to me in my official position, and the progress which he was making in business. In fact, I said everything that I could to obtain what we both so ardently desire. What a pleasure it is for me to give you pleasure! I shall always try, in any case, to obey your commands. The result does not rest with me.

I hear nothing of Apraksin's departure. Why is there no

court to-night? What are they doing at those everlasting conferences? How is everyone with you? I am told that the Empress went yesterday to the Nevski.

There is much talk about a treaty to be made between Holland, England and the King of Prussia, but I have no information of it from my court.

My daughter has received the Georgian costume, which you had the kindness to send for her. She is enchanted with it, but does not know that it came from you. You know how I adore her. Poniatowski will have spoken to you about her; and I confess that you could give me no greater pleasure than when you send me some little ornament for her. I do not blush at speaking to you in this way; your kindness to me and my tender love for her are my excuse. She writes to me that the costume was at once altered to fit her figure, for she is smaller than you, and that she is delighted with it.

From Sir Charles Hanbury-Williams

Thursday evening [October 24].

I am much obliged to you for your letter written after dinner yesterday. I have again very carefully thought over your position with regard to those who have your confidence and who say that they are your friends. This is my advice. If it is not judicious, at least it has been well weighed.

Poniatowski's return is what you have most at heart. This can only be secured by means of the Chancellor, for he alone knows the secret; but I imagine that it will soon come to pass of itself. Now, in this matter the Schuvalov can be of no use to you whatever. That family, however, look upon themselves as assured of your future protection. Apraksin has made them promises in your name; you have given all, and have obtained nothing in return. But you say that your promises were conditional, and that you will retract everything if they do not submit to your legitimate wishes. It therefore seems to me that through Apraksin you can discover their intentions of helping you in the following manner. Tell him in confidence that the Grand-Duke is extremely alarmed at the raising and the placing of the command of these thirty thousand men, and that you plainly see that his hatred and jealousy of the Schuvalov has increased of late: that the Grand-Duke also feels certain that it is they who are pressing on the negotiations with France, and that he is so irritated by these two circumstances that you are no longer in a position to quiet him. But that, if Apraksin could give you some assurance from the Schuvalov that they would mar and break up the present arrangements between Russia and France, you think that you might again be able to quiet the Grand-Duke and be in a position to give assurances through him (Apraksin) to the Schuvalov of his protection : but that without some step of this kind made by them in your direction, you would take back your word, and no longer be willing to hear anything more said about them : that you were weary of empty words and would require action, a point which had become absolutely necessary to you, because the Grand-Duke had made up his mind that the friends of France were the enemies of Russia, and you would never be able to get this idea out of his head.

Your good sense will make the necessary corrections in all this : you know Russia better than I do. But you see that all my advice is based on the recognized views of the Grand-Duke, so you can use them with effect without appearing on the scene yourself. Assure Apraksin that the views of the Grand-Duke with regard to France are unalterable, and that you yourself would not dare to attempt to change them.

The news by the post is that the Saxon army, amounting to sixteen thousand men, has joined, and been incorporated in, the Prussian army.[1] The King of Poland left for Warsaw on October 22, n.s. The Saxon officers on the staff have had leave to go wherever they think fit, having given their word not to serve against his Prussian Majesty or his allies during this war. I have received a letter from a man on whom I can rely,

---

[1] The figures are correct, but the soldiers were made to transfer under compulsion and proved of little value to Prussia, many units subsequently deserting wholesale.

who writes as follows:[1]—"Do not place the least faith in all the stories which have been spread about the bad treatment of the King and the Royal family of Poland or of the Electorate of Saxony. Never has an army under similar circumstances behaved with so much discipline and moderation as the Prussian army has done in Saxony. His Polish Majesty should now be convinced that his country, instead of being a sufferer, will return one day to his hands much improved by the wise administration which has been introduced and by the wise measures which have there been adopted. You may be sure that all I say is true."

I end by saying that you can boldly tell or send word to Apraksin, since he informed you that Peter Schuvalov was ready to carry out your wishes when he knew them, that the desire of the Grand-Duke and yourself is that he should break off negotiations with France.

The Chancellor does not send me back my book. God alone is aware how whole-heartedly I am your servant.

From Sir Charles Hanbury-Williams

Saturday [*October* 26].

You will see by the enclosed that your orders have been faithfully executed.

I assure you, Monsieur, that the Palatine of Russia and the Great Treasurer Flemming are two persons of the highest probity and pledged to the most profound secrecy.

I am not well, and am overwhelmed with business. Two enclosures will be sufficient for to-day. At least you see that my letter to my friend on so delicate a subject has been satisfactory. I hope that you approve of what I do.

---

[1] Probably from Mr Murdock, who was acting in Berlin for Andrew Mitchell during his absence at King Frederick's headquarters. His view was hardly the one taken by the Saxons.

From THE GRAND- DUCHESS

Sunday evening [October 27].[1]

I return you the letter from C.P., and I add an extract from his letter to me. I thank you a thousand times for the way in which you have put the whole matter. He has felt less worried about it than I feared he would. If you wish to see the note which his father has written me, I will send it ; but you must ask for it, or you will not get it. I hope to speak to Apraksin to-night, and I will tell you all about it when I return you your last letter. Do you know that Ivan Chernuishev goes to Dresden to the Queen of Poland ?[2] I have no answer from the Chancellor, nor have I seen Bernardi for two days. My gratitude and friendship for you are inexpressible. These letters have done me a deal of good.

From COUNT PONIATOWSKI TO THE GRAND-DUCHESS.

Extract from the letter from Count Poniatowski (written in Catherine's handwriting).

This is what it comes to. After questioning me tenderly, but with all imaginable skill, my mother understood clearly what made me so ardently desire to return to you. She even encouraged me, by speaking of the measures which I should adopt and follow to gain what the future promised to my ambition. When, encouraged by this, I pressed her more strongly to give her formal consent to my return, she told me with tears in her eyes, that she foresaw with sorrow that this affair would alienate my affection, upon which she had based all that was sweetest

---

[1] This letter is in Catherine's own handwriting.

[2] Sir Charles wrote optimistically to Mitchell on November 11, n.s. that he felt sure that he had convinced the Empress that the stories of Frederick's doings in Dresden were untrue ; but that she had sent Chernuishev to find out the real facts, and was likely to be more well-inclined to the King of Prussia.

in life, *that it was very hard to refuse some things, but that in the end she had determined not to give her consent.* Upon that, when she saw that I was beside myself, that I threw myself weeping at her feet to implore her to change her mind, she said, bursting into tears " This is just what I had expected." Yet, notwithstanding, she wrung my hand and went away, leaving me in the most horrible predicament that I have ever had to face in my life. I dashed my head against the walls, shrieking rather than weeping. I never closed my eyes all night. I looked like a corpse the next day. I forced my mother to pity me. Embracing me as she had never done before, she tried to pacify me, and, without thinking, said many things which were a great comfort to me afterwards when I began to reflect upon them. Then Flemming, seeing me discomposed, pale, sad, and hardly able to speak, pressed me so far that, half from exhaustion, half from the hope of assistance, I told him everything. He said at once, " Well, here is a pretty business. We must save you. I will help you with horses and money." While we were speaking, my uncle, the Palatine of Russia, arrived and, seeing that I was extremely agitated, asked me what was the matter. I told him that my mother would not allow me to return to Russia. He professed to be ready to help me in any way, provided that I would point it out to him, and to work on my mother's feelings, provided that he knew the reasons for her objections. I remained silent, till Flemming said, " This is no time for trifling. His bolt is shot, and *ours too, if he does not go back.*" " How is that ? " replied my uncle. He was playing the idiot, although he had already shown me, by the many questions which he had asked since my return, that he suspected the truth. Finally, Flemming said to him, " We shall lose the support of *Collette* (Catherine) and shall deserve her displeasure, if he does not go back." Then forthwith my uncle promised to keep my secret and to help me ; and at last, after much deliberation, we agreed that, if our King does not send me, being unwilling or unable to do so, I should go with my other uncle, the Chancellor (who does not know the secret), into Lithuania, and from thence go to you, writing to my parents that I had received letters, so urgent and so imperative for the good both of my country and of my family, that I had

started in the hope of their approval and in the fear of missing
the decisive moment. My father approved of this plan, and joy
filled my heart, when these letters came to stop me, as it were,
in mid-stream. I had difficulty in quieting my father's mis-
givings, but at last he made up his mind that I shall leave as
soon as the King has appointed me, or as soon as you all send
for me ; and the proof of this lies in the letter written with his
own hand which he handed me for you, and which is enclosed
with this. . . . But I will tell you that although in later conversations than the ones which I related, my mother again
repeated the same thing to me, always with many tender speeches,
yet she let drop more than ten remarks which clearly prove that
she really desires the matter settled, provided that she can say
to herself, " I never formally consented." . . . Oh *Poutres !*
(the Empress), You madden us. Die as quickly as you can !
Tell *Bonn* (Sir Charles) about my mother, and beg of him to write
to my father at the right time and place to ask him formally to
send me back, as he had need of me. For among other things,
she argued with me, that if he had had need of me, he would
again have formally asked my father for me ; and that " his
right arm " was only a compliment.

From SIR CHARLES HANBURY-WILLIAMS

Sunday [October 27].

You will be very much surprised at what I am going to tell
you. I had an hour's conversation last night with the Empress,
and afterwards I had the honour of supping with her. I spoke
business to her, I told her stories, I made her laugh.

This is how it all came about. I had said to Anna Carlovna[1]
at court that I begged her to inform her husband that I would
come to his house that evening. The Empress went to pay the
Vice-Chancellor a visit. I knew she was there ; but, nevertheless,
not knowing what to do, I went. She was actually there when I
arrived. Seeing her carriages at the door, I ordered my coachman

[1] Countess Voronzov.

to return home, but before we had gone fifty yards, they came running after me, and I was made to go in. The Empress came to me at once, made me sit down beside her, and talked to me for more than an hour; and afterwards at supper she treated me with marks of distinction.

I had a long conversation with the Chamberlain Schuvalov.[1] I was forcible and frank with him in all I said, and am pleased with the truths which I told him. I renewed the proposal for the mediation of the King and the Empress. I am bold enough to say that my arguments impressed him, and he said to me, "Have you proposed it to the Ministry? For (with a smile) you know I am not a Minister." I replied by another question, "Do you approve of the proposal, and do you wish for peace?" He assured me that he did. I replied, "In that case I shall propose it to-morrow; second my efforts, I beg you." He assured me he would do so. I spoke very little to the Vice-Chancellor, but I know very well what I am about with him. He was not at table with us: he is very ill. But it was whispered in my ear, "You will do nothing with the Chancellor; he is your enemy, and you will find him so to-morrow." If that is the case, I must pick a quarrel with him, and shall play my game elsewhere. All my support comes from you, my devotion is to you alone; therefore I wish to delay the meeting with the Chancellor until Wednesday, and I beg you to write him a note to-morrow in the terms which I have already indicated, and demonstrate, prove to him, that your protection is in my case a reality.

I owe the interview with the Empress in great part to Roman Larionovitch[2]; and you would oblige me, if you would send him word that you are pleased with the help he gave me.

Did M. Prasse,[3] the Saxon Secretary, write at your order, some time ago, from the Chancellor to your mother? Some such

---

[1] Ivan Shuvalov.

[2] Count Roman Voronzov.

[3] M. Prasse was Saxon *chargé d'affaires*, for which post he had been selected after Funcke, the Saxon Minister's departure. He became the lover of Countess Voronzov, the Vice-Chancellor's wife, but so carefully was the liaison conducted that no one suspected it at the time.

letter is in existence. I knew on Friday that Ivan Chernuishev was going to Dresden, and I can tell you some very strange things about his journey; but as I shall soon be able to tell you even more, I will put it off till another time. I am finishing this letter at three o'clock in the morning. *A vous plus qu'à moi-même.*

From THE GRAND-DUCHESS

Tuesday, after dinner [October 29].

I knew that the Empress had been at supper, but I did not know that I had to envy her the pleasure of a conversation with you. I am overjoyed at it. I believe that if it happened oftener, you would be on perfectly good terms. I will not fail to show my gratitude to Roman Voronzov. You will see by my letter of this morning that you will inevitably drag me with you, if you break with the Chancellor. It is the same thing to be on good terms or bad with him, one is treated equally in the same way. I do not even know who M. Prasse is, much less do I know about this letter to my mother. I only know his name from the *Pièces Justificatives,* and that is not to look at him in the best light. Do you know that since his refusal to sign, all is done at conferences without any communication to the Grand-Duke ; so his signature is dispensed with. If this was done to any private individual, what would be said ? I shall give you all the support in my power, and would that I had enough to tell you how much I honour you and how I value your friendship.

Apraksin told me that they say that Prince Troubetskoï used to come to see me disguised in a grey cloak. I replied that it appeared to me that some people's jealousy led to much imagination and falsehood. I have received from Bernardi two thousand ducats, a thousand imperials, and two thousand roubles. Did you know of this, and shall I have any more ? He says that it passes through your hands.

From SIR CHARLES HANBURY-WILLIAMS

Friday [November 1].

I have more business on my hands every day.   I work like a galley-slave.   I sent off a courier at two o'clock this morning. I have been at a conference all the afternoon.   But nothing makes me forget my duty towards you, my prime benefactor.

I must tell you that the King of Prussia has laid his plans so well, that, without anyone having had the least suspicion of it here, he has marched 50,000 men as far as Königsberg.   They are actually there, and threaten to attack your Empire.[1]   Your troops, alas ! are not in a fit state to march or even to mobilise. That is how you are served in this country.   That is the fruits of the reign of the Schuvalov and Apraksin.

The King of Prussia had had two thousand waggons built, each capable of carrying 15 men, and it is believed they are intended to form an army at a moment's notice in the heart of Livonia.

I shuddered on learning all this.   My love for the country where you will one day reign gets the upper hand of everything, and I swear to God that my devotion to you has played a great part in all that I have done.

I rushed to the Vice-Chancellor.   I painted in true colours for him a picture of the state of your affairs.   I called upon him as a good Russian to repeat this to the Empress.   I entreated him, for the love of his country and of the Empress, to hide nothing from her.   I told him that he would be a monster of ingratitude to his Mistress, if he did not point out to her the danger in which her Empire is involved, and to what a low ebb she is reduced by vile wretches : that his conscience, his duty, and his honour, all called him, and finally that I would proclaim him to the whole world, if he did not do so, as a man who joins with others to betray his country and his noble Mistress.   He was moved.   He felt the force of my words and the danger of the Empire.   He asked for my advice, and added that he was

---

[1] This intelligence was not entirely correct.

resolved to put all that I said before the Empress, truthfully and without reserve.

I replied that I was ready to help him, offering him for the last time the joint mediation of England and Russia to put an end to the differences between Austria and Prussia, and I entreated him to propose it at once to the Empress. He replied, " I will inform the Great Chancellor of our talk. But under any circumstances I will tell the Empress everything and will support mediation." After this conversation, I went in all haste to the Chancellor. I repeated to him my talk with the Vice-Chancellor, and I proposed mediation to him. He said clearly, " I shall propose it myself to the Empress." But they both asked me whether I had no letter of credentials from the King of Prussia. I answered that they were obliged to believe all I said as English Ambassador. They agreed. You can imagine with what impatience I await the result of all this.

Notwithstanding all my business, I have forwarded two of your letters by my courier, and wrote one of ten pages to Poniatowski. Nothing can exceed my friendship for him. I also wrote to his father and mother in the strongest terms. Thus, you have no further need of me.

I see, or rather foresee, that when you wear this crown, you will have a heavy burden to bear. Some change is needed in all this, and I see how necessary it will be for you to have a disinterested friend to help you. I swear to you that if you command I will give up everything to assist you for the first year ; and believe me, I am in a position to apply the remedy, for I see and know the evil.

I am going to make you laugh at my frankness. Your china is as ugly as it can be. If you have nothing more beautiful, and if you want some for a chimney-piece at Oranienbaum (to adorn it), I will send you some charming pieces, if you will give me the pleasure of your acceptance of them.

More news—the King of Prussia has actually raised another army of 30,000 men in Saxony, and in all he has now 200,000 men on foot.

I am very much pleased with the Vice-Chancellor. He has

shown his love for Russia ; and I beg you to make him feel on Sunday that he is not out of favour with you.

Everything that the Great Chancellor communicated to you on the subject of the exchange of plenary powers between this court and that of Versailles is false.   I believe that the intention to make an alliance with France is over.

Pray God to bless my schemes ; they have no other aim but peace, a good understanding between the King and the Empress, and the prevention of Russia cutting a sorry figure in Europe. I remain certain that I am high in your good graces, because you tell me so.   Should I lose them, I shall be the most miserable of men, but you are too true and I am too loyal to fear such a loss.

I have not yet had time to answer your letters.   The moment I have the news that mediation is accepted, I shall send it to you.

From THE GRAND-DUCHESS

Saturday [*November* 2].

I hesitated to answer you, for fear of increasing your difficulties, but on consideration I felt that I owed you too much gratitude to postpone.   I have also to congratulate you upon your skill, which surprises and delights me : too happy shall I be, if some day you will reward my good intentions with your assistance, the value of which I assure you that I fully appreciate.   You will shape and point out to me the road to glory.   You will prevent me from wavering.   Here is a note of what the Chancellor says.   He sent to assure me, just as you tell me, that there had been no exchange of plenary powers.   He says also that you do very wrong in speaking business to everyone ; that the day after you had had supper with the Empress, or the one following, she had sent to ask him what your proposal was, and that he did not know what to tell her : that the offer of mediation is looked upon as a sign of fear on the part of the King of Prussia, and that you should leave him free to act.   He said that he had long been a Minister, and would bring everything round to the point which you desire, but that you must not persecute him.

He still maintains that he and Apraksin have dealt a mighty blow at the pro-French party. I hear much talk about this party, and I begin to be uncertain who belongs to it, for Peter Schuvalov asserts on his oath that he does not, nor even Alexander Schuvalov, who grows milder towards the King of Prussia, and wishes, apparently in order to damage the Chancellor with me, to send me the King of Prussia's memorial with the *Pièce Justificative*. He assured me, two days ago, that he was a great Prince, who knew his own interests well and made no mistake about them. There was a conference this morning, of which I suppose you were the cause, for it is an unusual day for one. Never tell me that I have no more use for you, for I believe that it would be difficult for me to get on without a friend like you. I shall call on you to keep your promise, and you will not be absolved from it so easily.

I will show the Vice-Chancellor and his brother my satisfaction at their conduct. May Heaven bless your good intentions; I wish this most sincerely, and with all the friendship which you deserve.

From Sir Charles Hanbury-Williams

[Sunday, November 3.]

Here is something to amuse you to-night. I implore you to return them to me to-morrow morning, for I am in great need of them. Then I will send you some more, which I have just received. This Prince writes as well as he fights.

I am ill, but shall come to court. I am sinking under the weight of business. The King of Prussia loads me with kindness and friendship, of which he gives me striking proof.[1]

Sunday. Hand this packet to the Grand-Duke, but ask him to keep the fact of having seen it perfectly secret. The Chancellor would never forgive me.

---

[1] In response to Sir Charles's earnest request for some ready money to be used in case of need to further Prussian interests, Frederick sent him 10,000 ducats without further delay. (A. Mitchell, October 24, n.s. 1756.)

From Sir Charles Hanbury-Williams

Sunday, 2 o'clock in the afternoon [*November* 3].

I have just received your letter, for which a million thanks. I have already written to you this morning.

With regard to the Chancellor's news, I believe it to be quite true. But I dare not mention it to him, for fear that he should discover the source whence I received it.

It is certain that if they accede here to the Treaty of Versailles, all union between England and Russia will be at an end. We want no guarantee for Hanover on those terms.

All I have to beg of you is to cry out against this treachery towards us all, to declare to the Chancellor that the Grand-Duke will oppose it in every possible way, and that you will look on all those who lend themselves to such a work as the enemies of Russia. The Chancellor has never had so much influence as at present, and all depends on him. It is useless for him to contradict it.

From Sir Charles Hanbury-Williams

Monday [*November* 4].

Bernardi told me yesterday, and the day before as well, that the Chancellor had ordered him to beg you from him to speak to me yesterday at court, and to ask me to write and prevent anything more from appearing in print which might affect him.[1] I beg you to tell Bernardi, or better still to write to the Chancellor, that you have spoken to me ; and that I have answered you, that since I have been at this court I have tried by all manner of means to win his friendship and confidence, and that I will again do what I am asked to do at present : but that after all I clearly saw that I have secured neither the one nor the other, and that it was impossible for me to make any progress with

---

[1] In any further documents which were to be published by the King of Prussia.

him, as he seemed to have forgotten England and his ancient system. You will add that I appeared to be in a very bad temper, as indeed I am. If your letters for Poniatowski are here by to-morrow evening, they will be in time You can keep the King of Prussia's books several days.

From THE GRAND-DUCHESS

Monday, after dinner [November 4].

You will have received the letter from Count Poniatowski. He says that he has delivered all that he was entrusted with for the King and for Brühl.

The Hetman told me yesterday that for three days consecutively the Empress had grumbled about you at meals, and that it was the Chancellor who did you harm in what he wrote. He did not tell me exactly to what these remarks and writings referred.

The Grand-Duke heard that while the Chancellor was talking to the Empress and Esterhazy yesterday at court, he assured the latter that Her Imperial Majesty would faithfully assist her ally, and would support their interests by everything in her power ; from which the Grand-Duke concluded that there will be a winter campaign. Good-bye to the good schemes for peace! When one believes that everything is at its best, everything is upset. I am truly very shocked, Monsieur, at this lack of stability ; I assure you that my friendship for you will never suffer from that trouble.

From SIR CHARLES HANBURY-WILLIAMS

Monday [November 4].

I am delighted, Monsieur, from the bottom of my heart, at the letter which you have received. I already knew that you had one, but the contents are just what I hoped for. The rest will follow of itself.

In answer to your letter of yesterday, I beg you to write to the

Great Chancellor that ever since I came here, I have been in his hands, that I speak of business to no one but the Vice-Chancellor, and that by his own instructions.   As for my conversation with Ivan Ivanovitch, there was no means of avoiding it, and I said nothing to him that I would not say to the first comer.   You can begin your note by saying that you told me everything at court which he had announced to you.   Add that I have never done anything without his approval and that I defy him to quote any instance ; that the assurances he gave me with regard to France have pleased me very much, and that I told you that I was very satisfied with them.

All the conversation between the Empress and Esterhazy yesterday evening consisted in congratulations on the fact that the Prussian army has gone into winter quarters.

Swallov is in a hurry to leave.   I will write to you at more length to-morrow.   I await Poniatowski's return with impatience.   He will come the first possible day, you may be certain of that.

I will send you back all your letters together.

From THE GRAND-DUCHESS

Tuesday, 8 o'clock in the morning [*November* 5].

A very bad headache and all kinds of other things have prevented me from writing to you to-day, as I had intended.   This is what I have to tell you.   I was talking to Apraksin Sunday at court, at first on indifferent matters, but when he recommended me to show favour to the Schuvalov so that I should then have nothing to fear from them, I spoke out :—"After the assurances which you have given them, I think that they ought to be pleased, but I warn you that the Grand-Duke is so annoyed about the 30,000 men and about their intrigues with the French, that I shall never be able to influence him in their favour unless this stumbling block is removed.   You have told me repeatedly that Peter Schuvalov would do everything I wish.   You can tell him that, if he does not break off all union with the French,

I can do nothing for him with the Grand-Duke, and that he will never be forgiven by him. You know yourself how he has at all times hated the French." He paused a little, and said to me, " They are aware that this is laid to their charge, but they are too deep in the mire; and I am leaving in two days." I replied, " You still have a day for speaking to them ; and if the Chancellor is sincerely opposed to the French, this should please him and is a method which I provide for him." He reflected and answered, " Ivan Chernuishev is going to Dresden, and I have indications that he is instructed by the Schuvalov to make some arrangement or other with the King of Prussia. Consequently, they will have less need for the French." " Is this a secret from the Chancellor," I replied, " or have you heard it from him ? " " No," he answered, " they keep it from the Chancellor." " Well then, it is all nonsense," said I. " They have not enough skill ; yet I wish you to make known my views to them." He promised me to do so.

He came yesterday, Monday, to take leave of me. I was unwell, and was a good hour with his wife before his arrival. She was weeping; and I mellowed under a million tokens of friendship. At last, I discovered from her that her husband had only received 6,000 roubles for his journey and 700 a month, while Münich had 25,000 and a thousand every month in old days, and Ivan Schuvalov usually had 100,000 for his birthday. Peter Schuvalov had offered them a substantial sum by way of loan, saying, " When I am poor, you will help me in my turn," but her husband had only accepted 5,000 saying, " You want to buy me." On going to take leave of Peter Schuvalov's wife, the latter had reproached her, saying that she and her husband, though on the best of terms with me, never did hers any service : that it must be from lack of wish to do so, for it was in their power, and that Ivan Schuvalov had said the same thing to her husband. After this she related to me that her husband was going to command an army without officers or cavalry, and that when he had told the Empress of this the other day, she grew angry, and then went to Peter Schuvalov and said to him, " You overestimate my forces to me, and deceive me, without fear of God. Apraksin assures me that I am short of cavalry." In

o

consequence, Peter Schuvalov has never allowed the V.M. (Field-Marshal), to speak to the Empress for a week ; and Ivan Ivanovitch reproached him for alarming Her Majesty without due regard to her health. After this, Apraksin told me that he had spoken to the Chancellor about what I wished Peter Schuvalov to know, that he had found that it was too late, in view of the fact that plenary powers were already exchanged for an accession to the Treaty of Versailles : and he straightway again told me that the mission of Ivan Chernuishev diminished the necessity for France's friendship and added, " There must be someone here who excites your fears." I answered, "I am alarmed by events, and am reassured only by words ! " Thereupon he named numerous persons whom I could trust ; and after dinner the Chancellor sent me a list, in which are noted against the names the duties which it was suggested that they should undertake, in the event of them helping me. Certain it is that the Schuvalov will prevent everything, and that the Chancellor is perhaps more pro-French than they are, in consequence of his Austrian leanings. It would be very easy to learn the secret of Ivan Chernuishev's mission from him himself If I wished it, one single conversation with him would suffice for me. I sent my congratulations yesterday evening to the Chancellor by Bernardi on this happy exchange of plenary powers, adding, that, as he and his friends advised me to ally myself with Ivan Schuvalov, I was going to do so, but that he must know me well enough to realize that I was out for all or nothing. Ever since the day before yesterday Alexander Schuvalov has been asking me for a secret interview. He said to Naruishkin, and to an old woman, who is in my service and of whom I am very fond, that he wished to gain my confidence, and that I did not realize how much he was willing to do and could do for me. I have not yet granted him this audience. Tell me what to do, and help me. All the three Schuvalov make me more flattering speeches than ever. My arm is raised ready to strike, for I am tired of being deceived. But remember that this road is also slippery. The Chancellor wants me to write him a note to show to Maltzahn. He will send me the rough draft, and I will translate for you a letter from Korff.[1] I shall always consult you like the Delphic Oracle, and I hope that you will remain obscure, in view of your friendship for me. Here is my letter for Count Poniatowski and some very ugly Chinese charms. If you do not like them, I shall put up very lightly with your frankness.

I have still a thousand things to tell you, but the arrival of the Grand-Duke may prevent me.

From SIR CHARLES HANBURY-WILLIAMS

Tuesday [November 5].

I thank you with all my heart for having sent me the letter from Gross to the Great Chancellor.[2] I had already foreseen

---

[1] Nicholas, Baron Korff (1710-66) Senator and later Chief of the Police, a Courlander in the Russian service.

[2] COPY OF A LETTER FROM

MONSIEUR GROSS TO THE GREAT CHANCELLOR BESTUZHEV.

Monseigneur, While still at Dresden I received the letter which your Excellency confided for me to Count Poniatowski, Stolnik of Lithuania. Although the King and the First Minister were still shut up in the camp at Struppen, I found means to prepare them for the requests concerning this young nobleman, who, in consequence, on his Majesty's arrival here,[a] was received in a manner of which he has every reason to feel proud. On my own arrival, I found nothing to do beyond making strong representations to Count Brühl, that the high recommendations which the Stolnik has brought with him should without loss of time produce the desired effect, and I have the satisfaction of making known to your Excellency that this Minister has positively assured me that he has already influenced the King to send the Stolnik to your court on a mission from him, and to invest him before starting with the blue ribbon on behalf of the Republic. He could only be sent by a resolution of the Senate, which is a long-winded affair, with no certainty of success. Therefore, in order to hasten his return to St Petersburg, the Stolnik himself raises no objection and prefers to be sent with a commission from the King. He hopes, however, that, in order to uphold his dignity, his credentials will not be sent from the Chancery of Saxony, but from that of the Grand-Duchy of Lithuania, following the precedent of what happened in the year 1744, in the case of the present Grand Treasurer, Count Flemming. To gain this point, I shall render him all the assistance in my power. Meanwhile, I have the pleasure of confirming to your Excellency, that, in consequence of my previous representations and the exalted intercessions

[a] Warsaw.

its contents; indeed it could not be otherwise. My delight about it is very great.

Your court always acts according to events, not by policy or settled plan. If the King of Prussia had beaten the Austrians instead of going into winter quarters, I should have been petted and not scolded. That is the fate of Ministers. It is not what we deserve, or do not deserve, which makes us successful or unsuccessful at foreign courts. But everything is governed by chance and temper.

I am quite convinced that the Great Chancellor does me harm with the Empress. But what can I do? I have never given him cause to be my enemy. I wish to be his friend, but not his slave: and I see that his friendship can be won at no other price.

I have just at this moment received another letter from you, dated this morning, which I shall answer, although I am in the midst of my post.

You can send the letter, as it is, to the Chancellor, although I should have preferred that the resignation of the coadjutorship should have been demanded as a preliminary article. However, it is always possible to put so many stumbling blocks in a treaty

of Her Imperial Majesty, the Princes Czartoryski and their friends are now received by the King in a most gracious manner, and that Count Brühl and his son-in-law[b] appear to live with them on most friendly terms. To remove all ancient bitterness, the First Minister assured me again yesterday, that there was nothing that he desired more than that, by some means or other, they may themselves endeavour to end the unhappy affair of Ostrog,[c] assuring me that for whatever scheme, which they might adopt in order to secure this object, the court would grant every possible facility. Your Excellency may feel satisfied that I shall take care, with all the enthusiasm of which I am capable, that these good intentions may not grow cold, and that they may produce at the earliest moment the results which we have reason to expect from them.

Meanwhile, I have the honour to be, with the most respectful attachment, Monseigneur, your Excellency's humble and very obedient servant,

Gross.

Warsaw, November 4, 1756.

b Count Mniszek.

c A *cause célèbre* in Poland, which, in the year 1754, was within an ace of plunging the country into the horrors of civil war.

like this that your letter pledges you to nothing, and I return it to you. You shall have all your others to-morrow.

You can say about me in your letter to the Great Chancellor, that you know that I have always been his friend, and that he promised you his friendship for me

From SIR CHARLES HANBURY-WILLIAMS

Wednesday [*November* 6].

I knew that the Great Chancellor was doing me harm with the Empress. No one but he could do it; I have given him no cause for it. I have always done him good, not evil. I could have done him harm with you. But I do not like doing harm; and the one thought that some day he may be of use to you has smothered all my complaints against him. I look to you for everything, and to him for nothing. I trust to your position— that is my sheet anchor.

I congratulate you, as well as myself, upon the arrival of Poniatowski, but I implore you on my knees to use all caution imaginable after his return. The Chancellor has already obtained the Hetman's removal; he is trying to embroil me with the Empress, and in that way to force me to ask for my recall: and some fine night he is capable of having Poniatowski locked up. He is capable of everything that is blackest; believe me, I only speak the truth.

I shall turn over in my mind how to arrange for your interviews. I shall give Poniatowski my ideas and you shall decide.

As for the thanks of the Empress or her grumblings, so long as I do my duty I have no ambition for the one nor fear of the other. But the fact that the Chancellor tries to undermine me with her by lies revolts me. How much he has received from the court of Vienna I do not know, but I have full information about the sum which Apraksin has drawn. In any case, the Chancellor is entirely in the hands of Esterhazy. I shall deplore the departure of the Hetman; it is true that I love him dearly, and do not forget in the future that, if some courtier should speak ill of him to you, it is the chief request of your devoted servant that you should protect that worthy man and do him a good turn. You may rely on it that the Chancellor is being well paid for the exchange of Holstein ; but I repeat again that, before anything is done, the coadjutorship must be renounced in favour of your family. Insist upon it, and you will get it ; for I am not thinking of your interest alone, but I do not wish you to lose any of your dignity.

True it is that on Sunday your court was fully determined to help the House of Austria, but on Friday they held different views. That is what happens at courts which are governed by events rather than by settled plans and well-founded policy.

I intrench myself behind my honesty and loyalty to my Master. I do not believe that Russia is in a condition to make war. I have said so : I shall say so again. If you continue your protection, all else here is indifferent to me. I am yours ; do what you please with me.

From THE GRAND-DUCHESS

Thursday, 3 o'clock [November 7].

I sent the Chancellor this morning a note in German, in answer to a rigmarole in the same language, in which I had an opportunity of putting very clearly everything that you laid down for me to send him. I attached to the whole a solemn oath that you were not his enemy, as he very frankly told me though in closely veiled language. I added that I had never noticed any spark of this feeling in you, and I assured him that I would not fail to warn him if I ever did perceive it. I considered this last promise very necessary for many reasons, and I am daring enough to hope that my note will make some impression on this man of iron, who wishes to have me under his sole control without interference from anyone else. He sent me this strange note,[1] with a letter

---

[1] Apparently the following memorandum from Count Volkov, the Great Chancellor's secretary. It is attached, in M. Goriaïnov's text, to Sir Charles's letter of November 16, to which it does not refer in any way. It bears the date, November 7.

FROM COUNT VOLKOV   *November 7.*

Her Imperial Majesty has ordained that the nomination of Count

from Count Brühl, in which it was stated that Count Poniatowski would leave in ten or eleven days with the blue ribbon and his instructions. That letter was of November 6 [n.s.]. The letter tracing the Chancellor's scheme for the coadjutorship business was sent to his house this morning, after what you wrote me yesterday that I must not make any difficulty about writing it. I sent him a message by word of mouth that it is out of consideration for him, and that my own feeling was that the renunciation should be made, purely and simply to win me over, and to induce me to influence the Grand-Duke in favour of the exchange.

I shall follow your advice about seeing Count Poniatowski ; and since I have felt certain of his return, I have intended to speak to you about the dangers which have to be foreseen.

The Hetman is the man at the court on whom I can most depend. You may be certain that I shall never fail him ; with me he has two great stays, your recommendation and the gratitude which I owe him for his loyalty. The Empress went to shoot black-cocks the day before yesterday, but was taken so ill that they despaired of bringing her round. She came back, and is better.

Poniatowski as Minister is displeasing to Her Imperial Majesty, owing to his great friendship with Monsieur Williams, and that, in consequence, his Excellency the Great Chancellor is to inform the Secretary of the Saxon Embassy, Prasse, by word of mouth, that although Her Majesty has given the said Count Poniatowski a letter of recommendation to his King, his nomination as Minister to the post here would be displeasing to Her Imperial Majesty ; that the aforesaid favour was granted solely at his request, in the hope that His Majesty would not take it ill, and that in this same hope Her Majesty desired the Saxon Envoy to come here without delay at the close of the present Diet of Sweden, and still more that Count Gersdorff[a] should be sent here once more, since His Majesty the King of Poland would be better served by his own subject, and since he would inspire more confidence with us. But if, notwithstanding all this, it should be found impossible to prevent the arrival of Count Poniatowski, all care should be taken to discuss no business which might tend to prolong his stay here.

VOLKOV.

[a] Count Gersdorff had already served as Saxon Minister in Russia some ten years before this date.

I am sorry that I wrote that letter to the Chancellor on the Danish affair, but what else could I do ? If my friendship can be any consolation in your troubles, you should suffer none, for there is nothing to equal my regard and respect for you.

The arrival of Count Poniatowski should have been announced on Tuesday by that M. Prasse, whose name I did not know. Tell me, I beg you, what is that letter to my mother, of which you spoke to me a week ago ? Do you remember also that you promised me some further writings of the King of Prussia ?

From Sir Charles Hanbury-Williams

[Undated, November.]

I intended to write you a long letter this morning, but I have such a bad headache that I must limit myself to one subject.

The form of your bond to Wolff is no bond at all. This is how it should read :—

" I have received from the hands of Baron Wolff the sum of forty-four thousand roubles, which I promise to repay him or to his order, when he asks for them."

It would not be in keeping with your honour to give a worthless bond, as it would convert into a gift what is only a loan. Send word to Wolff to send you your money in gold little by little. He can always get five or six thousand roubles in imperials, and in three or four instalments you would receive the whole. The sum which you have to send me will amount to two thousand six hundred crowns. Send them to me by Swallov. This will be refunded to you, when the debt is paid off.

You will receive a long letter this afternoon in my own handwriting or in that of my secretary.

From THE GRAND-DUCHESS

Friday, at 6 in the evening [November 8].

Bernardi has just brought me word from the Chancellor that, when Prasse was speaking to the foreign Ministers about Count Poniatowski's arrival, Douglas was much alarmed, as also was Esterhazy : but that he had shut their mouths. He requested me at the same time to write a note to the Count, to beg him not to put up at your house on his arrival, so that, as he says, the others may not protest. I answered that it was a mistake to advise any act of ingratitude, but that, as I believed that Prasse, or you, perhaps, had taken a house for the Count, the difficulty would be automatically removed.

The Empress is very ill ; but they have just come to tell me that she is better.

I am hurried, and I have only time to repeat to you the assurances of my friendship.

From THE GRAND-DUCHESS

Saturday, 3 o'clock in the afternoon [November 9].

The Chancellor believes himself to be on better terms with me than ever. He has sent me a million nice messages. Count Poniatowski has written him a letter which he can show, to ask him for a house, because Gross holds the rent of a quarter paid for by the court. They want to put him into the house of Marco, the singer, a very nice one and quite new, opposite the Church of Kazan. The Chancellor again assures me that Peter Schuvalov confides in him his fears, and begs him to put him on good terms with me ; to which he replied, that he begged him to make Alexander Schuvalov speak to me in his own (the Chancellor's) favour, for he was not aware of being so well with me as all the world made out. Peter Schuvalov promises free access to the Empress for the Grand-Duke and myself, especially in the event of illness. The Chancellor adds, " Fawn upon them and you will reign ;

but before you reign, do what you wish with them." I replied to all this affected austerity, that his Excellency the Chancellor would doubtless win the execration of the public by his intimate relations with Peter Schuvalov: and on the questions which concerned me personally, I said, as they were reeled off one by one, "I understand. I shall see. Nothing is impossible."

It is true then that you are anxious to have my receipt for the money ; there are still 4,000 roubles to come. Count Poniatowski must be as gentle as a lamb and try very hard to catch that slippery eel, the Chancellor ; for say what you will, he is to be caught. I know further from the same source—a matter which gives reason for caution, that Buturlin desired representations should be made to prevent Count Poniatowski's arrival, but that the Chancellor objected, and said that it would only add to the anxieties of the court of Poland and affront a family which was useful to them there ; that Peter Schuvalov supported this opinion, but that when Buturlin returned to the charge another day and was again silenced, he said to console himself, " Well, I will set a sub-officer of the Guards to spy closely on him." In this there is only one little slip of memory—that is certain Buturlin could never have said that, for these Guards are under Alexander Schuvalov, who commands the Petersburg Division. Therefore, my dear and faithful friend, they lie right and left, in the most subtle and clumsy manner, to such a degree that even my well-known simplicity in believing things which I am meant to believe, notices it—and that is going very far, for I am very stupid on these points.

Bernardi told me that you were in a bad temper. I beg you to comfort yourself with the comfort given by Condoidi. He said to an old woman, who, in order to keep the Empress awake and to enliven her, had not slept for two nights, and was in the depth of gloom, ' A little patience, I implore you. You have not much longer to wait. She cannot live."

I shall not dare to say a word to you of my inward feelings, though, as a rule, the mouth overflows with that which fills the heart. I shall confine myself to telling you that the gratitude which I feel towards the pilot who steers the bark will end only with my life.

From Sir Charles Hanbury-Williams

[Sunday, November 10.] *Dictated.*

Monsieur, I am so ill of a fever, with a very bad headache, that I am unable to answer your last letter with my own hand, and it is with difficulty that I dictate this.

Everything will go as the Chancellor desires. The Hetman will leave immediately. I am forced to ask for my own recall, for fear it should be asked for by the Empress ; and Poniatowski will only be allowed to remain here for the time necessary for him to pay his respects, and even then he will be so closely watched during his stay here, that, as your best friend, I advise you not to think of seeing him but patiently to await happier times. Such, Monsieur, is the treachery of the man in whom you have placed so much confidence ; but his treachery has no limit. Your honour, your personal safety, and that of your friends, all cry out together that you should break with him. Take steps at once to do so : consult Alexander Schuvalov. Tell him that you place yourself entirely in his hands and in those of Ivan Ivanovitch, so long as he has no common ground with the Great Chancellor, declaring that he has ill-used and betrayed you too often for you ever to be able to trust yourself to him again.

The four thousand roubles which are still due to you are at my house ; and I beg you, for love of me, to give your bond to Bernardi in the form which I indicated to you, so that he may take it to Baron Wolff and so that I may be clear of everything which has to do with the Great Chancellor.

Recollect and be assured that the Chancellor's whole credit proceeds solely from the credit which the Schuvalov believe him to have with you. By that he has controlled the Schuvalov for some time past. If, then, your credit is to control the Schuvalov, control them yourself.

Try to arrange through Alexander Schuvalov to obtain a secret interview with Ivan Ivanovitch. Ask him for everything, promise him everything.

From THE GRAND-DUCHESS

Tuesday [*November* 12].

This is what the Chancellor has just sent me, produced at the last council but one by the Vice-Chancellor.

Extract from a letter of Monsieur Rouillé[1] to the Chevalier Douglas of September 4, 1756[2] :—

" If various intelligence can be relied upon, the King of Prussia has taken too much part in all that has just happened in Sweden.

Nothing is more worthy of the Empress of Russia than the advice which she has sent to the States of Sweden, not to carry things too far.   His Majesty[3] is convinced of that Princess's sense of justice, for she knows too well the rights of sovereigns, a fact which will restrain her from going beyond this advice in a purely domestic matter in Sweden.

The disturbances in that kingdom appear sufficient to destroy the false impressions which many persons have wished to spread about your journey to St Petersburg.   In attributing to it views contrary to the interests of their Imperial Highnesses, the Russian Ministers should remember the ardour with which, a few years ago, His Majesty supported the independence of Sweden, and the declarations which he made to oppose the designs of those same Ministers, who maintained that their sovereigns had the right of interfering in the government of that country.   Can it be that His Majesty, who at that time gave such public evidence of the interest which he takes in the constitutions of each State, could wish to stir up trouble in Russia, and is it probable that he can be seeking to destroy a settlement made by a Princess for whom he has always felt true affection ?   This language is disseminated by many, and was doubtless suggested to them by the English Ambassador.   That restless Minister is piqued

---

[1] Minister for Foreign Affairs at the court of Versailles, from 1754 to 1757.

[2] The correspondence between Rouillé and Douglas during the latter months of 1756 are missing from the series of diplomatic documents in the *Archives des Affaires Etrangères* in Paris.

[3] Louis XV.

and annoyed at seeing a diminution of his influence. He is perceived to be looking about for every possible means of regaining it by the immense offers which he makes. But after the King of England has so openly broken his first treaty by that of January 16,[1] can he believe that fresh credit will ever be placed in his proposals, and can St Petersburg count on the durability of a new arrangement with this Prince, when he so easily breaks the old ones? This alone must ruin the Chevalier Williams's influence. The King of England may be annoyed with his Minister and recall him; but although his recall would punish conduct which lacks circumspection, it would not justify the Treaty of London, for which the responsibility rests solely with the King of England and his Ministers, and not with his Minister in Russia. It is of decisions taken in London, therefore, that the Empress of Russia should beware."

From THE GRAND-DUCHESS

Wednesday after dinner [*November* 13].[2]

Your health makes me anxious, and that is why I am sending Naruishkin to your house. For the same reason I am afraid that the reading of a long paper may worry you. After thinking things over yesterday and this morning, I have decided to speak to A.S. this afternoon. My line of conversation is prepared; but, as he is extremely stupid, I shall also put the substance of what I have to say in writing, and Naruishkin will take it to I.I.[3] I felt doubtful, but my resolve is taken: and I hope that

[1] The Treaty of London, between England and Prussia.

[2] Letter in Catherine's handwriting.

[3] This is what I am thinking of writing to Ivan Ivanovitch:—

" You will be astonished, but you can feel pleased, for this paper may be likened to the Peace of Westphalia, which serves as a basis for everything that has since been done. Here is the substance of what I have said to Alexander Schuvalov, of which he should inform no one but you. You are the centre of all that I wish. I have seen his tears and listened to his speeches, I have heard of your own about your present anxieties and your fears of uncertainty. This conduct seems to me sincere: I have felt that my confidence should respond to your advances. I have pondered over it for

you will be pleased with me, and that your advice will bear fruit. Above all, postpone your recall, and calm yourself. We shall see changes I am sure; and what is there that I shall not do in return for all the friendship which you show me.

From SIR CHARLES HANBURY-WILLIAMS

Wednesday evening [*November* 13]. *Dictated.*

Ill as I am, Monsieur, I have not failed to weigh your business with all the attention and careful thought of which I am master.

As you have let drop a word to Alexander Schuvalov of your dissatisfaction with the Chancellor, the secret will be already known to Ivan Ivanovitch; but the noble and open manner in which you express yourself to him should answer your purpose completely, by banishing his fears, by restoring his tranquillity of mind, and by the certainty which you give him of good fortune in the future.

The manner in which the last paragraph is expressed is admir-

three days, and I have decided to put this act of sincerity into effect. What follows will still further convince you. Alexander Ivanovitch says to me, 'You attribute to us all the harm which is being done. Yet it is not us, but the man whom you believe to be your best friend; he has done it, and continues to do it.' He adds, 'In time you will see that we are loyal to you, and that they are not.' I rely on these words, and you will see that I am sincere by what I now tell you in confidence. Doubtless he speaks of the Chancellor. This is what it comes to. I have regarded him for four years with the confidence and all the friendly feeling of which I am capable, without one single recollection of the injuries which he did me in the old days. He has only repaid me with deceit, and even with treachery. I could relate you twenty instances. I should give him up for any one of them, and I throw myself into your arms. Have nothing to do with him, if you wish to retain me. I ask you for everything at the moment, and I promise you everything in the future.

One sentence for your ears alone, of which Alexander Ivanovitch knows nothing. Do you remember what made us come to blows? A similar reason may re-unite us for ever. I knew that in former days you had feelings of honour. These feelings will comprehend the generosity of my action."[a]

[a] Catherine speaks of friendly feelings towards Ivan Schuvalov, shortly after her marriage. He was then a page in her service. She refers to this upon more than one occasion in her autobiography. The actual cause of their estrangement is not clear.

able, and is worthy of you. Dare I suggest a word in conclusion, to say that you beg him to remember that confidence of this kind can only lead to bonds of true friendship or of eternal hatred ?

I conclude by imploring Heaven to bless your enterprise, approving of all that you are about to do, and vowing myself to your service. What gratitude must I not express to you for all the kindness which you show me ? I promise you that the question of my recall shall be yours to decide ; but, in continuing your kindness, put me in a position to defend myself against the blackest and most ungrateful of men.

Arrange an interview with Ivan Ivanovitch, if it is possible.

From Sir Charles Hanbury-Williams

Friday [*November* 15]. *Dictated.*

Swallov has come to my house, and tells me that the Grand-Duke is worried about some falsehood with which he had been primed about the King of Prussia—that that Prince designed to unite himself with the King of Denmark, who would then help him to take Holstein.

You have already seen a clear refutation of this lie in the King of Prussia's pamphlets. But if you think that something more explicit is necessary, I am ready to obtain it for you from the King of Prussia himself.[1] My love of truth makes me favour that Prince more than ever, since I see that only by inventions and calumnies can he be discredited.

Do you know that Monseigneur is in great difficulties for 1,600 roubles ? He begged Swallov to get them for him, but the poor devil, not having a penny, came to me ; and I will help him. Will you forgive me for taking this step, as I think it is a present intended for one who bears the name of mistress ?[2]

Imagine how anxious I am and in what uncertainty I shall

---

[1] Sir Charles wrote to Mitchell on November 27, n.s. asking for some such assurance. (*Frederick, Polit. Corres.* xiv. 149.)

[2] No doubt Countess Elizabeth Voronzov, daughter of Count Roman Voronzov.

remain, until I know the result of your negotiations. You have comforted me by telling me that you are sure that there will be changes. I trust you in everything.

I am sending you a new paper of the King of Prussia, but I am not yet in a fit state to answer your letters, nor, consequently, to return them to you.

The Grand-Duke shall not know that I have lent the money to Swallov.

From THE GRAND-DUCHESS

Friday morning [November 15].

The whole of my lecture to Alexander Schuvalov, so wisely combined, so cleverly argued, so eloquently spoken, so excellently sustained, in one word, the highest achievement of my perspicuity, would have been thrown to the winds, as I had foreseen, owing to the man's extreme stupidity, but for my letter to Ivan Ivanovitch. Picture to yourself a man about to be hanged, who received his reprieve just when he believed that death was certain. Such was Ivan Ivanovitch's condition on reading that heaven-sent letter. Naruishkin thought that he would have a stroke. He was beside himself. Naruishkin bolted the doors to prevent him from committing any imprudence. Finally, he dashed into an oratory, and there remained in a trance for over half an hour, beating his head on the ground and his hands on his breast. The other allowed him to pour out his gratitude to God, but did not take his eyes off him. He returned, set to work to read and re-read my letter, then kissed the bearer's hand, and finally, after tearing up about ten sheets, wrote as follows:— " All the confidence which you have placed in me will be repaid on my part by eternal gratitude. I am extremely sorry that the letter which you have sent me is a little obscure at the end, where you speak of what has caused us to be on bad terms. ' A similar reason may reunite us.' Explain, Monsieur, whether it is the same reason which caused our misunderstanding, or whether it is another of the same nature ; and be assured that

I shall never fail to prove to you the devotion which I feel towards you."

He then showed great impatience to know everything, spoke of the Hetman, and promised to help him. He never stopped re-reading my letter. At last, after an hour and a half quite alone with Naruishkin, he went out into his ante-room. When spoken to, he did not answer. He was asked what was the matter ; he complained that he had been writing ever since dinner, which was untrue. As my letter had been returned to me, and his was to be sent back to him, I wrote under what he had written, " I have no time to say more. Do not jump at conclusions. Everything will be explained to you in good time " —so that he should not mistake the Hetman for what he is not,[1] nor fall back again upon the past. I shall, however, take no step without your consent. I spoke strongly to Alexander Schuvalov about the Hetman ; and he has my conversation in writing, to which I refer you.

In the course of yesterday afternoon I received a letter from the Chancellor in his own hand-writing, a sign that the matter was of importance. He says that he sees with very great regret that I take him for a rogue, that if I will no longer place confidence in him, I shall drive him to go and plant cabbages on his estates. He said that he has been more careful of my interests than of his own soul, and that, if that had received as much attention from him, he might have believed himself in heaven with the prophet Elijah. Here is my answer. I would not trouble you, if I did not think that it would make you laugh.

" I understand the heads of your accusation. I believe that you are sincere with me ; but I am too much so, not to tell you quite frankly that I do not find you the same to my friends, who are just as truly devoted to me. If it distresses you to hear the naked truth, far worse it would be if I sank to pretence. My nature is incapable of that, and I could not believe that anyone would wish it. So, moderate your cruelty towards my friends, whom you are making miserable, or promise me to put up with my frankness. One must live and let live."

[1] i.e., her lover, which Cyril Rasumowski never was, though he was deeply in love with her some years before.

P

I was delighted yesterday to think that you were feeling a little better. I hope to hear that this improvement still continues.

As I am on the subject, at the risk of wearying you I must tell you of some ameliorating circumstances regarding Count Poniatowski's stay here, and that the Chancellor has given Prasse the three following points, to be used as an answer to meet their objections :—1. That the court was sending Count Poniatowski here, because it was taken to be the acceptable thing to do, after the recommendation which he received from here. 2. That, as he had already been here, he was in a better position to serve his Master than a new delegate. 3. That, in consideration of the rank and importance of his family, the step was looked upon as a friendly one to that court, and one which might prevent a numerous family, who were of use, from becoming discontented. All this is better expressed in Russian—and can pass muster.

The Empress was talking the other day to the Chancellor, and said, " People at court will think that I am in love with Poniatowski," and added in a very low voice, " Why do they send him ? " and immediately gave orders that a good house should be got ready for him.

Bernardi gave me some message or other from you, to be read to the Chancellor. I answered, " Very well." But it is wrong for anyone to write so long a paper to an invalid, and especially for one who is very deeply interested in that person's health.

From Sir Charles Hanbury-Williams

Saturday [*November* 16.]

Monsieur, I have only time to tell you that I am delighted at the conduct of Ivan Ivanovitch towards you. He has himself furnished you with an expedient for putting his sincerity to the test. Hold him to the offer which he makes you to assist the Hetman by preventing his journey into the Ukraine,[1] and send

---

[1] Some letter or copy of a letter appears to be missing, for no mention is made of the terms of Schuvalov's offer.

him word, that, if he renders you this service, you will look on it as a most real proof of his devotion to you, and that afterwards you will give him your entire confidence.

You will have a long letter from me to-morrow with all yours. *Saturday*.

From Sir Charles Hanbury-Williams

[Sunday, November 17.] *Dictated.*

Believe me, Monsieur, that my admiration for you increases every day. Your secret negotiation has throughout been marvellously well conducted; and the kindness which you continue to shower on me fills my heart with devotion and gratitude.

I own to you that I am anxious about the answer which Ivan Ivanovitch will give you about the Hetman's affair. I look upon that young man as all-powerful, and if he shows you this mark of his devotion, there is nothing but good to be looked for from your union with him. But until now you have had nothing but words. When I see one single thing done to help you, I shall be satisfied.

In conformity with your advice, I have not failed to write all that you have told me to the English Minister at the court of the King of Prussia, and I can promise you in advance that the answer will be very satisfactory. I have at this moment received a letter from that Minister, telling me that he had just learnt from various sources that the health of the Empress was very bad, and that they were very anxious at the Prussian court about the views of their Imperial Highnesses the Grand-Duke and Grand-Duchess. So I am requested to inform them of all that I know on the subject.

I learnt to-day that a Dutch vessel, which arrived at Riga, brought 86,000 ducats in gold for Count Esterhazy. You see, by that, how flourishing is Russian trade!

I shall strictly obey your orders about the money which I hold; and you should tell Bernardi that you wish this money to remain in my hands until you require it.

I have just received the letter which Ivan Ivanovitch has written to you.[1] The only doubt I have is whether he is acting sincerely or not. I should like to believe that the affair had gone too far for him to be able to stop it, and I think that you have gone too far in this affair not to pretend to trust what he says. Certainly, with his assistance, the Hetman can be brought back from the Ukraine in a short time. Send him word therefore that you are satisfied with his answer, and that you have no doubt that, if he had been able to help you in the affair in question, he would have done so.

My doctor does not wish me to go out yet ; so I shall not have the pleasure and honour of seeing you to-night.[2] But I cannot finish this letter, without repeating again my gratitude for the

---

[1] FROM THE GRAND-DUCHESS TO IVAN SCHUVALOV.

(Fragment of copy).

I accept your offers, and I am willing to test your tenders of help. After that, you will have my complete confidence. Prevent the departure of the Hetman ; all the reasons given to you to support his departure contradict your arguments. Peter Schuvalov's bitterness against that worthy man is inspired by the Chancellor, who cannot bear that I should be friendly with anyone but him.

FROM IVAN SCHUVALOV TO THE GRAND-DUCHESS.

Monsieur, I am in despair at being unable to execute your wish by preventing the departure of your relative. Believe me, Monsieur, by all that is most sacred in this world, that I am telling you on my honour the simple truth—I am not in a position to do so. The necessity for his departure has been so strongly represented, that two orders have already been given, upon the three recommendations of the Council. I have not dared to interfere in this matter, but had I been able to look ahead, I might perhaps have helped to carry out your orders. I have already tried to do something, but it is useless, and only one thing remains, for him before his departure to ask for permission to return, should the position of affairs not require his presence. Then, being on the spot, he can see how things are, and come back. During his absence I shall leave no stone unturned and shall neglect nothing which may help towards his return. I have given this advice to one of his friends. The misunderstandings of my relations do not concern me. I look upon the Hetman as an honest man, and one who liked me. I hear that he continues to do so, and that increases my regard for him. Believe, on my honour, what I am putting forward. Your very humble and very obedient servant,

I. S.

[2] At court.

daily marks of kindness which I receive from you, and without giving you the strongest assurances of my affection, my devotion, and my eternal gratitude.

From THE GRAND-DUCHESS

Monday morning [November 18.]

I spoke to Peter Schuvalov at court yesterday. I placed myself in such a position that everyone should see that he was talking to me. He harangued me for a good half-hour. I let him have his head and listened. In the end, I was obliged to say something to him. My answer was, " I shall see whether your promises are sincere by the results which they produce." He replied with emphasis, averring that all would be well. He talked on again for half an hour, and said at the end (apparently the passion for talking carried him away, and he no longer knew what he was saying), that for my sake he would even overcome his prejudices. I took him at his word, " I will give you a riddle to solve, to see if you speak the truth." He answered, " What is it ? " " Well ! since it is a riddle, you must guess it. Think ! What prejudice could you conquer to satisfy me ? " He considered, and said, " You speak of the Hetman ? " " Monsieur, I mention no one's name ; but as you say it, I will not contradict you." He was rather embarrassed, and said, " In making my peace, you wish me not to leave out the man who has a share in the advances made to me and to advise him about it, in order that he may share in them." He wanted to enter into details and to explain the matter, but I interrupted him, saying, " How does your promise stand of conquering your prejudices for my sake ; here is the first thing which I show you that I desire ? " " Very well," said he, " that is true; you will see that I can do anything when you wish it." I replied, " I shall see ; this answer, which I have so often repeated to you this evening, cannot offend you, since you assure me that it will turn out to your advantage."

Troubetskoï related to me that they spoke on Thursday of the accession to the Treaty of Versailles, that Austria does not relax her efforts for a moment to draw us in, and that the College of Foreign Affairs had received orders to draw up a scheme for accession, but that this had not yet been done.

Ivan Ivanovitch, in conversation with Naruishkin, said that he would try to put me on good terms with the Empress, and that he would help the Hetman. He was very cheerful on hearing that I had not been offended at his refusal about the Hetman's departure.

Now I am going to answer your question about the attitude of their Imperial Highnesses towards His Prussian Majesty, in the event of the decease. This, Monsieur, is what I know of it. The Grand-Duke, from his military inclinations, is Prussian to the death ; and this goes so far that it has become a prejudice and is engrained in his disposition. It is almost useless to speak of the Grand-Duchess, since it is not settled that she will then have much authority ; but we will satisfy your curiosity. She will never advise anything which she does not believe will contribute to the greatness and interests of Russia, for which she has as strong an affection as a Spartan had for Lacedæmon ; and also she recognises the necessity for the country to be well governed internally.

I am very sorry not to have had the pleasure of seeing you yesterday, but as it was for the good of your health, I sacrifice to that my desire to see you.

When do you expect Count Poniatowski ? Forgive the bad writing.

From Sir Charles Hanbury-Williams

Tuesday [*November* 19].

I felt sad when I read all Peter Schuvalov's fine speeches. Here is a man who promises everything and will do nothing. And, after all, you ask very little. You ask them to cease persecuting your friend, who has committed no crime but that of being your friend ; for you must feel convinced that there is no more necessity for sending him into the Ukraine than there is for sending him to Japan. I am sorry that you have allowed Peter Schuvalov to talk so much to you. Keep to Ivan Ivanovitch. He is the best of the family; and take the first opportunity of making Peter Schuvalov feel that you are weary of his compliments and fruitless declarations.

I believe all that Troubetskoï told you. Enmity to the King of Prussia must cement Russia and France, and will end by the destruction of that friendship which has existed between this Empire and Great Britain since the time of Ivan Basilevitch.

One must always tell you the truth; but I begin to think that this subject wearies you. Tell me frankly if I guess aright; and it shall be the last time that I shall speak of it to you. In any case, always remember that I have never asked you anything about these matters, and that in all my correspondence with you, my interests have never been any stumbling-block to the least of yours nor to those of your friends. I believe you to be disposed heart and soul to the triumph of Russia; but what triumph can it be for Russia to follow blindly the prejudices and vengeance of Austria and France, to crush a Prince who has never done the least thing against Russia, and in doing so to abandon a defence contracted for with her most faithful and her oldest ally?

I am quite of your opinion on everything which the Chancellor sends you word about in connection with Poniatowski, and I fail to understand why he delays his departure. All this will not make him more partial to France; and yet it is our enemies who deal this blow at him. In my inmost heart, I have already given up thoughts of the pleasure of seeing him often when he comes. I always sacrifice myself for my friends; and once more, believe me that I am disinterested, and that to help my friends I am always ready to forget myself.

Make one addition to the Grand-Duchess's ways of thinking and I shall be satisfied (for it seems to me she has often said it to me) : that is, that she will always remain a true friend to England, and that she believes that the alliance between the King, my Master, and Russia is natural and useful, and of at least as much importance to this Empire as any other.

My health is very bad. I am suffering a deal of pain and I do not sleep; I have a constant low fever which is the result of my complaints. You shall have your letters to-morrow; but I am in my room in bed, and I dare not move from it to fetch them. I will also send you the Prussian Memorial to France on their present quarrel.[1] In the end, these two courts will be at daggers drawn, thanks to the good offices of that of Vienna.

From THE GRAND-DUCHESS

Tuesday morning [*November* 19.]

Yesterday the Chancellor sent me a number of letters which had arrived from Warsaw, a narrative from Gross, a letter from Count Poniatowski for me, and one, from what he said, from the Castellan of Cracow, Count Poniatowski,[2] to which he begged that I would reply, saying that he was raising difficulties about letting his son go, and that he, the Chancellor, would write whatever I conceived to be best. When I opened this letter, I found that it was from Count Sapieha, Palatine of Smolensk.[3] I returned it to him instantly, and on thinking it over, and remembering that in the letter from Gross to the Chancellor it was stated that he, Gross, thought that they were delaying the departure of Count Poniatowski, until they knew how his nomination would be received here, I came to the conclusion that there must be a great desire to delay or possibly even to prevent his arrival. In consequence, therefore, I sat down to write to the Chancellor in withering terms, declaring that I would certainly break off all connection if I was deceived on these points, and

---

[1] This dealt with de Broglie's conduct. The French Ambassador in Dresden had made use of wild expressions upon Frederick's entry into Saxony, and failing to get into communication with the King of Poland after the battle of Lobositz, had tried to force his way through the camp, only to be stopped by the Prussians. (A. Mitchell to Sir C. H-Williams, November 9, n.s. 1756.)

[2] Poniatowski's father.

[3] Brother-in-law of Count Flemming.

that, knowing by this what to make of things in future, I should consider the matter as settled.

Gross's narrative for the Empress contained an account of the intrigues of Durand to prevent the King from nominating Count Poniatowski, which went so far as to collect all the partisans of France, so that they should demand an audience of the King, in order to beg him to send anyone else but the person in question. The King, having learnt what was in course of preparation, sent for Count Poniatowski to his closet, and told him that he was sending him to Russia as his Minister. Durand loudly expressed his annoyance, and announced that the Ambassador, Broglie, would take it very ill. To this he adds that some days previously the King had wished to send a certain Sacken and a man named Aloa with despatches, and that again Durand would not allow it, excluding them definitely. Gross further reports that Durand says openly that his court will be very annoyed about this, and that he also had approached him (Gross) : but that he had answered that Her Imperial Majesty, having always given her protection to the Poniatowski family, and in this last case having particularly recommended this member of it, could not fail to accept him as envoy. Count Poniatowski writes to me that Gross is helping him very loyally ; but that he is very taken with France, especially with Brühl : and that he fears that this may do harm to the Russian party.[1]

The Chancellor wrote me another letter with his own hand, in which he says that he is doing everything in his power to help me, and that these new difficulties, which I shall realize from the papers which he is sending me, will show me that he is being given new work to do. As a matter of fact, I can find no difficulties in these documents, and I believe that they are solely in his imagination. I told him so quite plainly, adding that a letter by a courier from Prasse to Brühl, to hurry on the departure of Count Poniatowski, would finish up everything to my

---

[1] Gross had been a good friend to England in days gone by, when Sir Charles was still in Dresden. But after the latter's personal influence was removed, the Russian Minister appears to have drifted more and more into the opposite camp.

complete satisfaction. I comfort myself by relating this to you; give me your advice, I beg you. These letters are of the 14, n.s.

Count Poniatowski makes no mention of any dissatisfaction; on the contrary he says that his father and mother are agreed.

From THE GRAND-DUCHESS

Wednesday morning [*November* 20.]

I begin with a subject which vexes me—that you beg me to make additions to my ways of thinking. As I had once told you that the alliance with England would always be sacred to me, that I thought it useful and necessary to Russia, and after that had given you proofs, although, alas, they have borne little fruit, that I upheld and would uphold the cause, I believed that it was scarcely necessary for me to repeat anything so self-evident I could tell you, if I was in the humour to say nice things to you, that it might well be possible to feel less secure of the King of Prussia as a powerful and formidable neighbour, than of you or of the King, your Master. But strike out this paragraph; I do not wish to make you such pretty speeches. I am much too put out, and shall speak of things which I do not understand. Always tell me anything you like; I shall never be tired listening, and shall eagerly follow your advice. I know the extent of your generous feelings to the full, and shall never grow weary of helping you, in any way that I can, with all the gratitude which I feel for you. I shall never forgive myself if I fail you.

The Chancellor has sent me his answer to Gross. It is satisfactory; and he recommends him above all to pass round the word to every court that confidence is to be placed in Count Poniatowski and that in his reports he takes care to make the best of the Count. In a note to me, the only remark that he can make about you is that you are *pigheaded.* Your state of health is a great worry to me. I hoped you were better. Baron Wolff told me, on Sunday, the cause of your sufferings. *Mon Dieu,* what would I not do to relieve you from all your troubles!

I am in no anxiety about my letters; I believe that I know you better than you know me.

The Prussian Memoirs will give me pleasure, for I read the writings of the King of Prussia with the same avidity as those of Voltaire. You will think that I am making up to you, if I tell you to-day that I am a profound admirer of His Prussian Majesty.

My letters are often very confused; but you must remember that you have forbidden me to use rough copies, and that I believe them myself to be needless in writing to a friend.

From SIR CHARLES HANBURY-WILLIAMS

Thursday [November 21.] Dictated.

Thank you so much for your last letter. When you speak to me of England, you always give me comfort; and of that I have great need, for this morning Bernardi gave me a message from the Chancellor—that the Empress was in a hurry to accede to the Treaty of Versailles and was pressing him to prepare the documents. This corresponds exactly with everything that Troubetskoï told you. This puts an end to the alliance between Russia and England. All that is left for me, therefore, is the hope of one day seeing it take life again under your auspices.

The Great Chancellor has also sent me word by Wolff, that the court of France is making a present of eight to ten thousand roubles to the Vice-Chancellor for having arranged the exchange of ambassadors between the two courts.

The third thing will certainly be, to drive me from hence. I think, therefore, that you will no longer disapprove of my action in asking for my recall.

Although I am very ill to-day, I thought it my duty to tell you all this.

Only tell me that you continue to respect me and to protect me; and all else that can happen to me here will be of complete indifference to me.

Remember my letters, which said long ago, " Your friends will be sacrificed." The Hetman first, myself next, and I tremble for Poniatowski.

From THE GRAND-DUCHESS

Saturday morning [November 23.]

If you approve of the enclosed note,[1] I will write it to Ivan Schuvalov. I have thought proper to make it obscure, as it actually is, so that he could not say that I had spoken to him of business, for that point is rather a delicate one for me.

I am very unhappy about your anxieties. The last words in your letter pierce me to the heart. Would it not be possible for Count Poniatowski to win over the Chancellor by his conduct towards him ?

I promise you that I shall firmly rebuild all that they are now pulling down, if the decease ever gives me the opportunity.

How are you ? Will you go out to-morrow or the day after ?

From SIR CHARLES HANBURY-WILLIAMS

[Saturday, November 23.]

My obligations towards you, Monsieur, increase every day. Thank you exceedingly for the offer which you make me to write to Ivan Ivanovitch, but my devotion to you does not permit me to allow you to address yourself to him on my business, being fully convinced that these people will never render you any essential service. Perhaps you already know the story

---

[1] " Though you have refused me the first request which I made to you, to your own detriment, my sincerity towards you inclines me to make you a second. Find means to prevent the connection which is desired by the makers of fashion. Everything does you harm, nothing does you good. I repeat, give me arms to fight for you. I assure you that this deserves most serious consideration on your part. I know infinitely more about it than I tell you. Decide your own fate and my conduct towards you. Yours shall govern mine. Open your eyes ; I shall not let you stumble. No answer, please. Your actions will speak for you."

which I am going to relate to you. After all the splendid declarations which Peter Schuvalov has made you, even going so far as to say that he would sacrifice his prejudices to obey you, he has done just the reverse, for he has tried to gratify his prejudices at the expense of your request. He has plainly declared that he would be the friend of no one who was not the friend of Apraksin. He has insisted that the Hetman should at once write a letter to Apraksin, to ask his forgiveness for having treated him badly, and to ask for his friendship; and after that he was to go to Prince Kurakin to apologize for having slandered his wife.[1] But what is more astonishing still is, that Ivan Ivanovitch maintains that Peter Schuvalov is right in what he propounds. If the Hetman were ready to take such a step, he would lose a great deal of my esteem, and, I imagine, of yours too; and I believe that it is to render him unworthy in your eyes that he proposes this subservience. You can see by all this, how much higher the family of the Schuvalov puts the friendship of Apraksin than your request, and believe me, Monsieur, that your only course is to be very cold to Peter Schuvalov to-morrow and the evening after; and if, notwithstanding your coldness, he still persists in speaking to you, give him a curt, sharp answer, and put an end to the conversation.

My health, far from allowing me to see you to-morrow, is in a sad way. I shall send for Condoïdi and consult him; my stomach is in bad state. It is a fortnight since I have eaten bread, and I only live on a little gruel.

I send you a paper of the King of Prussia, which will give you a true notion of the quarrel that France has stirred up for him.[2] He is at daggers drawn with France, and I pride myself that this will not lower him in your estimation. I have just received an answer to things which I have never done nor said, set out in most malicious terms, and calculated to do me all possible harm.

---

[1] Apraksin's daughter, and mistress of Peter Schuvalov.
[2] Mitchell wrote to Sir Charles on November 29, n.s., that he was sending him the *Rélation*, which was just printed.

From THE GRAND-DUCHESS

Monday, 4 hours after dinner [*November* 25.]

The fatigue of yesterday prevented me from writing; and I seize the first opportunity at my disposal to enquire after your health.

I arranged for the King of Prussia's writing to be read to the Grand-Duke, and I read it with the satisfaction which one feels when one reads the truth.

Do not think that it is a bother to me to write to Ivan Schuvalov. None could exist, when it is a question of helping you. He has commissioned the Hetman (whom he takes for what he is not with me) to persuade me to adopt the new system. I answered that the Grand-Duke would certainly never adopt it, nor would he forgive those who would try to make him do so. The Hetman should have given him that answer to-day. Peter Schuvalov did not show himself yesterday, but, as he sent me his excuses and made use of the very words which you communicate to me, I received the whole message very coldly, and replied that I should despise the Hetman if he was capable of cowardice; and that as for him, Peter Schuvalov, I had known for a long time that there was a great difference between his words and his actions.

The Empress—for it is very right that I should speak to you of her in a manner which will comfort you a little, is in a pitiable state. She went out yesterday evening just as dinner was served. She came to the Grand-Duke and me, and said, " I am feeling well, and have no more cough nor shortness of breath, but I cannot put on a tight dress on account of great pains in my stomach." As she had previously spoken of oysters, I said, " Madame, that pain may come from having eaten too many." " No," she said, " I have had it for a year and a half, and it never leaves me." I beg you to realize that she could not speak three consecutive words without coughing and without being out of breath, and that, unless she thought us both deaf and blind, she could not tell us that she was free from those complaints. As this made me smile, I tell it to you. It is comfort for those who have no other comfort.

Count Poniatowski has just written to me. His letter is of the 26th, new style. He says that on various pretexts Brühl will not let him depart, and that they are waiting for a courier who has been sent here, and who is due to return on the 28th. His greatest vexation is at the part which he will have to play towards you, and I assure you that I am in despair, when I think of the troubles which I shall bring on you both. He hopes, however, to find some honourable course, without failing either in friendship or in duty : and he begs you to love him. He adores you, and I esteem and reverence you.

From SIR CHARLES HANBURY-WILLIAMS

[Tuesday, November 26.] *Dictated.*

I am sure, Monsieur, that your kindness to me will cause you to learn with sorrow that my illness continues the same. Condoïdi assures me that he will pull me through in time ; but I doubt it, for my liver no longer does its work, and my digestion is so ruined that I have eaten nothing solid for nearly a month.

I am sorry that Count Poniatowski worries himself about me. I am his friend ; I brought him up, and I shall prove to him that my friendship for him makes me love him. It matters not that we shall not see one another often. We shall find means of communicating our thoughts to one another, and I am so certain of his devotion to me that I think only of how to help him. This is what I think about him. I flatter myself that, one day, you, Monsieur, and the King of Prussia as your lieutenant, will make him King of Poland.

I am sure, from the letters which I have received by the last post, that His Prussian Majesty is fully disposed to do all that can be pleasing to the Grand-Duke and you, Monsieur. He gives me a free hand to say everything that I wish to you on that subject.

As for your court, it is so governed by the court of Vienna, that an Englishman is become a monster at Petersburg. Lieven sent me word on taking his departure, that he dared not come to my house to take leave of me. He was half-dead(?), but he begged me to believe that the Great Chancellor and Apraksin had been carried off their feet and were forced to do all that they were doing at the moment, and that they detested the alliance with France ; but it was Wolff who brought me this message, and I have my suspicions that he spoke more from the Chancellor than from Lieven. You have told me, and I have no doubt whatever of your sincerity, that you hold the King, my Master, in high esteem, and that you love England. Russia makes a treaty with France ; and at the same moment, France receives with open arms a Minister from the Pretender, in order to plan the invasion of Great Britain. If you were in your place, you would not allow this. You would see all these things with your own eyes.

Under no circumstance whatever shall I allow you to embark upon a negotiation with Ivan Ivanovitch on my behalf. Look upon me entirely as a person who is bound to you by love, regard, and affection, and as one who will never allow you to do yourself harm in my interests. I trust in the future. I trust in your word. I trust in your opinion of the best interests of Russia.

I know on good authority that the Schuvalov laugh at the Grand-Duke, that they say that he is drunk every day, and that he cannot live long.

I have not yet got the King of Prussia's papers to send you. They have not yet been returned to me ; but as I have made up my mind to communicate nothing more to your court, you shall in future have them the very moment that I receive them.

Do not forget, Monsieur, I pray you, all my conduct towards you. Gauge it impartially. I should wish to help you from inclination, were it in my power. That is the strongest of all links. My reward, from a heart made like yours, will be your approbation and your support. That is all I ask.

Before finishing this letter, I cannot refrain from telling you that I am in great anxiety about Poniatowski's journey. All is treachery here, and things are whispered to me which I will not believe.

I must tell you that I have a snuff-box, set in brilliants, which is a kind of nick-nack that I do not care for. I had given it to Bernardi to exchange for me for some sort of aigrette for my daughter. He told me that the snuff-box would please you; and I told him that it was the same to me whether you had that or another one. I beg you, therefore, to return it if you do not like it, but I thought that I ought to tell you what had happened.

Adieu, Monsieur, give me your constant protection; I always look upon myself as your protégé, and I glory in the title.

From Sir Charles Hanbury-Williams

[Thursday, Friday, November 28, 29.] Dictated.

Monsieur, My health remains bad. I am forbidden to read or write, but where you are concerned, rules are as naught. I am certainly in a bad state, but I hope to be better soon. I am delighted with Condoïdi. He is a man of talent and much knowledge, and speaks sense to me. Since I have known him, I have greater faith in all that he has said about the Empress. You will soon have a new and charming paper of the King of Prussia. May heaven preserve you.

From the Grand-Duchess

Tuesday morning [December 3].

Although you have been forbidden to read or write, a longer silence on my part might make you anxious, so I break it. I am delighted to hear that your health is better. I am in mortal terror about Count Poniatowski. I dread some intrigue, of which I have no knowledge or even indication, to prevent his arrival.

Yet, on the Feast of St Andrew, the Chancellor let drop the following words to me, " If he does not come, for ever call me scoundrel instead of Bestuzhev." But then he tried to make me believe that the delay in his arrival could only be the fault of the Count himself, which has made me so suspicious, that since then I have always persisted in saying that I blamed the Chancellor, and that I was almost convinced that he was contriving some counter-plot to prevent the Count's arrival. This is what I believe to be the truth. When Brühl received the answer from here about the nomination[1], he would have put off his departure, but a week later the Chancellor's letter to Gross and another from Prasse, of which I have seen copies, perhaps put things straight again ; and I now believe that the Count has started. I continue, nevertheless, to urge the Chancellor to write, which he and Prasse have again done. Advise me, help me to get to the bottom of this cursed man.

Peter Schuvalov dares not show himself to me, having failed to keep his word, and that is the reason which kept him at home during the festivities. I hear this from the Hetman, who was assured of it by Ivan Ivanovitch. Esterhazy related to the Chancellor that Douglas had received letters from Durand, in which he said that Count Poniatowski, when speaking to Durand, had called Douglas a rascal. The Chancellor detests Esterhazy, complains of him, and said to me the other day, " We must get rid of that man from here at any cost."

I have regretted nothing so much as having lost the chance of seeing you, and of having been unable to assure you by word of mouth of the continuance of that high esteem and sincere friendship for you, which are my pride.

From Sir Charles Hanbury-Williams

Saturday [*December 7*].

By the last post I received news from Dresden, and I am instructed by the King of Prussia to assure their Imperial High-

---

[1] Perhaps Volkov's letter. See *ante* p. 214.

nesses, in the warmest terms, of his affection and regard, and to say that he will be delighted at all times to give them proof of it.

I have since received orders from the Grand-Duke to ask His Prussian Majesty for a permit for an officer who is in the service of his Imperial Highness. In consequence of this order, I have written to the King of Prussia about this permit. I would have made full use of my credit with His Prussian Majesty in this matter, did I not know already how anxious that Monarch is to please the Grand-Duke in everything which is in his power.[1]

I asked that, as soon as the King of Prussia had signed the permit, it should be handed over to the English Minister at Berlin, to be forwarded to me by the first courier who comes here, because it is not safe to risk such papers in the post.

I shall be only too happy if his Imperial Highness approves of what I have done. I send you two printed papers to amuse you.

From SIR CHARLES HANBURY-WILLIAMS

Sunday [December 8].

Here is one of the nicest books I have read for a long time If it pleases you as much as it has pleased me, I shall be very delighted. I have a very bad headache to-day, which prevents me from troubling you further, but I cannot hide from you my suspicion about Poniatowski's arrival. Is it not possible that Prasse, the Saxon Secretary, may be acting in an under-hand manner at the request of Esterhazy and Douglas, with a view to prevent his mission to this court ? This is what I suspect ; your judgment must decide. I am yours. Show this book to the Grand-Duke from me.

---

[1] See *Frederick, Polit. Corres.* xiv. 188. Louis de Zweiffel, a Prussian officer, had had to flee the country six years before, because he had unintentionally killed a *Chasseur* by striking him too hard a blow.

From THE GRAND-DUCHESS

Sunday evening [December 8].

The Grand-Duke thanks you most heartily for what you have done for his officer, and is as much distressed as I am to know that you are so ill. I am still further grieved to hear you often repeating, *my departure, my departure*. I hate that word, and I beg you very earnestly not to use it. Spare me the vexatious thought as long as possible.

Bernardi has just left me. Speaking to him of the delay of the affair in question, I added, " I am afraid that Prasse may engineer some plot to prevent it, at the instigation of Esterhazy and Douglas." He answered, " Do not believe it. His personal interests will prevent him from doing so. The Chancellor has promised to get him nominated Resident ; consequently a Minister from Saxony would be a nuisance to him, and unless Poniatowski is sent, he could never be sure that one may not come ; instead of which, as Count Poniatowski is only in charge of Polish affairs, he will feel easier." I offer this for your consideration, and wish you speedy relief and perfect prosperity. You shall have your printed papers when the Grand-Duke has read them. Yesterday's pleased him very much.

From SIR CHARLES HANBURY-WILLIAMS

Monday [December 9].

I am too happy to be able to please the Grand-Duke in any way. The kindness which his Imperial Highness has always shown me since my arrival at this court, calls for infinite gratitude from me, and I shall never fail to prove it to him when the opportunity arises.

I am delighted to learn that the printed papers which I sent you yesterday have given pleasure ; you shall have all which reach me.

I am not so well to-day ; I am very feverish and in much pain. The interest which you deign to take does me more good than all the medicines which I swallow ten times a day.

From SIR CHARLES HANBURY-WILLIAMS

Monday [*December* 9].

Would that I could give you comfort about Count Poniatowski's arrival. Nothing that Bernardi has told you of the Chancellor's sentiments gives me any reason to do so ; he is as resourceful in contrivances as any man is who has no scruple in overstepping the limit of truth. Prasse has not the talents of Funcke, but he has all his roguery, and he is as dangerous a man as a fool can be. You have seen specimens of his honesty in the King of Prussia's printed papers, and you see there how he follows his master Funcke step by step.

You do not wish me to speak to you of my departure. You tell me, nevertheless, that you have regard for me and that you are interested in all that concerns me. Can you then conscientiously wish me to remain in a country where I am daily exposed to calumnies without being able to defend myself, surrounded by enemies who have neither shame nor sense of truth, and finally exposed to seeing my King and country treated in a dishonourable manner ? My friends should not wish to see me in such a position.

There is a little thunderbolt about to fall on Peter Schuvalov. The chief magistrate and a great number of the inhabitants of Narva are coming here, to throw themselves at the feet of the Empress to demand justice from her. That town is entirely ruined by the prohibition to sell wood, and this was obtained by Peter Schuvalov to encourage a trade in wood which he carries on his own account on Lake Onega. There are actually at present five hundred thousand roubles worth of wood lying rotting in the streets and on the quays of Narva ; while the merchants dare not sell a halfpenny's worth of it, and the whole town, with the exception of four families, is reduced to beggary.

The army begins to complain loudly of what Peter Schuvalov is doing. You know that, to raise his corps of thirty thousand men, he is taking away a certain number of men from each regiment in the whole army. He takes the best ; and that causes this discontent.

How is the Empress ?

From THE GRAND-DUCHESS

Tuesday, after dinner [December 10].

I send you your printed papers read and approved. In wishing you to remain here, I am considering my own interest. You are too good a counsellor not to be regretted ; and one moment may alter everything. I knew of the murmurings in the division and garrison of St Petersburg, but I was not aware of those in the army. In all the taverns they drink to tearing Peter Schuvalov to pieces ; and the fury against him is great. His illness is feigned, his anxiety far-reaching ; he knows how much the public hate him.

The Chancellor has just sent me a letter from Gross, in which it is stated that Count Poniatowski will leave in 4 or 5 days, and will be here by the end of the year. This letter is of November 5, new style. Gross is personally very troubled about the appointment of Prince Volkonski, who they intend should be his colleague. He says that the multiplication of Ministers from here in Poland will do no good, and will give rise to the idea that they are displeased with him. Tell me, please, how long it takes for a Minister to come here from Warsaw, for I know it takes an ordinary person 8 days.

I trust that this scrap of paper will find you better. The interest which I take in your condition is very real.

The Empress remains much the same, very distended, coughing and breathless, and with pains in the lower part of her body.

From Sir Charles Hanbury-Williams

Wednesday [*December* 11]. *Dictated.*

I am much obliged, Monsieur, for your letter of yesterday evening. When that moment which can alter everything arrives, you have only to give your orders, and I shall be at Petersburg in three months. I pride myself that in those happy days you will not forget your faithful servant.

I had a very bad night, and I am so weak to-day that I can scarcely drag myself about my room ; and I begin to doubt whether I shall go out of it before my audiences for taking leave.

If M. Gross's letter was written on the 5th, n.s., and if Poniatowski left Warsaw five days after that letter, he should be here by now, for in 13 days one can do that journey very comfortably. So you may expect him at any moment. Perhaps Apraksin may have kept him a day or two at Riga, or, supposing that his carriage has broken down in Lithuania, he might remain there for three or four days before it was mended.

As soon as I am in a condition to do so, I shall not fail to write you a very serious letter on the subject of his arrival. I shall give you advice, I shall tell you what I think, I shall not even hide my fears from you. I am too much devoted to your interests and to your reputation not to take this step. I am delighted to find that I am in so much favour with the Grand-Duke ; and it is to you that I owe the kindly feelings which he has for me.

From the Grand-Duchess

Friday morning [*December* 13].

No. 1. We shall not keep the fête on the 18th. The Empress goes to the country. She wishes to worship at Christmas, and our customary week of preparation begins on the 18th. I think that we shall also be sent to the country, for if we remain we should certainly have to take part in the fête.

No. 2. The day before yesterday, at half-past eight o'clock in the evening, a conference was held in the presence of the Empress and the Grand-Duke. The prescribed form for accession to the Treaty of Versailles was there put forward ; it is very short. It is stated in it that they accede, it is particularly stated in it that they make no engagement to succour France, even if attacked, and equally that they desire no assistance from her. After the paper had been read, the Empress put it in her pocket.

The Grand-Duke said, " When I saw that this bound us to nothing, and that things had gone as far as this, I was unwilling to draw her ill-humour upon me needlessly." An opportunity arose, however, for him to make some remark against it. There was a moment of wrangling between the Empress and him, but they parted good friends. Many narratives of the position in Saxony were read, and much venom was shown against the King of Prussia.

No. 3. Condoïdi is again very insistent that she should continue the treatment which did her so much good this autumn, for, he says, the spring might be fatal ; but she will not listen.

Count Poniatowski has written a letter to Prasse, which the Chancellor has sent me, also of the 5th, in which he expects to leave the Thursday following, and to be here within three weeks from that date. This letter is about wine, purchases and servants. I have also seen two extracts of letters from Brühl to Prasse ; one is the answer to the representations made from here on the subject of Poniatowski's nomination. He says that taking into consideration the notification which he has received, they must have persuaded themselves that it would give pleasure, that it was an accomplished fact, and nothing could either be changed or his place filled up in the near future without offending some of the most distinguished persons in the Republic ; that his family had guaranteed his loyalty, and that half the public had accepted this choice and took a great interest in the Count. He adds, however, at the end, that Sacken remains designated as his successor. I make a face at that.

The second paper is a personal note to the Chancellor, in which Brühl makes excuses for having detained Poniatowski until now, saying that he had waited for the Ministers from V.(Austria) and of Ver. (France), so as to remove the feeling of offence which they had taken at the appointment of the Count, who would arrive without fail in a few days.

Now this is just what annoys me about it ; for neither Broglie nor Sternberg will leave Dresden,[1] and if Brühl does not change his mind, months will pass before we see our friend. I am satisfied that the Chancellor fools me about this difficulty, for I see that the letters from Brühl, Gross and Prasse all agree in raising the very point which I made to him, and that he makes them say what suits him.

Swallov told me that he thought that you went out yesterday. I hope it did you good. My regard for you will end only with life. I await with impatience the letter and advice which you promise me.

From Sir Charles Hanbury-Williams

[Saturday, December 14.]

Thank you for your letter, which I received last night. You ask for the advice which I promised you ; here it is. I am too much afraid of the tricks and treachery of nearly everyone here not to beg of you on my knees to be extremely careful when Poniatowski arrives, for I cannot divest myself of the idea that the Chancellor is resolved to keep you entirely in his own hands, and that he will allow no one to share your favour with him. You can have no doubt that he is capable of anything to reach his end. And things, though done expressly by his orders, seem to the eyes of the public to be the work of others, as for instance Poniatowski's mission. The Chancellor says in public that the Vice-Chancellor has arranged it, because the letters of recommendation from the Empress to the King of Poland passed through the hands of the Vice-Chancellor, and not through those of the

---

[1] Count Brühl was in Warsaw.

Chancellor. And believe me, if any misfortune befalls Poniatowski here, even though it is the work of the Chancellor, he will know how to hide his game in such a way as to deceive the whole world, and you more than anyone.

Be very circumspect, therefore, Monsieur, in your interviews with Poniatowski, and above all see him at his own house or at that of a third person, but *never at your own*.[1] If you go out at night and are recognized, it will only make the world talk and create suspicion. But, if he were caught entering your house, the game is up, and his fate is sealed beyond repair. My fears and my zeal tell me this ; and I feel so sure that I am right, that I beg you again on my knees to think it all over calmly and maturely. I shall answer your letter to-morrow. You would do me a great service, if you could manage to obtain information about the contents of the papers which were read in council regarding the accession to the Treaty of Versailles.

From THE GRAND-DUCHESS

Monday [December 16].

We are leaving to-morrow for Oranienbaum, as I had foreseen, and we shall come back immediately after the fête. I send you enclosed with this a packet for Count Poniatowski, if he arrives in my absence, which is scarcely unlikely, as he left, according to the letters from Prasse, on the 15, n.s. Please have it given to him, if you have anyone who can do so. If not, keep it till I return. I shall follow your advice about the interviews. I have sent to ask the Chancellor for the paper which you covet.

Something suggested to me by the Hetman runs in my head, though the possible consequences alarm me. It is this. To put in writing the whole of the grievances which the public feel

---

[1] In view of this advice from Sir Charles, it is of interest to note that in February, 1758, Poniatowski was arrested at the Grand-Duchess's very door leaving a pavilion in the gardens of Oranienbaum, which the latter occupied on the excuse of taking baths, and where they were in the habit of meeting. (Poniatowski's *Mémoires*.)

against Peter Schuvalov, as the Empress complains that no
one will tell her the truth about him and to have the paper
handed to the Empress by the Grand-Duke. This last point
is very difficult and may not strike home. I will compose and
write it with my own hand, with the approval of, and with the
corrections which all those who call themselves my friends, like
Troubetskoï and Buturlin, may wish to make. I will get the
Grand-Duke to sign it. I shall sign it; and the Grand-Duke will
hand it to the Empress. Against me alone will the hatred of the
Schuvalov be directed, but I shall have made my name with the
public. I suggest that you should think this over. If you disapprove, nothing more will be said of it; otherwise, I am
going to set to work instantly upon it. Yesterday she was in a
strange condition.

From THE GRAND-DUCHESS

Saturday morning [December 21].

I returned last night, but there is still no Count Poniatowski.
He certainly keeps us waiting for him; he is said to be at
Riga.

You have expressed satisfaction each time that I have shown the
concern which I take in all that happens to your country; and
this induces me to speak to you of it to-day. Allow me to begin
by congratulating you upon the profound good sense which pre-
vails in your King's speech at the opening of Parliament. I have
read nothing for a long time which has struck me so much. May
God preserve and help His Majesty. It is as much my respect
for his person as my affection for your country which fathers this
wish. I regret with you and for you the loss which you have
sustained of a friend in the Ministry. I remember having heard
you say that Mr Fox was one.[1] If you are well and if you have

---

[1] Henry Fox, afterwards created Lord Holland. He had resigned his post
as Secretary of State for the Southern Department because he found that
Newcastle, the Prime Minister, was not acting up to his promises, and
that it was impossible to work with him. Pitt succeeded him as Secretary
of State, and Newcastle resigned a few days later.

the time, I beg you to explain to me the crisis in your country. Do the changes which have been made augur well for the coming year ?   Tell me something about this Mr Pitt, who is now at the helm and who is completely opposed to the court. You know my curiosity, so make believe that I am talking to you.   If I could do so more often, I would not trouble you to write,

You shall have the copy of the paper about accession, when the Chancellor sends it to me.   Meanwhile, he has sent me word that it was there laid down that no assistance would be given to France against England, nor by France against the Turks, but that mutual assistance would be promised in other quarters.   It was in that sense that I ought to have taken the Grand-Duke's words.

The Russian merchants are beginning to feel the effects of the coolness between your court and ours.   All contracts for sales were concluded in former years in the month of December, and not only at this moment have they not been begun, but there is no mention even of them being discussed.   Apparently you think like the Russian proverb, " Those who will not hear must feel," and you touch us on the tender spot.

I will compensate for your daughter's pearls.   I hope your health is really better, so that I may have the pleasure of telling you in person how much I esteem and honour you.

From Sir Charles Hanbury-Williams

[*Sunday, December* 22.]   *Dictated.*

Monsieur, Thank you very much for your letter of yesterday. I am delighted that the speech of the King, my Master, pleases you.   I hope that God will preserve and help His Majesty, to whom Russia becomes more hostile from day to day.   Ivan Ivanovitch said in public at Tsarkoïe Selo that he did not know how it came about, but that I had information about everything that happened here, that I ought rather to be looked upon as

Prussian Minister than as British Ambassador, and that, as war was as good as declared between Russia and Prussia, no good Russian should hold intercourse with me.

When Ivan Chernuishev went to the Great Chancellor to take his leave, the Great Chancellor said nasty things about Poniatowski and me.

I expect Poniatowski to be here to-night, and I hope by some means or other to see him at once. I think that it would be best to write you a special letter (when I am free from the headache which to-day prevents me from writing with my own hand), to give you the facts about our Ministry and the intrigues at our court. Surely, the Chancellor cannot pretend that it could be taken in England as a meritorious action, that they would not aid France in the present war against her; but France will make plenty at Constantinople of the fact that she has not bound herself in any way to assist Russia against the Ottoman Porte. This sign of friendship from the Chancellor is only paralleled by many others which I have received at his hands.

I am indeed sincerely obliged, Monsieur, when you express kindly feeling towards my country, and I cannot say how flattered I am when you mention my daughter. The Hetman dined here yesterday, and we had a long talk. He agrees with me that Poniatowski cannot be too much on his guard on his arrival here. I do not yet know when I shall be able to pay my respects to you.

I shall be very much obliged to you for the paper which you have asked the Chancellor to send you. It seems to me that the Hetman told me that you had said something about Apraksin's return here for the New Year or for the Grand-Duke's birthday. But as you never made any remark of the sort to me, I imagine that he must have misunderstood you.

Adieu, Monsieur, my only comfort in Russia proceeds from you.

From THE GRAND-DUCHESS

Tuesday morning [December 24].

Doubtless you know of Count Poniatowski's arrival.[1] He writes the following for me to pass on to you :—" This is my plan for settling my affairs, which are in a very bad way at court. At my visit to the *patron* (the Great Chancellor), which is arranged for between 11 and midday, I shall profess entire devotion to him, and shall make full use of your special pleading. Next, my second object will be to win over Esterhazy, and this I hope

---

[1] Poniatowski had preceded his arrival by an unsigned letter to Sir Charles, which is amongst his papers at Cheltenham.
" My dearest friend,
Notre ami commun (Catherine) will be able to tell you all the thoughts which pass through my mind, and which the feelings that I owe you, and shall owe you all my life, inspire in me. It is enough that anything far or near should make you happy or afflict you, for me to feel it most vividly. I am sorry that I cannot venture on some story which would have a happy influence on all that concerns you. You gave us an example, without parallel, when you took so deeply to heart our sad situation and misfortunes. I can never forget your helpful kindness, and shall ever honour and love you as long as I live. Slening. December 20, 1756."

Two further letters accompanied the one forwarded to the Grand-Duchess by Sir Charles. One from Poniatowski's father, the other, attached to it, from Stanislas himself.

COUNT PONIATOWSKI, CASTELLAN OF CRACOW, TO SIR C. HANBURY-WILLIAMS.

December 3, 1756.

My very dear, and very honoured Seigneur,
I know all that my son owes to you. The hearts of his father and mother are filled with the deepest gratitude towards you. If no unforeseen accident nor cunning enemy betrays his destination, he will set out. Pray Heaven that circumstances may remain favourable, and that he will be of use to you ; we wish it from the bottom of our hearts.
Cursed be those who were the first authors of the change in the ancient system. Your prediction that things will return to their old course, comforts us a little. Count on my word of honour, that at all times, or wherever we can be of use, we shall give our assistance with zeal, be it from near or far.
Adieu, my dear and worthy friend, I honour you as much as I love you.

will be as easy for me as it is absolutely necessary. Once I have his approval, Douglas's yelpings will soon come to naught. I shall avoid all appearance of intercourse with *la sagesse* (Sir Charles), whom I implore you to convince of the absolute necessity of this for the good of all three of us, and in order to be able in

On the same sheet :—

STANISLAS-AUGUSTUS PONIATOWSKI TO SIR C. HANBURY-WILLIAMS.

I cannot thank you tenderly enough for your letter of the 11th of last month. Count on my gratitude. Indeed, it is due to you. *L'homme* (Catherine) to whom I beg you will hand the enclosed, will inform you of the contents. As it is very long, I have put it all in the same envelope, to avoid repetition. I hope you will be pleased with me. At least I desire it most truly, for I am your faithful friend. I hope we shall see you soon.

We have thought fit to include one further letter in the series which belongs to this date. M. Saul, one of the leading Ministers under Brühl at Dresden, had invariably shown himself a good friend to England and to Sir Charles, during the latter's official connection with Saxony. His complaints of the hard treatment which that country was undergoing at the hands of the King of Prussia, do not seem exaggerated ; and *Frederick's Political Correspondence* bears ample witness to the King of Poland's efforts to avoid hostilities. Frederick doubtless believed, rightly or wrongly, that treachery was in the air ; but he was far more justified in his attack on Austria than he was in turning upon the Saxons. The court of Vienna had already gone far along the road to alliance with France, the aim and object of Kaunitz's policy ; so the suggestions here made by Saul, that England should have warned the Empress-Queen before concluding her treaty with Prussia, would probably, if carried into effect, have made but little difference to the future.

D. L. DE SAUL TO SIR C. HANBURY-WILLIAMS.

Warsaw, December 12, n.s. 1756.

Monsieur, His Excellency Count Poniatowski has handed me the letter which your Excellency kindly confided to him for me, and I profit by his return to reply to it. I was very flattered by the further proof of the continued kindly feeling on the part of your Excellency towards me. I implore you always to continue it, and to remain persuaded that I deserve it by the genuine reverence which I feel for the person of your Excellency.

Your Excellency asks me whether I could have believed that so innocent a treaty as that made between the King of England and the King of Prussia should have produced such changes, as those which have been witnessed lately in Vienna ? I will answer him frankly, that I think and should have hoped that these changes could have been anticipated,

time to become even useful to him, a service which I certainly owe him from gratitude, and one which I wish from the bottom of my heart to perform. It is hard for me and very cruel to be forced to act in it like this, but I appeal to his honesty and at the same time to his good sense. Both will speak for me." I should believe myself to be doing a wrong to your character,

if England had warned the court of Vienna of what she intended to do, and if she had confided to her the plans which she had in view. This would without doubt have reassured the court of Vienna ; whereas the great mystery with which this negotiation was surrounded, added to the manner in which that court was treated, made her distrustful to the point of believing that England had changed her whole system as far as she was concerned ; and she could, therefore, only do the same towards England. I shall suspend my judgment upon it, and shall not enter further into the matter. I shall only dwell shortly on what concerns us personally.

After the new alliances already mentioned, our plan was to take no part, to interfere in no way, but to remain neutral, and to profit quietly by the advantages of commerce, while others recommenced to fight. A clear proof that this was our intention showed itself in the fact that, when peace was first threatened, we were still cutting down our army. Shortly afterwards, we recalled the rest of those troops from their quarters, and assembled them in the camp near Pirna, because we were led to fear that they might be interfered with in the passage that the King of Prussia intended to make through Saxony. We had provisioned the camp on a moderate scale, feeling confident that the King of Prussia would not halt, more especially as we were ready to give him all the security which he could possibly require, both for the free passage of the Elbe, as well as in relation to our army. Your Excellency will, perhaps, tell me that he could not, or rather would not, trust to our promises and to our pledges, however solemn they might be. But we wanted to go much further and to place in his hands every imaginable security ; for he was to leave his garrison at Wittenburg, Torgau and Pirna with Sonnenstein, and all our generals were to undertake, under oath, that not one of them would serve against him during the war. Besides this he was offered hostages. Was not this enough ? And should not the King of Prussia have agreed to such security? I would have wagered my head that he would have done so, and I confess that I constantly maintained he would, but I was mistaken. He left us no other course but to ally ourselves entirely with his party, and to make common cause with him. Now, as this would have been against the honour, and against the conscience of the King, he preferred to run the risk of all the disasters which threatened him, rather than to allow himself to be forced into a dishonest action.

This, Monsieur, is an abstract, but it is the truth of how things come about. Does this merit, Monsieur, the treatment which we have received ? Your Excellency cannot conceive what poor Saxony suffers, and without being able to see any end to our troubles. You know, Monsieur, that I have always been true to the English ; but your Excellency will not think it strange that I now range myself on the side of the French party. The

which I have learnt to know, were I to add one word in support of these lines.

I have sent to ask the Chancellor for the reason of his lectures to Ivan Chernuishev.

What I said to the Hetman about Apraksin's arrival was what the latter told me when he left, that, if he saw that his presence with the army was not an absolute necessity, he would take a turn round here during the winter. I think I told you this at the time; and, as the 6th of January, Twelfth Night, is a festival on which generals can show themselves to their troops, and as Apraksin has never missed that day, I imagined at the back of my head that he would perhaps come for that day; for as the senior lieutenant-colonel of the Guards he has the precedence over Buturlin, a fact which he usually never forgets, and one which causes their ill-feeling.

Adieu, Monsieur, I am more than ever your friend. I am in despair at causing you pain about Count Poniatowski.

From Sir Charles Hanbury-Williams

Thursday [*December* 26].

Thank you for your letter of Tuesday, and for the assurances which you give me of your protection.

I have no reply to make to your communication from Count

harm is done us, without reason and without mercy, by England's ally, if not at her instigation, at least by her connivance, and we cannot hope for deliverance or compensation, except through our old friends the Russians, and our new ones the French. Your Excellency does not believe in the durability of the new alliance between Vienna and Versailles into which we find ourselves forced to enter; but I am of opinion that it rests in France's power alone to make it last, for neither the court of Vienna nor ourselves will fail her, so long as she does not fail us. Being no longer able, therefore, I confess, to be a partisan of the English system, while affairs remain on the footing on which they are, I heartily wish that the two crowns may be reconciled, so that we can be the friend of both. But whatever the state of politics, it will never influence me nor change my feelings of reverence and devotion, with which I will never cease to be, Monsieur, your Excellency's very humble and very obedient servant,

D. L. De Saul.

R

Poniatowski.   His plan is already formed ; and I wish him successful results from the depth of my heart.   I should myself have advised him to avoid any appearance of intimacy with me. He alone could ever convince me that he would give up my friendship.   Indeed, I shall look upon myself as the greatest fool on earth, if I am mistaken about his heart. · He says that it is hard and cruel for him to behave like this to me.   Tell him from me that even the appearance of a coolness between us causes me pain.   But, being convinced that this course is serviceable, and even necessary, to him, I give my approval to it instead of blaming him.

I hope that you and he will be quite pleased with what I have just written.   I do so with difficulty, for I am very ill to-day.   I own that I have a great longing to see *le cordon bleu* (Poniatowski).

From THE GRAND-DUCHESS

Saturday Morning [*December* 28].

Count Poniatowski hopes to have his audiences to-morrow. He has sent me the enclosed letter from Flemming to impart to you.   The Chancellor, speaking of the Grand-Duke's hatred for the French, said, " Let him go on in the same strain, for we shall soon have need of it."

Count Poniatowski begs me to tell you that his heart bleeds for you, and that he is partly obeying your own advice by avoiding you.

Peter Schuvalov, so the story goes, has handed in a petition yesterday against Roman L.V. (Voronzov).

I hope and trust that all may be returning to its natural course ; my business is to honour you, to listen to you, and to give you proofs of my friendship.

The *cordon bleu* is marvellously well.   I send my best wishes for your health.

From THE GRAND-DUCHESS

Monday, 7 o'clock in the evening [December 30].

Believe me, my vexation is very great ; I am humiliated and ashamed at being the cause, though an innocent one, of the troubles which you and Count Poniatowski are experiencing. In fact, Monsieur, I shall look upon myself as the most miserable creature in the universe, if heaven does not place me in a position to repay you my debt. It is difficult, I think, to find a situation so changed, and an affair which has turned out so differently from what one would have expected. *Mon Dieu,* what do I not owe you, and how I wish that it was in my power to express it to you.

Here is the answer from Count Poniatowski to your note which I sent him. Take trouble to read the whole, for at the end he speaks of Prasse : and return it to me. Your anxieties pierce me to the heart.

From SIR CHARLES HANBURY-WILLIAMS

Tuesday [December 31].

Although it is post day and I have much to do, I sent away my secretary the moment that I received your note.

Calm yourself, Monsieur. I am too deeply touched by your sorrow not to tell you that you are causing yourself needless distress. Nothing in this world will persuade me, after the assurances which you give me of Poniatowski's feelings, that he is not my dearest friend for all eternity. I shall receive him as my son. I shall not speak one word to him of politics. Our conversation will turn on you, on himself, on his family. I know beforehand that tears will come into my eyes when I embrace him. He has only to do and to say what he wishes. I am satisfied that he loves me, and that is enough.

He would have deserved my contempt and entirely lost my

friendship, if he had not accepted his mission, even on the understanding that he was forbidden ever to see me or speak to me again. In my view, he owes you too much not to sacrifice everything (except his honour, for that would make him contemptible in your eyes) to throw himself at your feet. He would not lose his honour by giving me up, because I should be the sole judge of that matter, and should not only have acquitted him, but would have even justified him to the whole world. I am honest and impartial. Those qualities are given me solely to help my friends.

Do all he asks you. Put on a good face to Prasse, I beg you.

Further, if there is anything in my power that I can do to make you and Poniatowski more happy, point it out to me ; and you shall joyfully and promptly be obeyed.

I do not know how to forgive myself for being the cause (however innocent) of giving you one moment's sorrow or anxiety.

For charity's sake, send me word that you are easy in your mind. I share in all your troubles, and shall always take a part in what gives you pleasure. I am yours unreservedly, and swear eternal devotion. I embrace Poniatowski from the depths of my soul, and love him as my son ; if he were my son, I should force him to act exactly as he is doing. Think for a moment that if I suffer it is for your sakes, and that my merit is sufficient comfort to me. In a case like this the friend shows himself in a true light.

To read this letter might make Poniatowski's visit, which he has to pay me, less distressing for him. I beg you, therefore, to send it to him, if you agree with me.

Dare I implore you to let me know as soon as possible that you are content ? I shall be unhappy until I hear this.

From THE GRAND-DUCHESS

Tuesday evening [*December* 31].

Ah, Monsieur ! How clearly your letter reveals the generosity of your mind ! I must tell you, without exaggeration, that you are worthy of respect. Overcome with emotion, I wept, and marvelled at your fortitude. I sent your letter at once to Poniatowski. You can count on me for ever, Monsieur ; I shall raise statues to you, and the whole world shall see how highly I prize merit. I shall make it my boast.

Since you desire to know if we are happy, I say, Yes, and that there seems to be no difference between the present and the past. To-day's audiences won praise for Count Poniatowski for his eloquence. He speaks nobly, and it becomes him admirably. Even the Empress admitted it ; so says the Vice-Chancellor, who had put off the audiences for two days, but when old Münich was called upon to reply instead of the Chancellors, the Vice-Chancellor left his house at once. N.B.—He said he was ill in bed.[1]

From SIR CHARLES HANBURY-WILLIAMS

Monday [*January* 6, 1757].

I return you your letter with the enclosures. Everything that you were told was told to the Great Chancellor by the

---

[1] On the back of the leaf on which this letter is written, and on the opposite side, are these words in Williams's handwriting :—
  " Dear Friend and Kinsman,
        The bearer of this M————"[a]
It is the beginning of a letter—a further proof that Williams copied Catherine's letters at home before returning them to her, and that the collection of copies of Catherine's letters have been saved for us by Williams's care.—G.

[a] These words are in English.

Envoy from Holland.[1] He has rather embellished what I told him confidentially, as I was sure that he would repeat it to the Great Chancellor ; and yesterday he came to my home again to wheedle me.

I certainly have every right to repay the tricks and treacheries of which I have been the victim, without violation of the laws of justice or honesty. But, if what Bernardi told me from you this morning is correct and you wish me to stop, I will no longer listen to the voice of reason nor to that of my resentment. But remember, Monsieur, that when you approached him in my interest, he did not listen to your request, and dealt me a blow which he believed to be mortal, but which did me no harm at all.

I shall finish as I began, always maintaining the same gratitude for your kindness and the same obedience to your wishes.

You see how eagerly I seize on every opportunity to prove to you my sincerity and my devotion. I realize how you are situated and the need which you have of this man. I pity you—but that is not sufficient ; I must also help you.

The Chancellor sent me word a long time ago that France would not attack Hanover, unless the troops of that Electorate joined the Prussian army. That proposal was made to France without the knowledge of my court and is an insult, not a favour. We have never taken instructions from the court of Versailles, and we shall make use of our armies as the King wishes, not as His Most Christian Majesty prescribes. We have asked Russia to defend Hanover in the event of it being attacked by France, but never will my Master ask France not to attack it. It is true that I am much roused by this affair. Your accession has gone to Versailles. But what is claimed to have been done on our behalf makes me much more angry than all that has been done against us. I beg you to let me know if you really sent Bernardi to me to-day.

Field-Marshal Apraksin's wife is with child at Riga.

[1] M. van Swart. Mitchell wrote to Sir Charles from Berlin to warn him against him.

From THE GRAND-DUCHESS

Wednesday, after dinner [January 8].

Bernardi spoke to you in the Chancellor's favour by my orders. Whatever the man is, he is devoted to me, the only one that I have with a head, the only one who can be of use to me. What do you expect to gain by ruining him ? The Schuvalov, less able, quite as mischievous, equally dishonest, and with far greater ill-feeling towards me, would only reward you with new treacheries. Would that miserable Vice-Chancellor be his successor ? Know him for what he is. He is quite unworthy of your regard, and only gains your approval by the hypocrisy beneath which he knows how to hide his real character. In fact, if you ruin the Chancellor, my fate is certain. He is an enemy of Prussia, but not of England. I know from various sources, and amongst others from Count Poniatowski, that he supports her on all occasions, and says quite plainly in every court that Russia must remain the friend of England. Your talents may cause him jealousy ; he cannot like you, but be assured that he is in no way the enemy of your country. I feel, however, the justness of the high line which you take on the question of the attack on Hanover. The spring may easily bring forth means to put everything back into its proper order ; and once I am there, I can guarantee you friends who will be as grateful for your friendship and your personal assistance as for the sacrifice of your animosity, which you will make for my sake, and which can only prove to the advantage of your country and your cause. I shall be able to say that each step which you take makes me feel more and more attached to them. My friend, my counsellor, it is decreed that the whole of your generous nature will be expended on me.

Again I address you with the attached paper. It is the answer from Bernstorff (and it makes me indignant) to the letter which the Chancellor begged me to write to be shown to the late Maltzahn,[1]

---

[1] See *ante*, pp. 87, 88. Maltzahn died of a chill at the end of 1756.

and this is the answer which I think of sending.[1] I weary you; you do everything for me and I do nothing, but I hope that I shall not die before the earth realizes the full extent of my friendship for England.

I am asked to make thousands of nice speeches to you, one more affectionate than another, the least of them being that he adores you, that he was entrusted with the commission that you know of, from which there was no escape : in fact, that no one is unhappier than he, that everyone has sufferings, and that such an extreme case is a torment from which there is no relief.

[1] COUNT BERNSTORFF[a] TO M. D'OSTEN.[b]

[*January* 8.]

Monsieur, The King is so moved by the sentiments expressed by the Grand-Duke in the letter which she (the Grand-Duchess) has written to his Excellency the Great Chancellor, that he has ordered me to despatch this courier to you at once, to hand you the letter which, at his command, I am addressing to the Chief Minister ; and which you will find, from the copy which I send you, conforms entirely with the desires of his Imperial Highness.

It is, in fact, so worthy of the good heart and the spirit of enlightenment of this Princess to rise above the prejudices which others have perhaps attempted to inspire in her, and to surrender them for two such important objects as to destroy to their very source the calamitous quarrels which until now have torn asunder the House of Holstein, and to prove to the powerful nation over which she will reign that she prefers the true welfare of the Empire to all other tastes and all other considerations, that the King, seeing that she adopts this policy, could not fail to conceive a great opinion of her talents and genius. The treaty of exchange and of agreement, therefore, becomes more than ever desirable to His Majesty, since it will furnish him with the means of forming an honest and intimate connection with a princess, who had the ability, from what we see, to rise to great achievements, and who is worthy of his hearty regard. The King, then, delighted at the hope of establishing a real friendship with her, and sincerely anxious to prove his desire to do what is pleasing to her, as well as to those who belong to her, has resolved to offer to the Dowager Princess of Zerbst[c] an annual pension of 6,000 crowns for the duration of her life, to commence from the day of the conclusion of the treaty of exchange. And as it is further possible that, under present circumstances, the Grand-Duchess herself may have expenses to meet, the King, who asks nothing better than to show her how concerned he is in her importance, her comforts and her advantage, from the moment that she becomes his friend, commands and authorizes you to tell Count Bestuzhev that we are making arrangements with the Sieur Pierre, His

a The Danish Prime Minister.
b Danish *Chargé d'Affaires* in Russia, afterwards Minister.
c The Grand-Duchess's mother.

From Sir Charles Hanbury-Williams

Friday [January 10].

Your commands have annihilated my resentments; and they are given up to please you. Perhaps I think worse than you do of the Schuvalov, and at least as badly of the Vice-Chancellor.

agent and banker to His Majesty at Hamburg, to hold in readiness a hundred thousand roubles for the use of her Imperial Highness, a sum to the amount of which you, or merchants living at St Petersburg approved by yourself and the Great Chancellor, can draw on your note of hand from time to time, in accordance with the instructions of that Chief Minister, and that you will then hand it over to his Excellency, so that it may reach the Grand-Duchess through his hands. As there is no court of exchange directly between Petersburg and here, and as it would doubtless be more convenient that this part of the business should remain as secret as possible, we can scarcely make use of any better channel than that which I have indicated for remitting the money. I venture to hope, Monsieur, that the Grand-Duchess will decide by this sample how the King looks at things and what his friendship is and might become.

It would indeed be deplorable, if so great a Prince and so great a Princess, whose blood is the same and who seem made to exalt all the world over the august name which is common to them both, should always remain disunited; and that so small a matter as that which divides them, should compel them to continue to oppose one another in every thing and mutually to obstruct their power and greatness.

I am well assured, Monsieur, that you will lose no means of bringing home the truth and force of this reflection. No one, it must be allowed, has ever known it better, no one has less lost sight of this great object than Count Bestuzhev. If the treaty which is to produce so much good succeeds, it will be his work; and the two nations, whose harmony will be assured by this agreement, will have reason to laud his name and his administration for ever.

You will have no difficulty in realizing my impatience to hear from you. For nearly six years, I have been occupied, to the extent which you know, with the affair of which I speak. I have never hoped for success until the day when I knew that the Grand-Duchess had declared in its favour. If, in spite of that, it fails, we must never think of it again. I have the honour to be with much attachment, Monsieur, your very humble and very obedient servant, BERNSTORFF.

Copenhagen, *December* 20, 1756.

PROPOSED LETTER FROM THE GRAND-DUCHESS TO THE GREAT CHANCELLOR.

I have received Monsieur de Bernstorff's letter which you have sent me. After the tokens of regard which this letter expresses to me from the

Only a week ago, speaking about him to the Hetman, I said that the Vice-Chancellor was the one man in Russia whom I could not forgive.

As for the Great Chancellor, I shall never make advances to him. When the business of the King necessitates, I shall go to him. If he treats me properly, I shall always answer him cordially. But that is as far as you should ask me to go, although I tell you frankly that you have complete dominion over me in everything. In obedience to your orders, I have made known to the King of Prussia Monseigneur's request for the permit for his officer, and his doubts and anxieties about the designs against Holstein.

The answer from the King of Prussia is as polite as it is amiable. He says, " I did not allow one moment's delay in sending off the desired permit. It is already in the hands of your Minister, and will be sent to you by the first courier. (Our Minister, who is in Berlin, tells me that he has the permit.) On the question of Holstein, as his Imperial Highness makes me the offer of his friendship I accept it and give him mine wholly

King of Denmark, I did not expect to find in it evidence of such marked contempt as this offer of a hundred thousand roubles. I beg you, Monsieur, to tell Monsieur d'Osten of this letter, and to show it to him, in order that he may inform the King, his Master, that my manner of thinking is not as unworthy as his court imagines, that what I have done was out of love for Russia, that in the future I will take no step of which the Grand-Duke is not informed, and that were it not for the regard which I have for you, Monsieur, I would inform him at once of the offers which they have dared to make to me. As both the King of Denmark and I are married, the one worthy offer which he could make me is impossible, and I can receive no other which would not do me injury. If His Danish Majesty desires our friendship, that of the Grand-Duke and me, and if he wishes for the treaty in question, these are the conditions, which are unalterable. It is my last word :—

Oldenburg and Dalmenhorst to be raised to the rank of Duchies, with the same seniority, votes, etc. at the Diet of the Empire.

The coadjutorship and the Bishopric of Lübeck granted in perpetuity.

All the Grand-Duke's debts paid, without any restrictions or cost to the Grand-Duke.

One and a half million crowns or ducats paid here to the Grand-Duke without deduction or charges. The eventual succession, etc., etc.

I do this because I love Russia, and also that the King of Denmark should know that that is the only reason. I have too good an opinion of Count Bernstorff's worth, not to believe that he will give it his support.

I am, etc., etc., etc.

in return, as much for his own sake as for that of the Grand-Duchess, assuring him that in all that concerns Holstein and Slesvig I will make no treaty with anyone but the Grand-Duke." I shall make no comments on this answer; it is clearness itself.

I expect to pay my visit to Poniatowski on Monday at six o'clock in the evening. I have something to say to him which will surprise him; but he need not feel uneasy.

When you tell me that your fate is bound up with that of the Grand-Chancellor, you tell me something which astonishes me, but something which reminds me at the same time of everything that I have so often wished for you.

True it is, that never in my life have I read such a letter as M. de Bernstorff's. To make such an offer to a person like you, and to dare to name the sum, is the last degree of stupidity. I very much approve of the commencement of your reply. But I would not yet name conditions, and I should merely say that I was ready to listen to what they had to offer; and afterwards abide by your conditions. Now, I am convinced it is in the power of Denmark to hand over to you the Bishopric of Lübeck, for the election is at present at the absolute will of the chapter.

Before finishing this letter, and after having promised you to conform to your wishes about the Chancellor, allow me to ask you upon what grounds you wish me to believe that the Chancellor is the friend of my country. For more than fourteen months he has done us more harm than he could have done us had he been our enemy. He has had our confidence, without any return on his part; he has made me a thousand promises without fulfilling one. Lastly, under the name of friendship, he has prevented us from providing for our own safety, while he was doing all that our enemies asked of him, and has finished his performance by uniting France and Russia. In little things which personally concern my Master, in a small personal favour which the King asked of the Empress,[1] he does not deign to answer, and yet accords the very same favour to Sweden. The treatment which

[1] Permission to ship a small quantity of grain from Livonia to Hanover.

we have received from the Chancellor on the Treaty of Commerce (so lucrative to Russia) is even worse than the rest.[1] At foreign courts Russian Ministers carefully avoid those of England. Yet, notwithstanding all this, you shall be obeyed.

From THE GRAND-DUCHESS

Tuesday [*January* 14].

I owe you too much ever to be able to repay you my debt. The Grand-Duke, too, is most grateful for the assurances of friendship which you have procured for him.

I know of your yesterday's visit,[2] and I am much astonished at the malicious indiscretion of a certain person. Here is a draft of a letter, better expressed than mine. I beg you to give me your advice on it.

You have known how to turn the natural feeling of friendship which I had for you into a sense of duty. I shall try to convince both you and your country of it, if God so wills. Count Poniatowski begs me to ask you to search amongst your papers for a paper which Ogrodzki[3] had written and given to you on your departure from Dresden for Russia, explaining the reasons of their party's conduct and their refusal to accept the so-called reparations, etc., etc. He asks you to have a copy made of this paper, and to return the original to Ogrodzki, who has kept no copy of it.

---

[1] Bestuzhev had been delaying the conclusion of this convention for months, by pretending to refer it to various Government departments and Chambers of Commerce.

[2] To Poniatowski.

[3] See Poniatowski's *Mémoires*, p. 186. Ogrodzki had spent his youth in the elder Poniatowski's house, and had superintended the studies of his sons. In the course of a long life he had shown much aptitude for the study of foreign affairs, and was selected at this time to accompany Poniatowski to Russia as his official secretary.

From Sir Charles Hanbury-Williams

[Wednesday or Thursday, January 15 or 16.]

Before answering your letter, I must tell you that your court has refused point-blank to give permission for the exportation of a little corn from Livonia into the States of Hanover, which are in great need of it ; although this favour has already been granted to Sweden, and although the King asked it as a personal favour from the Empress.

I am delighted that Poniatowski was pleased with my visit on Monday. I did not wish to tell you the story of that malicious indiscretion, but it is perfectly true.

I had approved of your proposed letter to the Chancellor, but I must own that I have changed my mind under the circumstances. The Chancellor is too useful to Poniatowski, and Poniatowski is equally useful to him on account of his influence with you. But I advise him to husband his power and to create frequent small difficulties, for, to be in favour with that Minister, one must be good for something. Do, therefore, what Poniatowski wishes, but should you ever come to negotiate, stand firm for your interests, for the advantage to Denmark is very great.

Poniatowski asks me for a paper, but he does not give me the title of it, and without that it will be very difficult to find it. He would do well to ask Ogrodzki what it is.

I am delighted to have restored his peace of mind. I have not many friends ; I should scarcely know where to turn for more, but those whom I have cultivated have always been pleased with me ; and he will always remain so. I had already anticipated his wish for my picture. I had a start made on it yesterday by Rotari,[1] with the intention of giving it to him.

---

[1] Count Pietro dei Rotari, a member of a noble family in Verona, appointed court painter to the Czarina in 1756. We have been unable to trace the whereabouts of this picture of Sir Charles.

I am pierced to the quick by this last refusal from your court about the corn ; and I thought that the Chancellor, if only from gratitude, would have granted so small a favour to the King.

From THE GRAND-DUCHESS

Friday [January 17].

The title of the paper which the Count begs you to look for is, the Statement of what passed with regard to the affair of Ostrog, before and after the Diet of 1754.[1]

Truly, I am very dissatisfied, Monsieur, at their refusal about the corn, and I shall make the Chancellor feel it very acutely. How can one bind that man, if not by the obligations which he bears to the King, your Master ?

Here is news which has reached me about the attempted assassination of the King of France, and which you doubtless know. A person named Jacques Damiens dealt him a blow with a knife in his side ; he is improving. The assassin made the attack in the midst of the guards at night-fall, when the King was leaving his daughter's house to celebrate Twelfth Night at the Trianon ; so that Bekteïev believed, when first informed of it, that they had only played some Twelfth Night trick on the King, for it was five o'clock in the evening. The assassin said, " *My greatest regret is that I have not killed him.* The greatest tortures will not drag any confession from me ; let them save *the Dauphin* " ; and two men were at once arrested in Versailles disguised as women. The wounded King said, " I hand the assassin over to the Dauphin ; he can do what he likes with him. I forgive him."

This is what they call pretending to pardon. It is terrible, and has made my hair stand on end.[2] Parliament, even the 180 who had left, assembled in haste and debated upon it.

Ivan Ivanovitch heaped a thousand insults on the Chancellor

---

[1] See *ante*, p. 212.

[2] Damiens was torn in pieces by horses harnessed to him.

when speaking to the Hetman, not mincing his words, and ended by saying that no one could ever trust him, and that he deceived everybody.

Count Poniatowski promises faithfully to follow the advice which you give him about the Chancellor.[1]

From Sir Charles Hanbury-Williams

[Sunday, January.[2]]   Dictated.

Monsieur, When returning your letters, I beg you to accept my thanks for all the kindness which you show me, as well as for the news from France, and for the great excuses which you make in Poniatowski's name for cancelling his dinner to-morrow. I am quite proud to be in the secret of the illness of his cook, and I am of opinion that he has done very well not to embroil himself with the Chancellor over this matter, all important as it is.

If I have missed my dinner, at least I have received your note, which contains three lines at the end which would repay me well for a week's fast. I count on making you my very humble bow to-night, and, if they do not play me any trick, it is my turn to play in your game, and that again is worth more than dining with Poniatowski. I beg you to tell my son, that, if he never gives me dinner, if he always shuts his door against me, and if I never see him again in my life (certain as I am that he is only acting in your common interests), I shall always love and serve him just the same.

From the Grand-Duchess

Monday evening [January 20].

The Countess of Essex, of whom I am very fond for her father's sake, will, I hope, forgive the bad taste which I see in one of the

---

[1] To do his best to give Bestuzhev his support, in view of the use the latter might be to the Grand-Duchess in the future.

[2] Probably January 18 or 19.

costumes that I send with this, and will put it down to the barbarous countries[1] whence it comes. I have never owned as much as this ; but what does one not do to preserve one's self-esteem ?

Here is something, too, which obliges Count Poniatowski to beg you to safeguard his innocence, which might suffer from a *tête-à-tête* with you, if you make him dine alone at his house without the guardians of his honour, Messieurs Prasse and Ogrodzki ; and, in order that his virtue, like that of a lily and easily soiled, should not suffer from the ill-mannered conversations of mischievous men, beg them all three to eat with you or no one. Forgive, Monsieur, the impertinence of this note. I assure you that it is the outcome of the immense regard and affection which no one can withhold from you.

From Sir Charles Hanbury-Williams

[Tuesday, Wednesday, January 21, 22.]

The father of the Countess of Essex thanks his benefactor on his knee, both for her magnificent present and for the kind sentiments which she expresses in speaking of his daughter. You may load me with honours and presents, yet I tell you that it is beyond your power to increase my devotion to you.

How comes it that Poniatowski could imagine that I was wishing to give him a dinner, as Minister, by inviting him to dine *tête-à-tête* with me ? Never has such an idea entered my thoughts ; and I promise you that he shall have the guardians of his person and character on either side of him. If he so wishes, I shall not set a single dish before him without asking Prasse for his permission, nor shall I offer him wine without Ogrodzki's consent. And so, to make him happy, I shall give him a good dinner and lots of bad company.

I have sent Poniatowski four volumes on the affairs of Poland, and amongst them the one for which he asked me. If he keeps

---

[1] By this expression Catherine clearly alludes to some joke.—G.

any of them, let him at least send me a copy.   Again I thank you for your generous kindness to my daughter ; it touches me in my most tender spot.   I have just received Poniatowski's note, which you sent me : I have already given my answer to Bernardi. Tell my son that I always love him very tenderly, and that I hope that those who are dazzled may become blind, because I wish to see you in the situation where you are worthy to be.

I am not well to-night.   I beg you to send me word of all you hear of this awful assassination of the King of France.

From Sir Charles Hanbury-Williams

Thursday [undated, 1757].

If your note, which I received yesterday, gave me pleasure, the one I have just received this morning has given me much pain. I protest, Monsieur, on my honour, that I am completely ignorant of what you tell me, and that not one of the letters from my court contains the least reason to make me believe that my court will send a fleet to the Baltic.[1]   The last letters from the King command me to assure Her Imperial Majesty, in the event of my taking leave of her, that, whatever the situation of affairs in Europe, his friendship for her will always remain the same, and he commands me to make the Empress understand that he is always most anxious to cultivate and increase this friendship. This is the wording of my instructions ; if I knew more, you should know it.   According to your orders, to which I shall always conform, I return you your letters, for nothing in this world will change my unalterable devotion to you.

This letter is short ; you shall have a longer one soon, but I

---

[1] The King of Prussia had been urging the English Government for some months past to send their fleet to the Baltic, as the decision of the Russian Government to detain neutral ships containing contraband was likely to be detrimental to countries which had trading interests in those waters.   A rumour had recently reached St Petersburg that the fleet was likely to be dispatched.

S

feel obliged to return your letter as soon as possible, as you seemed anxious about it.[1]

From SIR CHARLES HANBURY-WILLIAMS

Wednesday [*March ?*].

Monsieur, An order from you has been handed to me by a third person—to recommend M. Friesendorff, formerly a captain in the service of Sweden, to his Highness the Duke of Cumberland, for a post among his troops. If his Royal Highness had asked me to recommend someone to you, Monsieur, I should have taken the liberty of asking him if he would be responsible for him, or at least whether he had been recommended to him by someone on whose word he could rely.

Permit me, therefore, Monsieur, to ask you the same question with regard to this Swedish gentleman. And at the same time have the kindness to remember that Monseigneur is actually at the head of an army opposing that nation. Now, consider for one moment that the person to whom you have often promised your protection would be the unhappiest of all men, if he recommended an unworthy subject to his friend and patron the Duke of Cumberland. If you command me, Monsieur, after all that I have just said, Friesendorff shall at once have his letter of recommendation.

Adieu, Monsieur, my devotion and affection for you cannot become greater than they are. My affection is unalterable, and as soon as you tell me that I can boldly recommend this man, I will do so. But I am sure that you will commend me for acting with the same caution in the affairs of my Prince and my friend (Poniatowski knows that he is so) as I have always done in yours. Never forget me, I entreat you.

[1] This urgency, no doubt, prevented Sir Charles from taking a copy, for the letter is not included in the series.

From THE GRAND-DUCHESS

Saturday, March 21 [22].

Monsieur, In view of your generous conduct towards me, my conscience obliges me to warn you that a secret order, which is meant to apply particularly to you, has been given to open all letters of foreign ministers. Perhaps you may know it ; but I should have felt scruples in hiding my knowledge of it from you, all the more so, because it is aimed at you more than at the others. I hope that you are never in any doubt of the unexampled regard which I feel for you. I begin to understand English fairly well, and I study it three hours a day. I hope that I shall gain further credit from this in your eyes.

This intelligence comes to you from me, and from no one else.

From SIR CHARLES HANBURY-WILLIAMS

Saturday [March 22].

I thank you much for the enclosed, and look upon it as a further proof of the continuation of your goodwill and protection.

I assure you that for more than a year I have not received any letters by post without sure signs that, they have been opened, and I was prepared that, if there was any further order, it would be to stop them altogether. I shall be very much on my guard with regard to my correspondence.

I have been for ten days at Wolff's country house. The air of the place suits me ; I like its lofty situation. I often think of you here, and pray for the accomplishment of all that you can desire.

I am always better on the day when I receive one of your notes. I do not mention politics to you. I meddle with them as little as possible. I can do no good, and I do not wish to do harm. Your protection and goodwill is all I ask for in this country.

The wish is very near my heart, Monsieur, that your son should have a brother.   Dare I ask if there is one on the way ?

Adieu, Monsieur.   Look upon me as a little man (not in stature) in a corner, always ready to answer all your questions, to obey all your wishes, to carry out all your orders to the best of his ability, who will always carefully seek the means of gaining your regard, because he knows nothing so worthy of regard as you.

Ask Bernardi, I beg you, where I am at present, and if he has been to see me.   He has not paid me one visit ; and I have been here for ten days.

The fact that you learn our language does honour to it.   If you continue to apply yourself as you are now doing, rely on it, that in eight or nine months your efforts will be rewarded.   I shall soon send you the great dictionary of the English language, which is a *chef d'œuvre* : and as soon as you are in a position to read them, you must have a collection of our comedies, which are very good.

From the Grand-Duchess

Sunday [March 23].

I am marvellously well, and have good hopes ![1]   I send you this news, because you wish me well.   I have too much proof to doubt it, or ever to forget the gratitude which I owe you.   As to the reproaches which you seem to make me, the time will come when you will do me justice, and when I hope that you will be satisfied with me.   Neither my head nor my character will ever change.   Therefore, you may for ever rest assured of my friendship and my esteem.

How does my friend Griff please you ?   He is enchanted at your kindness, and says that you love me.   Is your health good in the country ?   I wish I could be with you there.

[1] En avancant.

From THE GRAND-DUCHESS

Monday, six in the evening [April].

There is a tall man, with legs like wood, with a head like those on which they dress your wigs, stupider even than ugly, and that is saying a great deal. The title of colonel gives him the excuse for wearing a red coat, because he has not the money to pay for anything else without the help of Messieurs Schuvalov. This barely human figure calls itself Brockdorff, a great nobleman of the pleasant and delightful country of Holstein, of which he is one of the chief figures.[1] Do you know him ? Fifteen lines on his account are not worth writing ; yet would you kindly tell me, *If you ever spoke to Monsieur d'Osten about him, and what you said : and whether you further said that you would speak of the same thing to Count Poniatowski, and that you would write to me about it ?* For M. d'Osten announced this to Count Poniatowski. In any case, I beg you not to let M. d'Osten see that you know this. This is a curious letter ; but we have a certain little question to clear up, to which end a frank statement from you would be of great help to us. I hope, Monsieur, that you will forgive the sauciness of my style, in consideration of the unexampled regard and friendship upon which it is so firmly based.

Another favour. Have the kindness to praise the skill (not that she pretends to have any, but it is well that it should be thought that she has), the spirit, the talents, the devotion to this country and to the one to which you belong, as well as the knowledge of their interests—you will praise the Grand-Duchess, if you please, to the Grand-Duke, advising him, as his true and faithful friend, to follow the beneficial advice of that excellent head. This will produce much gratitude on one side, and much good on the other. I own and confess to you with penitence the impertinence and imprudence of all this. Act as confessors do.

---

[1] Brockdorff arrived in Russia in 1755 to grace the Grand-Duke's household. He became friendly with the Schuvalov, and was employed by them to create ill-feeling between the Grand-Duchess and the Grand-Duke, over whom he had obtained much ascendancy.

From Sir Charles Hanbury-Williams

Thursday [*April*].

I have received your letter, Monsieur, and will answer all your questions.

My frank statement about M. Brockdorff, and about what I said of him to M. d'Osten, is, that never have I made, nor wished to make, the acquaintance of the former. I did not like his face, and I remember that, on arriving here, he spoke ill of Count Poniatowski's family. I have never spoken ten words to him in my life. What I said about him to M. d'Osten was this. We were discussing the exchange of Holstein. He was telling me that Brockdorff was opposed to this exchange, and that he was believed to have some influence over the Grand-Duke, to which I said : " This must be taken into consideration, it might be well to try to win over that man. I will think it over and will consult with Count Poniatowski." But I never said that I would write to you about it, for I flatter myself that we two alone, and Count Poniatowski, know that such a correspondence exists. Since that conversation, I have learnt that Brockdorff was in the hands of the Schuvalov, and that Peter had let him make a profit of over 20,000 roubles on the purchase of some horses ; and the moment I knew that, I never gave a further thought to mixing myself up with him, nor to winning him over, nor to speaking to Count Poniatowski about him.

There, your first commands are executed. The second shall meet a like fate, and I shall sing the praises of the person in question, as a general does those of an officer whom he wishes to raise at one bound over the heads of fifty others. And to all you say I shall add, if it please you, that the military department should be sufficient for him, without his interference in either domestic affairs or foreign politics. Nothing that you can say requires an excuse. My devotion to you is so whole-hearted and my conscience so clear, that there is no question which you have not the right to ask me, and to which I shall not always be ready to make an answer.

I shall try to be worthy of the continuation of your friendship and protection. Of your regard I am assured both in the present and in the future ; for you will never abandon uprightness and truth.

I am happy in the country, and I only think of what I please and never of politics, often of you with all the regard and consideration which you deserve and with all the gratitude which I owe to you. If you have any history of Louis XIII, I beg you to lend it me.

From THE GRAND-DUCHESS

[Undated, May.]

Monsieur, I owe you an answer. I do not know how to give it : on the one hand, much affliction at your departure ; on the other, a difficulty in telling you what I want and how to say it to you. I am not accustomed to take such steps ; it is no part of my character nor of my heart to act like this. Yet I speak quite openly. Arrange an advance for me (if you can) of a sum equal to the one which I received. If this is possible, let it be done even more secretly than the first time—could it not be brought for your own use or under some such pretext, without anyone here knowing that it is for me ? Tell me what you think of this with all the sincerity which I am accustomed to find in you, and recollect that your advice has been useful to me and has awakened in me friendship and the liveliest of gratitude ; and I hope that I may not die until I have made them manifest to all. You will be the link to tighten afresh the natural friendship which should exist between our two countries, and what link can be stronger than one founded upon a regard and confidence which is so fully deserved ? Together we shall tame our enemies.

From THE GRAND-DUCHESS

Monsieur, The translation of the letter which you have sent me has made me thoroughly acquainted with the flattering and kindly disposition of His Britannic Majesty towards us.[1] It would be impossible to feel a more lively gratitude than that which I beg your Excellency to make known to the King, your Master, on my behalf ; and I hope that you know me well enough to give him guarantees for the future of the effect of my present sentiments, as soon as it is in my power to manifest them. I look upon the English nation as the one whose alliance is most natural and useful for Russia ; and this idea is confirmed in me by the remembrance of the personal obligations which I owe, and which I shall always long to owe, to the King of England, because I am truly devoted to him. The contrivances of France will never deceive me, for I know them. Nevertheless, I shall listen with great satisfaction to, and desire to learn all that you are willing to tell me about them. Your uprightness, your judgment,

---

[1] The letter of the Secretary of State, Lord Holdernesse, to Sir Charles, dated January 25, 1757, n.s. (Record Office), runs as follows :—

" His Majesty would not omit the opportunity of expressing his esteem and regard for the Great Duke and the Great Duchess, to both of whom His Majesty has thought proper to write upon your departure. I send you enclosed those letters, and copies of them for your information.

The King thinks it most advisable to confine the letters to very general expressions of his friendship, so that they can be shown. But at the time when you present them, you may, by word of mouth, add stronger expressions of His Majesty's particular friendship towards their Imperial Highnesses, whose interest the King has greatly at heart. You will acquaint them, that whoever will be selected to fill your place, will be particularly instructed to consult with them upon every event that may occur, and upon all occasions to contribute by all means possible to whatever may tend to their honour and advantage. The King has the firmest reliance on the steadiness of their attachment towards him. And as the same rules which are laid down for your conduct when you take leave of the Empress and her Ministers are not intended to take place in regard to their Imperial Highnesses, you may enter freely and fully with them upon the present state of affairs, and endeavour to arm them against the artifices of the court of France, and beg their protection for the person who will hereafter be responsible for carrying on His Majesty's affairs in Petersburg."

and the important services which I have received from you, have won from me a friendship which will only end with life and a regard which reaches to the degree of reverence. It is a tribute which I cannot deny to your character. I shall willingly give my support to whomsoever the King of England may think fit to employ here, although I shall not be able to refrain from a grudge against him, from the fact that he will be replacing you. It will be your task to point out to me the safest channel. I reaffirm the assurances which have been given to you, to seize the first possible occasion to rebuild the ancient system, for I shall see that it is carried out. And I hope that the whole world will at last agree from all points of view, after the cards have been well shuffled, that new allies have not the same value as old ones.

Adieu, Monsieur, I wish you all the happiness that you deserve, and I wish that I may one day benefit by your counsels. I have profited by them too well not to desire them ardently, at a time when I shall perhaps need them even more than I do now.

CATHERINE.

From THE GRAND-DUCHESS

Wednesday [July 2].

You have no equal. That is what I said yesterday to *your son*, and I repeat it to you to-day with regard to your letter ; for the contents and the affectionate tone touched me very deeply. My friendship and my gratitude to you have reached such a point, that, in all truth, Monsieur, I personally shall remain in your debt for ever. Therefore, as soon as I can I shall repay my obligations towards you to the good of your country. Yes, Monsieur, never, never shall anything turn me from my master purpose, to set her again in her ancient position, in all the lustre which Russia, in her own interest, should wish for her. The arrival of M. l'Hôpital, far from lessening the value of that system which is so firmly established in my brain, only confirms it (if such trifles as those which I am going to recount to you can effect it). I feel an excessive dislike to the lack of sincerity in his character (to which, it must be owned, I reduced him), to the constant duplicity of his mind, and to the great freedom of his manners.   In a word, he displeases me supremely, because he is French, which to me means anti-Russian.   Neither can I make a good impression on him.   I shall always be a counterpoise to them, if it pleases God to permit it.   I am not mean enough nor cowardly enough to hide it from him.   All that I can do is to be silent.[1]   In this state of mind he found me at the ball on St Peter's day, when he wished to talk business with me, to sound me, and to make me talk.   I remained so silent, that he was the only speaker.   Monosyllables, or a look which implied, " Do you take me for a fool ? " were my only replies.   When he saw I did not respond readily enough to the eloquent pleading of his bad case, he went on to talk nonsense, which, I think, is neither his strong point nor mine.   And so, being both ill at ease, we could neither make a good impression upon the other.

I must tell you that I think that I have thoroughly shaken the Empress on the subject of Monsieur Brockdorff, and, far from my conversation being coldly received, she was never more friendly towards me ; and, notwithstanding the support of Messieurs Schuvalov, whose various phases of connection with the Grand-Duke I partially knew, I shall succeed in the end in getting rid of Brockdorff, who, by my endeavours, has already fallen greatly in the estimation of the Grand-Duke, on the ground anyhow of his supposed ministerial talents.   I am consulting

---

[1] L'Hôpital wrote after a ball given at court on St Peter's Day (*Aff. Etr. Russie.* July 27, 1757):—" The Grand-Duchess honoured me by speaking to me with much kindness and ease.   She has talent, and I realised that she was trying to prepossess me.   Our conversations turned on different subjects, which gave me the opportunity, however, of trying to prepossess her in my favour.   They speak of her as obstinate and romantic. If I can believe Count Esterhazy, she has behaved very badly to the Empress, whom she sees very little, as does the Grand-Duke.   It is even asserted that the Empress has made up her mind not to worry about their conduct any more, and that she allows them free rein.   But she gives them nothing ; and they are always at their wits' ends for money.   The Grand-Duke, on his side, has entirely lost the good-will of Her Imperial Majesty ; given to evil counsels—perhaps he is incapable of listening to good ones, he is the ape of the King of Prussia, who is his hero, but whom he can only imitate in things which strike the senses, such as his mode of dress and taste for soldiering. . . ."

the Chancellor in everything. I owe this confession to your uprightness. Once more, there is no one else in the world like you. I revere you, I love you as my father, I account myself happy to have been enabled to acquire your affection. The Schuvalov are afraid of me near the Empress, and, taking every thing into consideration, should some unexpected good fortune draw me more often nearer to her, and should she become more used to me, I do not know whether I could not really gain some influence over her mind. You will say that I write you trash ; it may be so. But I have had two conversations, in which I have convinced her of facts about which she was quite the other way of thinking. I owe you thanks for the good opinion which you have formed of the small amount of sense which Heaven has bestowed upon me ; perhaps you value it too highly from the friendship which you feel for me. Two things I know well : one is, that my ambition is as great as is humanly possible; the other, that I shall do some good to your country.

The last word in your letter pains me, although in it you promised me news which has always given me true pleasure. But the word *Adieu* will spoil it, although a political testament from you would be to me the most useful and desirable thing in the world. Speaking of this, I make so bold as to beg you to remember your son ; we grew silent yesterday, when discussing the difference between the new arrival, and the man whose departure will cause us such deep affliction and whose return would be regarded as Heaven's greatest favour. You see that I cannot stop when I begin to speak of you. Your word becomes my gospel.

INDEX

Adadurov, Basil, 137, 141, 163, 166-7, 169, 178
Adolf Frederick, King of Sweden, 18, 35 (note), 43, 45, 49, 74, 86, 88, 91, 152, 159
Amelot de la Houssaye, 99
Apraksin, Stepan F., Field-Marshal, 41, 48, 50-1, 53-4, 58-9, 63, 66-8, 70-1, 76, 89, 91, 101, 103, 106, 109, 110, 116, 126, 131, 139, 141, 161, 165, 176, 178, 182, 184-6, 188-191, 193-7, 201-2, 205, 208-10, 213, 237, 240, 247, 253, 257, 262
Augustus III, King of Poland, 14, 104, 116, 121, 142-3, 147, 150, 154-5, 177-8, 189, 195-6, 249

Bekteïev, Feodor, 40 (note), 63, 107, 270
Bernardi, Italian jeweller, 37-8, 41, 52, 54, 67, 69, 70, 75-7, 81, 84, 86-91, 93, 95-6, 109, 114-5, 117-9, 121, 123-4, 126-8, 130-3, 135-6, 138-42, 146-7, 156, 166, 178-9, 181-4, 188-93, 197, 201, 206, 210, 217-9, 226-7, 235, 241, 244-5, 262, 263, 273, 276
Bernstorff, Count, Danish Foreign Minister, 263, 266-7
— letter to M. d'Osten, 264-5
Bestuzhev, Count Alexei (Great Chancellor), 15-22, 24, 31, 38-41, 44, 46, 48-50, 53-4, 56, 58-9, 61, 63, 66-7, 71-80, 82, 87-100, 102, 105-6, 108-9, 111, 113-38, 140, 142, 144-8, 151, 155, 157, 159, 162, 164-6, 168-71, 173-9, 181, 183, 184, 186-94, 196-7, 200-1, 203-20, 222, 225-6, 228, 231-6, 240, 242, 244-6, 248-50, 252-4, 258, 261-3, 265-71, 283
— letter to Count Brühl, 146
— letter to Catherine, 69
Bestuzhev, Count Michael, 40 (note), 142, 166, 168, 180-1
Bestuzhev, Countess Alexei, 131
Betski, Ivan, 28-30, 32-4, 36, 40, 44, 46, 173
Bloudov, Count, 12-3
Bowles, Caroline (Mrs Southey), 23
Boyle-Walsingham, 176 (note). (See Hanbury-Williams, Charlotte)
Brahé, Count, 35 (note), 91, 99

Branicki, Great General of Poland, 37, 117, 175
Bressan, Grand-Duke's valet, 22, 60
Brockdorff, Count, 277-8, 282
Broglie, Charles Francis, Comte de, French Minister in Saxony, 154, 158, 232 (note), 233, 249
Brown, George, Count, 63
Brown, Maximilian, Austrian Field-Marshal, 160, 164
Brühl, Count, Saxon First Minister, 116, 121, 129, 146-7, 154-5, 159, 207, 211-2, 215, 233, 239, 242, 248-9
Brunswick-Wolfenbuttel, Duchess of, 164
Brunswick, Princess Caroline of, 164
Brunswick, Prince Edward of, 160
Brunswick, Prince Ferdinand of, 154, 164
Buturlin, Field-Marshal Count Alexander, 52, 57, 61-2, 76, 103, 141, 192, 218, 251, 257

Catherine, Grand-Duchess, passim ; the Correspondence, 11-13, 22 ; character, 17-21 ; marriage, 24 ; future position, 45, 59-61, 66, 180 ; money from England for, 64, 72, 74-5, 80, 91, 113, 130, 169, 216, 219, 279 ; and Apraksin, 102, 110, 162, 185-6, 208-9 ; and Great Chancellor, 173, 190, 224-5, 249, 263 ; her spies at court, 183, 188 ; presents to Lady Essex, 194, 252, 272 ; Hanbury-Williams's warnings, 213, 215, 250 ; attitude to King of Prussia, 230 ; friendship for England, 231, 234, 251-3, 280 ; learning English, 275-6 ; and l'Hôpital, 282
— letters to Great Chancellor Bestuzhev, 87-8, 128, 144
— letters to Ivan Schuvalov, 221, 228, 236
Cautemir, Prince de, 15 (note)
Charles XII of Sweden, 35 (note)
Cherkassov, Prince Ivan, 178
Chernuishev, Ivan, 197, 201, 209-10, 253, 257
Chernuishev, Zachary, 63, 69
Condoïdi, Peter, surgeon, 188, 218, 237, 239, 241, 248

285

Cumberland, William, Duke of, 274
Czartoryski, Prince Adam Casimir, 158, 175
Czartoryski, Prince Alexander, Palatine of Russia, 121, 153, 158 (*note*), 176, 198, 212
— letter to Sir C. Hanbury-Williams, 157
Czartoryski, Prince Frederick Michael, Great Chancellor of Lithuania, 153, 198

Damiens, Jacques, 270
Douglas, Chevalier Mackenzie, 17, 34, 36, 42, 47, 53-4, 61, 63, 89, 96, 99, 100, 107, 109, 137-9, 144, 154, 189, 191, 217, 220, 242-4, 255
Durand, François-Marie, French Minister in Poland, 152, 154-5, 157-9, 233, 242

Elisabeth, Empress of Russia, 14, 17, 19, 20, 24, 31-2, 35-7, 40, 46, 49-51, 53-4, 58-9, 62, 83, 93, 96-8, 104-6, 108, 110-1, 114, 116-8, 122-5, 130-1, 133, 137, 142, 148-51, 155, 161, 166, 168, 170, 173, 176-7, 179-94, 199-204, 207-10, 212-3, 215, 217-20, 226-7, 235, 238, 241, 246-9, 251, 261, 269, 273, 282-3
Elizabeth, Queen of England, 81 (*note*), 90, 99
Eon, Chevalier d', 30 (*note*)
Essex, Frances, Countess of Essex (Sir Charles's daughter), 139, 176, 194, 271-3
Esterhazy, Count Nicholas, Imperial Ambassador in Russia, 46, 142, 144, 152, 163, 207-8, 213, 217, 227, 242-4, 254

Flemming, Count George, Great Treasurer of Lithuania, 108, 116, 129, 143, 153, 175-6, 196, 198, 211, 258
Foussatier, French surgeon, 145
Fox, Henry, afterwards Lord Holland, 251
Frederick II, King of Prussia, 14-18, 27, 31, 34, 50, 58, 65-6, 76, 97-8, 100, 104-5, 110, 115-6, 128, 133-4, 137, 143, 148-52, 154-6, 159, 164, 170-1, 175, 177-9, 181, 189, 191-3, 202-5, 207, 209, 212, 220, 223-4, 234-5, 237-9, 243, 248, 266, 273 (*note*)
Frederick V, King of Denmark, 18, 84-5, 87-8, 92, 178
Frederick August of Holstein-Gottorp, Prince, 84 (*note*)
Friesendorff, M., 274
Funcke, Count, Saxon Minister in Russia, 95, 118, 136, 177, 245

Galitzin, Prince, 28 (*note*), 173
George, Prince of Wales, 164 (*note*)
Gersdorff, Count, 215
Gibson, Alexander, 77, 175
Glebov, Alexander, 31, 33, 42, 48, 54, 57, 71-2, 82, 94
Goriaïnov, M. Serge, 23-5
— Introduction by, 11-23
Gortschakov, Prince, 12, 23
Griff, 276
Gross, Russian Minister in Saxony, 94, 154-5, 174, 187, 217, 232-4, 242, 246-7, 249
— letter to Grand Chancellor, 211-2
Gyllenborg, Count Hening Adolf, 160

Hanbury, Major John, father of Sir Charles Hanbury-Williams, 13 (*note*)
Hanbury-Williams, Sir Charles, *passim*, the correspondence, 11-13, 22; residence in St. Petersburg, 14 (*note*); sketch of, 13-23; his letters, 39, 89, 93; and King of Prussia, 58, 97, 115-6, 175, 223; future position of Russia, 67, 82; bribes for Great Chancellor, 78-9, 116, 134; Great Chancellor's jealousy, 86, 111, 124, 135, 219, 267; ill-health, 95, 141, 145, 164, 216, 219, 228, 237, 239, 241, 247, 275; writes portraits, 100, 104-5, 172; will sacrifice himself for Catherine, 123, 127, 132; on European situation, 149, 171; his best friends in Poland, 158; and Poniatowski, 172, 255-60, 269, 271-2; to aid Catherine when Empress, 203, 283; loan to Grand-Duke, 223; his picture, 269
— letter to Grand-Duke, 55
Hanbury-Williams, Miss Charlotte (Sir Charles's daughter), 176
Hardt, Count, 91
Havrincour, M. d', French Ambassador in Sweden, 158
Holdernesse, Lord, 64 (*note*), 78 (*note*), 79 (*note*), 117 (*note*), 140 (*note*), 280 (*note*)
Holstein-Gottorp, Charles Frederick, Duke of, 18 (*note*)
Hop, Dutch banker, 134 (*note*)
Hôpital, Marquis de l', French Ambassador in Russia 14 (*note*), 137, 142, 166, 179, 181, 281
Horn, Count, 53, 172

Ismaïlov, Prince, 63, 139, 162, 165-6
Ivan IV (The Terrible), 81, 90, 99
Ivan VI, 44 (*note*), 62, 179